A Buyer's Life

A Buyer's Life
A Concise Guide to Retail Planning and Forecasting

DANA D. CONNELL

Columbia College Chicago

FAIRCHILD BOOKS
AN IMPRINT OF BLOOMSBURY PUBLISHING INC

B L O O M S B U R Y

NEW YORK · LONDON · OXFORD · NEW DELHI · SYDNEY

Fairchild Books
An imprint of Bloomsbury Publishing Inc

1385 Broadway   50 Bedford Square
New York   London
NY 10018   WC1B 3DP
USA   UK

www.bloomsbury.com

**FAIRCHILD BOOKS, BLOOMSBURY and the Diana logo are
trademarks of Bloomsbury Publishing Plc**

Third printing 2013
Reprinted 2015

Library of Congress Catalog Card Number: 2008943315

ISBN: PB: 978-1-5636-7771-7
        ePDF: 978-1-6090-1718-7

GST R 133004424

Printed in the United States of America

TP09, CH13

Executive Editor: Olga T. Kontzias

Associate Acquisitions Editor: Jaclyn Bergeron

Assistant Acquisitions Editor: Amanda Breccia

Editorial Development Director: Jennifer Crane

Associate Art Director: Erin Fitzsimmons

Production Director: Ginger Hillman

Associate Production Editor: Andrew Fargnoli

Cover Design: Erin Fitzsimmons

Cover Art: Coneyl Jay/Photographer's Choice/Getty Images

Text Design: TronvigKuypers

Production Service and Composition: Progressive Publishing Alternatives

BRIEF CONTENTS

EXTENDED CONTENTS

PREFACE

The purpose of this textbook is to prepare students to understand and formulate a six-month stock and sales plan for a retail business. Mastering the retail math components of the plan as they connect to one another will enable the user to more fully understand the interrelationships of the components. While many texts teach retail math formulas, they are done so in isolation. By integrating the formulas into the six-month financial plan, students are better able to understand the relationships while also becoming more proficient in their use and calculation. In addition, through the use of screen grabs, students are able to set up and implement Excel worksheets using formulas to improve their proficiency.

Corporate merchandising retailers such as Target, Sears, and others require applicants to pass a test of their merchandising math skills. This text will equip students with the formulas and basic decision making that positively impact financial results.

A Buyer's Life: A Concise Guide to Retail Planning and Forecasting will help independent retailers to gain essential skills in setting up their own plans using Excel, as well as providing them with a solid understanding of stock and sales flows to generate profit. These retailers often hire consultants to manage the financial plan. This text will allow independent retailers to gain the confidence to generate their own plans or to better understand what the consultants are presenting.

Account executives and multi-line representatives can benefit from this book through an improved understanding of financial planning and the constraints their buyers face. Establishing partnerships between vendors and buyers are essential to foster growth in business. The first step in establishing the relationship is to insure each member of the team has an equal understanding of the financial plans and expectations.

Users of this textbook should consider this an introduction to retail buying that puts the theory and the formulas into practice. The book introduces decision making at an entry level and is intended to expand thinking beyond fashion and shopping to consider buying as a means of running a profitable business.

A Buyer's Life is not intended for advanced levels of critical analysis including: plan manipulation, vendor and internal negotiation techniques, marketing initiatives, or strategic decision making.

To prepare students, as well as readers already working in the field, exercises within the chapters include Practice Problems, Application Exercises, and at the end of the chapter a detailed step-by-step guide, Create It in Excel! For instructors located in computer classrooms or smart rooms, there is a PowerPoint® presentation available that includes spreadsheets that can be used for in-class demonstrations. For those classrooms that are not equipped with computers, the spreadsheets from the Application Exercises are also on perforated pages at the back of the book. This allows the instructor to teach while students complete the worksheets in class using calculators and pencils. Whether buyers typically use computer or manual calculation, when they find themselves in the market without a computer they need to be able to pull out a calculator and run the numbers. This book helps students learn both manual and technology-supported methods.

The practice applications in the book can be used in a variety of ways. Instructors may use the problems as small group discussion and problem solving or as homework. Practice problems reinforce individual formulas and are presented as questions or decision making problems.

Application exercises apply each formula or concept into the whole of a six-month plan. Instructors are able to use the classroom lesson either as in-class Excel exercises or by using blank spreadsheets with manual calculator and pencil calculations. Each application includes one step-by-step description with the appropriate spreadsheet representing the concept. The step by step is followed by at least two additional examples and at least two examples to be used as homework. Instructors have the freedom to assign as in-class or homework, as appropriate to their individual class.

The Create It in Excel! feature in every chapter combines spreadsheets and screenshots to help readers create and become experienced in and comfortable with working with formulas and plans in Excel. This feature creates a six-month jewelry plan that is built with each additional chapter. Unlike the overall textbook where a variety of business examples are used, Create It in Excel! uses the same plan for every chapter while building the plan towards completion. By using the feature, students will become increasingly comfortable using Excel and entering formulas. Providing students with both visual images and hands-on practice will improve skill and proficiency.

The Search the Net feature provides Internet-specific exercises targeting specific sites as well as general types of sites, enabling the reader to work with current retail trends. Case studies and current retail events are excellent supplements to this text; in an age where technology is readily available in many classrooms, instructors and students are encouraged to visit the Internet for more in-depth discussion and additional classroom exercises.

Words and terms that are key to creating and working with six-month stock and sales plans are included in the chapters and gathered at the back of the book in a Glossary for easy reference. The back of the book also contains a perforated formulas page, a one-stop resource for formulas used throughout the book. Students can enter the formulas here, then pull out the page for easy use at any time.

The author of *A Buyer's Life: A Concise Guide to Retail Planning and Forecasting* has over 17 years of experience teaching retail buying and over 25 years experience as a corporate retail buyer for both regional and national stores. It is this real-world experience that she used to create the content and the structure of this book to make it a succinct and useful resource. While the basic formulas for six-month planning remain unchanged, the tools to implement those plans are ever changing. Use of the Internet, mobile communications, and improved technological planning tools have all enhanced the buyer's role and at the same time made it more complex than ever. Armed with the framework for interpreting the six-month financial plan will equip a wide range of students for the merchandising field.

1

Buying versus Planning

Becoming a retail store buyer might well be one of the most misunderstood careers in the retail industry. With promises of worldwide travel and multimillion-dollar spending power, **buyers** have the ideal dream job—or do they? Today, the career of retail buying requires strong analytical, statistical, and strategic decision-making skills as well as strong leadership and negotiation skills. Combining quantitative business skills with qualitative product-selection skills can be accomplished with a career path that embraces both buying and planning positions.

The path to buyer and beyond in a large-store corporate environment takes time, patience, and openness to learning something new every step of the way. Conversely, becoming a buyer or small-business owner for an entrepreneurial enterprise can launch a career in buying without the career path steps seen in large retail establishments. This chapter outlines various career paths and identifies potential decision-making challenges for small-retail entrepreneurs who may have an imbalance between intuitive buying and analytical planning skill. Large retail corporations follow specific career paths where skills in functional areas are learned and developed. Buyers have the opportunity to hone their skills as managers and financial planners before becoming buyers. For some corporations this is achieved through careers that promote cross-training. Cross-training

involves the movement of individuals from buying to planning to stores at entry levels and then back through the process at higher levels. For other corporations, individuals are identified for a specific path and are trained vertically in buying, planning, or stores. This process provides the individual with an in-depth knowledge or expert level of understanding in the specified area.

CORPORATE RETAIL

Multi-store corporate buying environments follow a structured career path that often incorporates a weekly classroom training component. Taking an educational classroom approach allows retailers to train small groups of employees about corporate computer and procedural systems and decision making. Trainers can present various real-life scenarios that better prepare employees for the work ahead and establish cultural norms within the organization. These classes are often taught by higher-level, experienced individuals from within the organization. A review of typical career paths and their positions, followed by descriptions of each role, helps clarify the responsibilities and skills necessary for success.

Throughout this text, several types of retailers are discussed. Although there are many similarities between retailers, each establishment follows a different path to support individual growth. Large retail stores tend to be structured through three branches. In some stores, these branches are integrally connected through teams. In others, they are independently linked by management. The three branches are as follows:

1. Stores organization
2. Merchant or **merchandising organization**
3. Planning organization

The **stores organization** is perhaps the most familiar because it is the group of people who interact with customers every day. Some retailers communicate regularly with the merchant and planning organizations, while other retailers have only limited communication. Stores organizations consist of regional managers, district managers, store managers, assistant store managers, and department managers. These roles are dispersed throughout the selling-floor functions as well as the operations functions (shipping/receiving, alterations, visual merchandising, and so on). This text focuses on the merchant and planning organizations.

THE MERCHANDISING ORGANIZATION

The merchant, or merchandising, organization is often admired but greatly misunderstood. The titles used in this chapter may not be indicative of all retailers. In general, position responsibilities are likely similar from organization to organization, yet the titles may vary. Consider these titles as a guide while focusing on specific responsibilities. Of course, entrepreneurial retailers and smaller retailers will wear many hats and have combined roles. Merchandising teams consist of **general merchandise managers (GMMs)**, **divisional merchandise managers (DMMs)**, **buyers**, **associate buyers**, and **assistant buyers**. Each team member is responsible for selecting the products seen in stores, negotiating with vendors, and being accountable for overall financial profitability. Managing the area of business responsibility while delivering the greatest profit margin is the primary goal of all team members. In most corporate retail structures, financial objectives can account for 80 percent of a merchant annual performance review. Figure 1.1 presents a hierarchical view of the merchant organization. Note that every organization is different and may interchange some titles, but the responsibilities are similar.

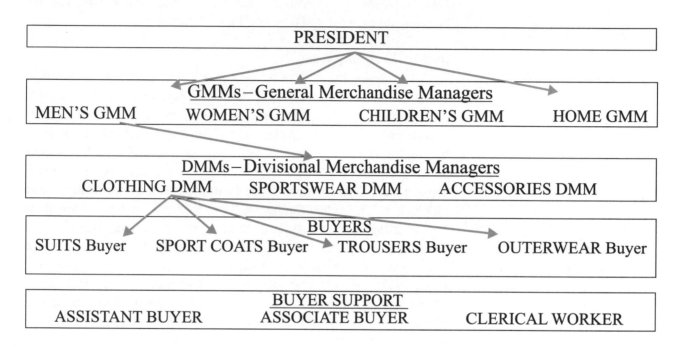

FIGURE 1.1 Merchant Organization.

Role of the General Merchandise Manager

The GMM reports directly to the company president and is responsible for a large general merchandise category. The GMM is involved in high-level, companywide decision making and strategic planning as well as delivering the overall profit margins associated with the general merchandise category. To deliver planned profit margins, the GMM must also engage in high-level vendor negotiations while providing leadership, support, and direction to the entire GMM team. The GMM is also critically involved in making career-path decisions. It is in the team's best interest to place team members in positions where they can grow and provide the greatest benefit to the team as a whole.

Role of the Divisional Merchandise Manager

The DMM's role is similar to that of the GMM, but the DMM has a smaller area of responsibility. DMMs oversee the performance for a specific division within the general merchandise category. DMMs typically have varied levels of responsibility that range in sales volume. For example, a new DMM might be responsible for a smaller sales volume area, such as special-size apparel (women's size and petites), whereas a more experienced DMM with a proven track record will be responsible for a very large sales volume area, such as women's sportswear. Strategic decision making for DMMs is usually limited to their specific area of responsibility or to the overall health of the GMM area. Each DMM directly oversees the buyer teams and is responsible for bottom-line profitability of their DMM area. Like the GMM, the DMM is also responsible for assembling the best team and providing growth and direction for that team.

Role of the Buying Team

The buying team is led by the buyer. Each buyer reports directly to the DMM and is responsible for specific departments within the DMM area. A buyer's department responsibility often ranges from two to six departments and carries a wide range of complexity. As with a DMM, the buying team has many levels of sales-volume responsibility. A new buyer will be responsible for smaller sales volumes and thus require a smaller support team. This approach gives the new buyer the opportunity to establish a track record that can be translated to larger areas of responsibility and subsequent promotions. In most cases, buyers have the ultimate say in deciding which products to buy. The exception to this is matrix retailers. Matrix retailers provide a list of approved vendors. If a buyer discovers a new vendor resource, most often he or she cannot buy from that vendor. Matrix buying is beneficial because it generates greater levels of partnership and overall profitability. However, such relationships can also result in stale assortments and lack of innovative products.

While buyers are responsible for product selection, the associate buyers, assistant buyers, and clerical workers all give support to the buyer. Their responsibilities can cover a broad range—tracking orders, placing orders, tracking sales, communicating both within the store and with vendors, and other miscellaneous tasks. Some associate buyers or assistant buyers may also have a small area of buying responsibility. Although the support positions do not have complete accountability for profit margins, individuals who are nearing promotion status may be given a small business or vendor to manage.

Because profitability is such a critical performance factor, buyers spend most of their time planning and forecasting sales. Sales are the driving force behind all decision making and the nucleus of all other financial components. As each chapter of this text explores the various components of the basic six-month plan, the primary component of each equation is sales. Besides planning and forecasting, buyers must also maintain vendor relationships and negotiate for the good of the business. For example, buyers with strong vendor relationships are more likely to be given priority shipping, new product launches, exclusive products, co-op advertising, and other marketing tools. Fostering mutually beneficial relationships can take a significant amount of the buyer's time each day.

CAREER CROSSOVER VERSUS CAREER SILO

There are two types of career paths in corporate retail: career crossover and career silo. The career crossover path takes a horizontal approach. In this path, the individual crosses over different parts of the organization and becomes cross-trained in various areas. This path is beneficial in that it gives the individual a broad perspective of the organization and connects the integration of each career with another. The second type, career silo, is vertical in nature, as it specializes in one career path whereby the individual becomes an expert in one area. This path leads to highly skilled individuals in specific areas but can limit an organization's flexibility.

CAREER CROSSOVER

The term **crossover career** refers to an organization that follows a career path by which employees advance as they cross over between two or three of the organizations (e.g., stores, merchandising, or planning). For example, a typical three-crossover career path (Figure 1.3) might move an individual through stores, merchandising, and planning, while a two-crossover career path

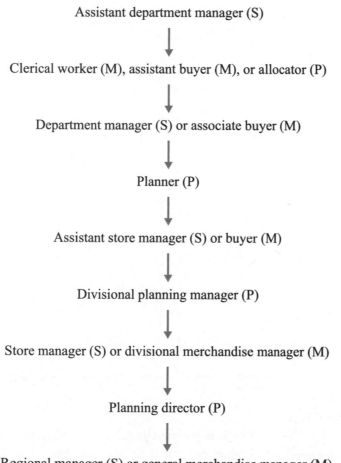

Assistant department manager (S)

↓

Clerical worker (M), assistant buyer (M), or allocator (P)

↓

Department manager (S) or associate buyer (M)

↓

Planner (P)

↓

Assistant store manager (S) or buyer (M)

↓

Divisional planning manager (P)

↓

Store manager (S) or divisional merchandise manager (M)

↓

Planning director (P)

↓

Regional manager (S) or general merchandise manager (M)

FIGURE 1.3 Three-Crossover Path: Stores Organization (S), Merchandising Organization (M), Planning Organization (P).

would move through stores and merchandising (Figure 1.4) or planning and merchandising (Figure 1.5).

The two-crossover career path can require more than five years to reach the title of buyer, but it results in a well-rounded retailer. This career path also provides many opportunities to identify and acknowledge one's strengths and weaknesses. Another benefit of crossover is that employees at the buyer level and above have greater appreciation for the work of their teams. By understanding the many constraints confronting each level, the manager is better able to lead the team with useful feedback and direction. A crossover organization has many benefits, but it also has two main disadvantages: (1) it takes time to progress through such an organization, and (2) individuals are sometimes placed in positions that do not correspond to their individual competencies.

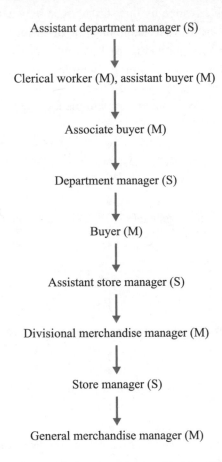

FIGURE 1.4 Two-Crossover Path: Stores Organization (S), Merchandising Organization (M).

SILO CAREER

In a **silo career** path, individuals progress through only one of the three organizations: store, merchant, or planning. This type of career path identifies individual strengths and subsequently fosters and directs those strengths toward the overall efforts of the organization. The crossover path gives the individual the opportunity to explore, and it gives the organization a view of the whole person. The silo path trains individuals for a career in each of the three organizational sectors and gives

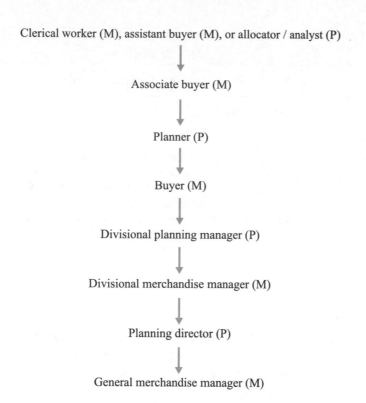

Clerical worker (M), assistant buyer (M), or allocator / analyst (P)

↓

Associate buyer (M)

↓

Planner (P)

↓

Buyer (M)

↓

Divisional planning manager (P)

↓

Divisional merchandise manager (M)

↓

Planning director (P)

↓

General merchandise manager (M)

FIGURE 1.5 Two-Crossover Path: Merchandising Organization (M), Planning Organization (P).

them the greatest breadth of knowledge within that path. The major downfall of the silo path is a focus that can be too narrow. A silo approach also lacks understanding across each organizational domain. Many large retail establishments employ high-level planners who have never worked on a selling floor.

TARGET

Merchandising/Buying/Planning

Gain broad exposure to merchandising while you lead and motivate cross-functional teams to drive assortment and marketing strategies. You'll have immediate general management responsibility and P&L accountability for a $100–$250M business for all Target stores nationwide. Plus, you'll interact with senior leaders in all functional areas.

MBA Recruited Role:

- General Management—Buyer

Skills We Look For:

- Interest in general or brand management
- Entrepreneurial spirit
- Superior leadership skills with passion for results
- Excellent strategic and analytical skills
- Creative problem-solving and risk-taking skills

http://sites.target.com/site/en/company/page.jsp?contentId=WCMP04-030890

WAL-MART
Merchandise Assistant, Audio Electronics

More Information About This Job:

General Summary:

The Merchandise Assistant manages the acquisition, coordination, and tracking of inbound supplier data, including all images and item-level content. He/she manages item page content, cross-sells, and accessories for the merchandise department. He/she assists the call center associates with customer service questions. This position will be responsible for managing the acquisition, coordination, and tracking of inbound supplier data.

Responsibilities:

1. Coordination of content and item setup (60%)
   - Supports the item-level efforts of all merchandise categories reporting to the Category Manager
   - Works closely with the supplier base to manage content acquisition
   - Works closely with the supplier base to manage the procurement and coordination of digital images and/or samples for the site
   - Coordinates with cross-functional departments
   - Coordinates with supplier base for item-level data, including images and samples as needed
   - Responsible for all item setup, cross-selling, and presentation of item page
   - Oversees the quality-assurance process as it relates to the item's preparation to go live on the site

2. Administrative and Tracking (30%)
   - Tracks all items coming in, out to supplier, or with cross-functional team to ensure all items go live in a timely manner
   - Item maintenance of all changes to content or imaging

3. Special Projects (10%)
   - Responsible for assisting in customer service problem resolution in a timely manner
   - Additional support of department needs as defined by the category manager

Qualifications:

1. Skills, knowledge, and abilities (SKAs):

   Functional Competencies:
   - Strong computer skills, particularly in Excel, and familiarity and comfort with database applications
   - Exceptionally detail oriented with ability to juggle multiple priorities simultaneously and process and track multiple inbound and outbound data requests without errors
   - Strong academic background in business or finance or a work history that demonstrates competence managing multiple information streams

Interpersonal Competencies:

- Schedule flexibility—ability and willingness to be on call periodically (including evenings and weekends) for timely resolution of supplier-related issues

- Friendly, personable, outgoing personality; quick learner; comfortable with ambiguity and a willingness to take initiative

Leadership Competencies:

- Understands and follows Wal-Mart's three core values: Respect for the Individual, Service to Our Customers, Strive for Excellence.

2. Experience:

- 1–2 years experience in a merchant assistant, customer service, project coordinator, or administrator preferred.

3. Minimum educational level:

- BA/BS preferred

http://jobs-walmart.icims.com/jobs/1563/job

SMALL RETAIL ENTREPRENEUR

Retail establishments with a single store or fewer than five store locations take an entirely different approach to buying and planning. In these stores, the buyer is often the business owner who must fulfill multiple roles within the organization. Establishing a hierarchy of stores, merchants, and planners is not financially or physically possible. Therefore, the owner is the store manager and merchant—but not necessarily the planner. Some retailers rely on their accountant or other financial consultants to provide financial advice. Other retailers hire consulting firms, which act as the planning organization for many small retailers. And finally, in some partnership establishments the partners each bring varied competencies to the relationship. One partner may have the product sensibility while the other partner has the financial sensibility. Regardless of the structure used, some form of planning is necessary for the long-term health of the store.

While there are multiple opportunities to address business issues in each of the three organizational areas, many small-retail owners do not take advantage of quantitative expertise. Perhaps the greatest challenge for these owners is managing a plan and forecast. Often these business owners neglect planning, which can result in too much inventory, not enough inventory, or unrealistic profit expectations. Often, when small-business owners enter into the venture, they are excited about store ownership and buying but have little or no knowledge of tracking and projecting sales trends. Hiring an appropriate consultant provides the ideal balance for external data analysis and forecasting with internal product selection.

FREESTANDING DESIGNER STORES

Freestanding designer stores are another avenue for buyers. Many designers open their own boutiques in key locations around the world. These organizations rely on their own internal buyers to provide for their stores. Unlike multi-brand retailers, these retail buyers have a unique challenge in working directly with designers. Assessing buying trends within the boutique while also gathering national sales information gives the designer-store buyer a unique perspective. The designer buyer does not have the opportunity to shop for outside product. To be successful, the designer buyer must analyze store sales to maximize the designer's strengths. Communication with the designer and stores is an essential component of a freestanding designer store.

KATE SPADE
Buyer

Overview:

With a playful chic aesthetic and a clean, graphic approach to design, American Accessories Company designer Kate Spade has become a modern American classic. She is known for her signature handbags, shoes, eyewear, stationery, and accessories for the home, including china, crystal, and flatware.

Buyers assume retail buying responsibilities (effective assortment, sales, and inventory planning for all Kate Spade product categories) with the sourcing and purchasing of unique products (current designers/manufacturers and vintage items) for the freestanding Kate Spade stores.

Responsibilities:

Essential duties and responsibilities to include but not be limited to:

- Identifying product opportunities, trends, and offerings that will impact the business and provide results
- Liaising with visual team to ensure that all products are properly displayed on sales floor for optimization
- Assisting during market with product selection and assortment
- Scouting and sourcing "collectibles" and special items for the stores
- Analyzing sales trends, key items, vendor profitability, and aged inventory as well as making recommendations for driving improved performance
- Liaising with production and planning teams to ensure availability and the timely delivery of merchandise
- Participating in meetings
- Being responsible for product setup and maintenance
- Ensuring all markdowns and in-store promotions are entered and set up properly in system

Qualifications:

Skills:

- Demonstrates initiative, is conscientious, and provides complete follow-through on all aspects of responsibility
- Ability to multitask and focus in a busy atmosphere
- Comfortable with team-based work structure, ability to demonstrate flexibility
- Excellent time-management and communication skills
- Familiarity with multiple resourcing venues (trade shows, private vendors, flea markets)
- High level of proficiency in Word, Excel

Required Skills:

Education and/or experience:

- College degree preferred
- 5 years experience in retail buying role
- Retail or specialty store background
- Ability to build line plans and assortments
- Possess strong presentation, listening, verbal, and written communication skills

SEARCH THE NET

➤ On the Internet, research and complete the following exercise:

1. Locate similar retailers, search position openings and determine their career paths.

2. Locate two different job postings for two similar retailers. Compare the requirements for each organization. Discuss how the requirements affect the customer in-store experience.

3. Identify your skills sets, and determine what you need to become both a buyer and a planner.

TERMINOLOGY

allocator: This entry-level planning position is also referred to as an analyst. Allocators or analysts are responsible for allocating orders to stores.

associate planner: The associate planner reports to the planner or DPM within the planning organization. This position provides analysis and forecasting to the planner and buyer.

assistant buyer or clerical: This entry-level merchandising position reports to the buyer and functions as support. This position often entails task-oriented duties of order distribution, order tracking, and vendor follow-up. There is limited decision making in this position.

associate buyer: The associate buyer reports to the buyer, often has a limited buying responsibility, and is involved in most decision making and negotiations.

buyer: The buyer reports to the DMM and has responsibility for a specific area within the DMM area. One buyer may be responsible for special-occasion dresses, while another is responsible for career dresses. The buyer has specific bottom-line financial responsibility to the organization, which can account for as much as 80 percent of his or her annual review.

crossover career: A corporate career path in which individuals move horizontally within an organization, attaining a mix of skills along the way. Crossover career paths cross an individual between stores, merchandising, and/or planning.

DMM: Divisional merchandise manager reporting to the GMM and having responsibility for a range of product within a broad area. For example, a DMM in women's might have responsibility for dresses. The DMM has significant financial responsibility.

DPM: Divisional planning manager reporting to the GPM and having planning responsibility for a range of product. The DPM is typically aligned with one or more DMMs. The DPM has significant financial responsibility.

GMM: General merchandise manager who oversees a broad-range merchandise category, such as men's, women's, or home. The GMM is typically a vice president, reports to the president or CEO, and has a high level of financial responsibility.

GPM: General planning manager or planning director who oversees the planning for broad-range merchandise categories. The GPM is typically a vice president, reports to the president or CEO, and has a high level of financial responsibility.

merchandising organization: Refers to all levels of product decision making and vendor negotiation. Members of the merchandising organization have a significant financial obligation to earn profit for the company.

planner: The planner reports to the DPM and has a close working relationship with the buyer. With the buyer, the planner forecasts and plans the business on an ongoing basis.

planning organization: Refers to the financial planning that affects the merchandising organization.

silo career: A corporate career path that places individuals in one specific silo or area of expertise. Individuals move vertically through careers in one specified area of merchandising, planning, or stores.

stores organization: Refers to the physical store where merchandise is sold to the customer.

2

WHO IS THE CUSTOMER?

Understanding the customer is the most fundamental task for any buyer. Having a great sense of style, fashion, or financial acumen are all irrelevant when directed at the wrong audience. A comprehensive analysis of quantitative and qualitative information coupled with a strong sense of the product category and the customer will enable the buyer to make comprehensive buying decisions.

Quantitative analysis involves statistical information gathered about the customer, such as **demographics**. It also includes analysis of **historical sales** results, which are discussed more thoroughly in Chapters 10–12. Qualitative analysis involves **psychographic** and **life-stage** assumptions based on quantitative information. Gaining thorough knowledge about the customer involves a four-step process:

1. Gather historical sales results.

2. Perform a demographic analysis.

3. Perform a psychographic and life-stage analysis.

4. Conduct **product decision making**.

STEP 1: GATHER HISTORICAL SALES RESULTS

Sales results are gathered and analyzed from previous years and seasons. Understanding what customers reacted to and what they didn't will help the buyer decide what action to take in the future. This analysis is essentially a review of what inventory sold and how much of it sold. Suppose that last summer the sportswear department had eight different collections over the season. In reviewing the sales results, the buyer notices that yellow tops were the weakest performer from most collections. Conversely, tops with blue in any form, patterned or solid, were the best sellers. When the buyer reviews collections for the upcoming season, he or she should avoid yellow and focus on blue.

On the surface, this example seems logical and would likely result in a decent sales performance. However, buyers need to give the customer a new reason to buy. Looking at new color options in the blue family, such as purple or aqua colorations, could yield a strong sales result. Identifying common themes such as color, style, price, brand, and so on when reviewing sales performance will be strong indicators of what, or what not, to buy next season. Another question the buyer might consider is why didn't yellow sell? A look into demographics could provide a clue. The answer could be due to geographic location or ethnicity. Customer skin tones could provide a clue as to what colors will sell and what ones won't sell. Later chapters in the book provide more details about decision making based on historical sales results.

STEP 2: PERFORM A DEMOGRAPHIC ANALYSIS

Demographics involve statistical information about the customer and about the geographic region where they are located. Some examples of demographics include (specific details are included in Table 2.1) the following:

- Location: country, state, city
- Climate
- Population and density
- Age
- Sex
- Marital status
- Educational level
- Occupation
- Income

Demographic information is essential to any buying decision. Even the seasoned buyer undergoes a periodic review to pinpoint shifts and changes that affect customer shopping habits. Local municipal districts, shopping districts, and shopping mall marketing personnel have access to demographic information. In the United States, this information is updated every ten years through the census. Buyers opening new stores in new locations also review demographics as a beginning point to understand the new market.

SEARCH THE NET

➤ Visit www. zipskinny.com to learn more about demographics by using zip code locations. Look up specific zip codes to compare and contrast.

TABLE 2.1. CUSTOMER PROFILE	
Market Segment/Bases	**Examples**
Geographic	
• Region	North, south, east, west
• City size	Up to 100,000, 100,001+
• Population density	Urban, suburban, rural
• Climate	Hot, temperate, cold
Demographic	
• Age	Up to 12, 13–19, 20–39, 40–59, 60+
• Gender	Female, male
• Household size	1, 2, 3, 4, or more persons
• Income	Up to $25,000, $25,001 to $50,000, over $50,000
• Occupation	Professional, blue-collar, retired, unemployed
• Education	High school or less, some college, college graduate
Sociocultural	
• Culture	American, European, South American
• Subculture	
• Religion	Protestant, Catholic, Jewish, Mormon
• National origin	Italian, French, Canadian
• Race	Hispanic, Oriental, African-American
• Social class	Upper class, middle class, working class, lower class
• Marital status	Single, married, divorced, widowed
• Psychographics	Achievers, strivers, strugglers
Affective and Cognitive	
• Degree of knowledge	Expert, novice
• Benefits sought	Convenience, economy, prestige
• Attitude	Positive, neutral, negative
Behavioral	
• Brand loyalty	None, divided, undivided loyalty
• Store loyalty	None, divided, undivided loyalty
• Usage rate	Light, medium, heavy
• User status	Nonuser, ex-user, current user, potential user
• Payment method	Cash, credit card, time payments
• Media usage	Newspapers, magazines, TV, Internet
• Usage situation	Work, home, vacation

STEP 3: PERFORM A PSYCHOGRAPHIC AND LIFE-STAGE ANALYSIS

The third step in gaining knowledge about the customer involves assumptions made based on the demographic information gathered. Psychographics involves making assumptions about personality, social class, and lifestyle. These assumptions can be translated into characteristics regarding customers: how they perceive brands, their shopping habits, and their cost-versus-benefit purchasing decisions. These characteristics are also referred to as behavior

TABLE 2.2. LIFE STAGE ANALYSIS	
Life-Stage	**Disposable Income %**
Tweens & Teens: This group has serious spending power because all of their income is disposable. Teens account for one of the largest growing spending segments. In dual-income or single-parent families, teens and tweens are the key shoppers for food, meals, and other miscellaneous purchases.	3%
Young & Single: Under Age 30 College students and those entering full-time work for the first time. Young singles are typically low earners and may have significant educational debt. Although this group's income is spent largely on needs, they don't hesitate to fulfill their wants!	8%
New Couples: Age Range 25–35 Unlike the young singles, this stage of life finds couples making major purchases such as home, car, etc. Disposable income is low but is spent with care and is directed at big-ticket items, leaving less for clothing and entertainment.	15%
New Families: Age Range 30–40 Raising a family brings on new expenses and responsibilities that can significantly hamper spending at this life stage. This is perhaps the most price sensitive life stage.	27%
Established Families: Age Range 40–60 These families have older children or no children at all. With fewer major expenses, these families are less burdened and have more disposable income than they did in the early stages of raising their families.	18%
Empty Nesters: Having children later, working longer, and living longer have all contributed to a large group that has tremendous spending power. The empty nesters are at peak income with low expenses.	29%
	100%

variables. Many of these decisions are subconscious, occurring with little or no thought. Study of how the human brain makes decisions and responds to stimuli by making a purchase is fascinating and is evolving each day. For the purposes of retail buying, buyers can learn from making psychographic assumptions and by observing customers in the store environment.

Life-stage analysis has gained significant importance in recent years. As people live longer and population increases, consumers are faced with new challenges that influence their buying decisions. During the 1950s it was common for women to run the household and make all of the buying decisions. Such women were generally in their twenties, had children, and held the job title of homemaker. Today there are multiple market segments made up of customers in various life stages. Consider that in a non-urban location, many of the households might consist of a married couple aged 25–35 and two or three children under age 10. This would typically be considered a young family. In an urban location, many households might consist of a couple aged 40–55 and two or three children under age 10. Is this also considered a young family, or is it a middle-aged family? Thus, life stage can be a more relevant indicator of spending patterns versus age.

Another concept associated with life stage is referred to as sandwiching. Many families are finding themselves caring for young children and aging parents at the same time. This situation has resulted in extended families living under the same roof. It has also resulted in changes in disposable income when younger family members must support older family members.

These nuances of life stage play an integral role in determining who the customer is and how that customer shops. Making assumptions about spending patterns is more insightful if life stage is viewed in conjunction with demographics and behaviors.

STEP 4: CONDUCT PRODUCT DECISION MAKING

The final step in understanding the customer is to combine historical sales, demographics, psychographics, and life stage into a comprehensive decision-making plan that addresses current product trends and availability. Maintaining a constant focus on factual information combined with historical and current performance and product knowledge will appropriately balance assortments and meet customer needs and wants.

Here are a few cautions for buyers to consider in understanding their customer.

1. What is your gut instinct? Often buyers will make product selections based on gut instinct or personal preference. Using instinct can be a useful tool, but only *after* the analysis is complete. If the analysis signals that the product is wrong, it probably is. However, if the analysis reveals that the product might be successful, trust your instinct and try it. Running a small test of product is often the best way to prove or disprove the product.

SEARCH THE NET

On the Internet, visit a variety of retail websites (include retailers you would not typically frequent).

1. Based on the website, compile a customer profile.

2. Visit a website for a competing retailer. Discuss how the customer profile might vary based on the Web presence.

3. If possible, visit the brick-and-mortar location. How is the physical store different from the website? What are the differences in the customer?

2. The sales representative keeps calling because the product is selling for your competitor. Should you buy it? Maybe not—ask a few more questions. Is the product selling for your competitor in your city? If not, maybe that product will not sell in your city, and that is why the competition has not bought it for that location. Find out if your competitor is really selling it. Sales representatives want to make the sale; they may have sold it to the competition, but is the customer buying it in your geographic location?

3. Your boss wants you to buy it. Why does your boss want you to buy it? If the company is working to grow a particular brand within the entire store and top management supports the growth, do it. But do it carefully. The brand wants to be successful, and so does management. Work out a buy that puts the customer first by selecting test products or small groups of product based on your customer.

These and other obstacles will arise from time to time and can easily derail a thoughtful buying plan based on the customer. Remaining focused on statistical knowledge and continuous analysis will ensure care in meeting customer wants and needs while also remaining profitable.

TERMINOLOGY

demographic: Statistical information about the customer. Demographic information is often obtained through government census or market survey.

historical sales: Analysis of past sales results, which may include specified time periods, past product performance, or past vendor performance. It could also include current sales trends as they relate to historical sales performance.

life stage: Considers factors related to family size and life cycle. Life stage can vary by geographic region and has a significant impact on disposable income.

product decision making: All encompassing decision making to buy or not buy product(s) based on overall analysis of demographics, psychographics, life stage, and historical sales.

psychographic: Involves the assumptions about a customer based on demographic information. Assumptions about a customer's personality, social class, and lifestyle are examples of psychographic assumptions.

has the potential to sell $1 to $2 million within 18 months. Your plan is locked into a top-down process.

What do you do? Consider the upside and downside of the decision. How will you negotiate for additional sales?

TRENDS

What is the meaning of the word **trend** for a retail buyer?

Retail buyers must concern themselves with three definitions of *trend*. The obvious definition is in relation to a fashion trend. What is the new style, color, or silhouette the customer is looking for? *Trend* can also refer to a lifestyle trend, such as a tendency for people to eat out more or travel to exotic locations. Lifestyle trends might also indicate exercise or eating habits. *Trend* also refers to the direction that business is likely to take based on statistical or historical information. For example, if sales were down 10 percent three weeks ago, down 8 percent two weeks ago, and down 9 percent last week, we could summarize that the trend is generally downward by approximately 9 percent and likely to continue on that downward trend.

Although the process begins with the big picture of the company plan, the buyer must also be concerned with the details. When the details are well analyzed and thoughtfully executed, they have a major impact on total sales. Identifying trends in fashion, lifestyle, or statistical patterns all influence the decisions a buyer makes.

For each decision, the buyer will first review historical sales. History can refer to last week, last month, or last year. Having an understanding of how to analyze sales history and make quantitative predictions is central to a buyer's decision making. The review can encompass an entire category, brand, or specific product stock-keeping unit (SKU). An analysis of historical sales will provide

TREND TRIVIA
This actress walked the 1997 red carpet wearing a stunning John Galliano dress.
•   Can you name the actress?
•   What was the impact of her dress and why was it reinterpreted?
When this celebrity aired her interview with Barbara Walters in 1999, the next day, a hot new lipstick trend emerged.
•   Can you name the celebrity?
•   What retailer sold the lipstick and how did it impact overall lipstick business?
In 2008, Michelle Obama took center stage on late-night television and adorned the covers of magazines.
•   What retailer saw a significant boost in sales?
•   This represented a shift in attitudes toward how women dress. What economic factors were also signaled in her fashion?
What do skirt lengths have to do with the stock market?
Identify a current trend. Where or why did it begin?

guidance for future decisions about what to buy, how much to buy, and at what price to buy. Analysis of historical sales plays a key role in planning for any business. Imagine you are the lipstick buyer for Club Monaco. The hot trend for the color Glaze will last for only a short time. Understanding what made the sales spike upward will guide the decision of how sales of the same product will move forward. While celebrity appeal works for lipstick, products like household cleaners will be affected more by national advertising or coupon campaigns. Bounty paper towels are not likely to have significant swings in sales performance unless they have an innovative new product function or decorative design. Whether a buyer is planning for a fashion business or a commodity goods business, the process of analyzing history and projecting forward sales is an important place to begin. Following are a variety of problems to practice making predictions of how much to buy.

SAMPLE PROBLEMS

Review the sales from last year for these two product categories. How might you project sales for this year? Apply the current sales **% change** trend in these categories (Table 3.1).

TABLE 3.1. CHARMIN BATHROOM TISSUE: CURRENTLY SALES ARE INCREASING BY 2.5 PERCENT			
Last Year Sales		**This Year Projected Sales**	
Units/Month	**Retail $ Sales**	**Units/Month**	**Retail $ Sales**
120/Jan.	$360	___/Jan	$ ___
183/Feb.	$549	___/Feb	$ ___
50/Mar.*	$150	___/Mar	$ ___

*Out of stock March 12: How does the year projection change based on the early stock out?

Currently sales are increasing by 12 percent; last year, they were increasing by 30 percent over the prior year. Apply a % change formula to project sales for this year (see Table 3.2).

TABLE 3.2. WOMEN'S FASHION TANK TOPS			
Last Year Sales		**This Year Projected Sales**	
Units/Month	**Retail $ Sales**	**Units/Month**	**Retail $ Sales**
100/Jan.	$2400	___/Jan	$ ___
217/Feb.	$5208	___/Feb	$ ___
635/Mar.	$15,240	___/Mar	$ ___

These two examples are simple and straightforward. Now focus on a fashion business that might require more thought. Look more closely at those tank

26 A BUYER'S LIFE

tops. This year the tank is updated with a small V-neck and has a contrast trim (except on white and black tanks) and costs $2 more at retail. In addition, the colors are not the same. Using your trend knowledge in fashion and historical data, make a sales projection (Table 3.3).

TABLE 3.3. LAST YEAR SALES: 952 UNITS AT $24 EACH = TOTAL SALES $22,848 ($22.8)				
Basic Tank—$24		**NEW UPDATED TANK with Contrast—$26**		
Last Year Sales by Color		**Project This Year Sales**		
White	381	White (self trim)		_____
Yellow	58	Black (self trim)		_____
Brown	72	Brown/lt. blue		_____
Pink	159	Pink/lime		_____
Red	95	Red/navy		_____
Purple	17	Orange/navy		_____
Black	35	Lime/yellow		_____
Navy	103			
Pale Blue	32			
Total Sales	$22.8	Total Sales	$	_____
Total Units	952	Total Units		_____

Follow the thought process:

1. Identify which SKUs from last year are the same as last year.
2. Identify which SKUs are most like the SKUs from last year.
3. Identify which SKUs are new trend color options.
4. Identify which SKUs are old and maybe no longer viable for purchase.
5. Use the history to project the future.

SEARCH THE NET
WWW.PANTONE.COM

It's relatively simple to name the current color trends, but what about predicting the future? Trend and color forecasters track trends and predict future trends. Research the Internet for current trend forecasting. What colors are up and coming, and what colors are on the way out?

HOLIDAY/EVENT SHIFTS

Some things may seem to stay the same, but they often do change. Take, for example, the traditional holiday shopping season. In the United States, Thanksgiving (the unofficial start of holiday shopping) falls on the fourth Thursday in November. The actual date varies each year. Thanksgiving begins the countdown to Christmas, which is always on December 25. Depending on when Thanksgiving falls, there can be from 25 to 32 "shopping days" until Christmas. These **holiday shifts** can greatly affect sales trends.

What other holiday shifts affect business?

Event shifts are another factor in projecting sales. The obvious example is the "After Thanksgiving Sale." If the Thanksgiving holiday shifts, so too will the corresponding sale. Consider other factors that shift sale events. In today's retail market, the players are changing every day. When one company buys another company, the parent company implements its sales strategy and eliminates the previous company's strategy. In doing so, the acquiring company must reeducate the customer. The reeducation process can take months or even years. The buyer must plan for the shift in events and project sales based on historical data and analysis.

APPLICATION

With the foregoing understanding of top-down and bottom-up sales planning, the next step is to develop a **six-month plan**. In this section you will calculate (1) a six-month sales plan and (2) a six-month sales plan with a holiday shift.

CALCULATING A SIX-MONTH PLAN

Apply the sales projection to the six-month sales plan using Excel Spreadsheet 3-A. See Appendix B for full-size versions of all Excel Spreadsheets, which can be pulled from the book and worked on separately.

1. Follow the step-by-step process:
   a. Last year sales: Add each month and enter the total sales—$332.0.
   b. Last year percentage sales by month: Calculate the total sales for each month as a percentage of the total season's sales.

   Feb.: $15.0 ÷ $332.0 = 4.5%
   Mar.: $22.0 ÷ $332.0 = 6.6%
   April: $40.0 ÷ $332.0 = 12%
   May: $75.0 ÷ $332.0 = 22.6%
   June: $95.0 ÷ $332.0 = 28.6%
   July: $85.0 ÷ $332.0 = 25.6%

2. Check your work:
   a. Add the percentages: 4.5% + 6.6% + 12% + 22.6% + 28.6% + 25.6% = 99.9%.
   b. Adjust the last month to 25.7 percent; the percentages should now equal 100 percent.

3. Now apply the percentages to Plan—This Year.

4. Calculate the total season sales: Last year total + 12.3% increase = $372.8.

5. Apply the monthly percentages to the total, and enter the monthly sales.

   Feb: $372.8 × 4.5% = $16.8
   Mar: $372.8 × 6.6% = $24.6
   April: $372.8 × 12% = $44.7
   May: $372.8 × 22.6% = $84.3
   June: $372.8 × 28.6% = $106.6
   July: $372.8 × 25.7% = $95.8

6. Add the total sales: $16.8 + $24.6 + $44.7 + $84.3 + $106.6 + $95.8
   = $372.8 (see Excel Spreadsheet 3-A).

   Your Turn

   In class: Excel Spreadsheets 3-B, 3-C.
   Complete the sales plan based on the percentage change shown.

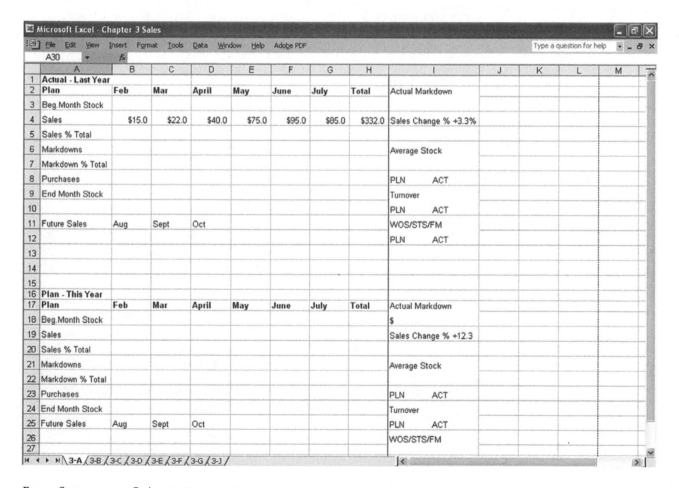

EXCEL SPREADSHEET 3-A Application with examples: Sales without holiday shift.

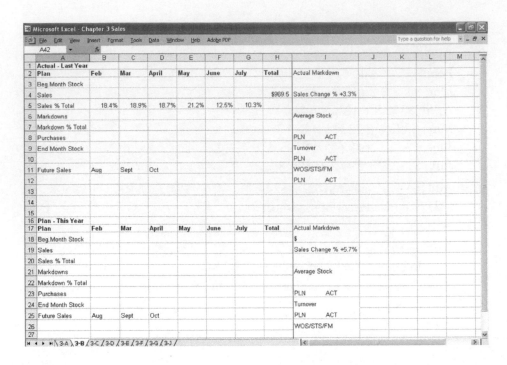

EXCEL SPREADSHEET 3-B Application: Sales without holiday shift.

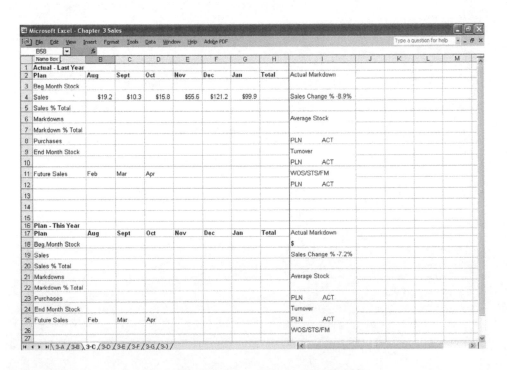

EXCEL SPREADSHEET 3-C Application: Sales without holiday shift.

A BUYER'S LIFE

Complete Excel Spreadsheets 3-F and 3-G for homework.

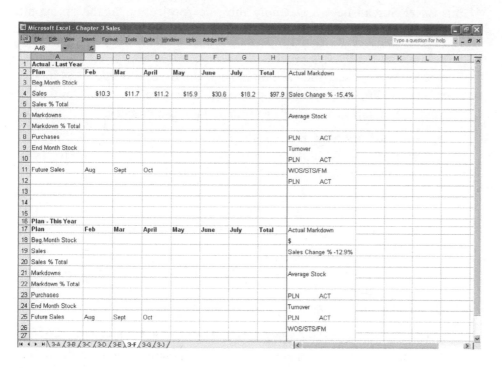

EXCEL SPREADSHEET 3-F Homework: Sales.

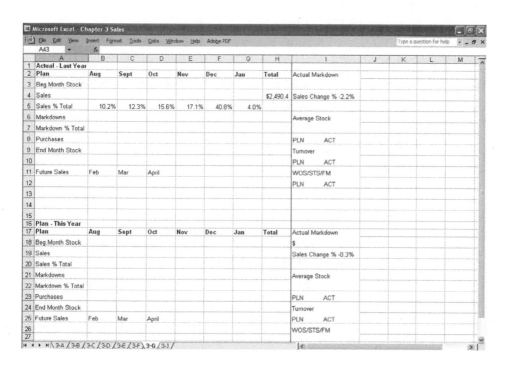

EXCEL SPREADSHEET 3-G Homework: Sales.

CALCULATING A SIX-MONTH PLAN WITH A HOLIDAY SHIFT

Using Excel Spreadsheet 3-D, apply the sales projection to the six-month sales plan.

1. Follow the step-by-step process:
   a. Last year sales: Add each month and enter the total sales—$456.8.
   b. Last year percentage sales by month: Calculate the total sales for each month as a percentage of the total season's sales.

   Aug: $27.5 ÷ $456.8 = 6.0%
   Sept: $38.2 ÷ $456.8 = 8.4%
   Oct: $41.1 ÷ $456.8 = 9.0%
   Nov: $73.6 ÷ $456.8 = 16.1%
   Dec: $255.5 ÷ $456.8 = 55.9%
   Jan: $20.9 ÷ $456.8 = 4.6%

2. Check your work:
   a. Add the percentages: 6.0% + 8.4% + 9% + 16.1% + 55.9% + 4.6% = 100%.
   b. Now apply the percentages to Plan—This Year.

3. Calculate the total season sales: Last year total + 4.2% increase = $476.0.

4. Apply the monthly percentages to the total, and enter the monthly sales.

   Aug: $476.0 × 6.0% = $28.6
   Sept: $476.0 × 8.4% = $40.0
   Oct: $476.0 × 9.0% = $42.8
   Nov: $476.0 × 16.1% = $76.6
   Dec: $476.0 × 55.9% = $266.1
   Jan: $476.0 × 21.9% = $21.9

5. Add the total sales: $28.6 + $40.0 + $42.8 + $76.6 + $266.1 + $21.9 = $476.0.

6. Last year Thanksgiving occurred in November week 3. This year Thanksgiving occurs in November week 4.
   a. Determine that last year sales were as follows:

   Week 1: 15%
   Week 2: 15%
   Week 3: 40%
   Week 4: 30%
   ——————
   100%

   b. Reapply the percentages for sales this year:

   Week 1: 15%
   Week 2: 15%
   Week 3: 15%
   Week 4: 40%
   ——————
   85%

   The remaining 15 percent can be attributed to Thanksgiving holiday sales.

7. Multiply 15 percent by the total month, and shift $11.0 into December.

8. Make the necessary changes on the plan this year by removing $11.0 from November and placing it into December.

9. Recalculate and apply the percentage to total monthly breakdowns for this year to the total season. (Refer to Spreadsheet 3-D.)

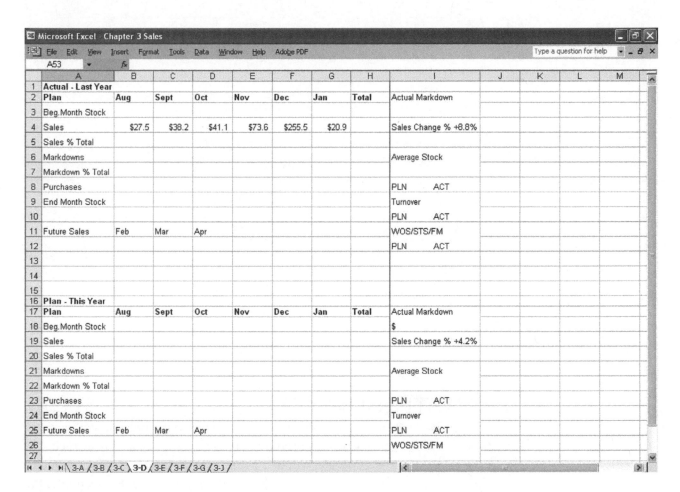

EXCEL SPREADSHEET 3-D Application with examples: Sales with holiday shift.

Your Turn

Use Excel Spreadsheet 3-E.

The After Easter Sale has a holiday/event shift from March to April.

The sale represents 14 percent of last year sales.

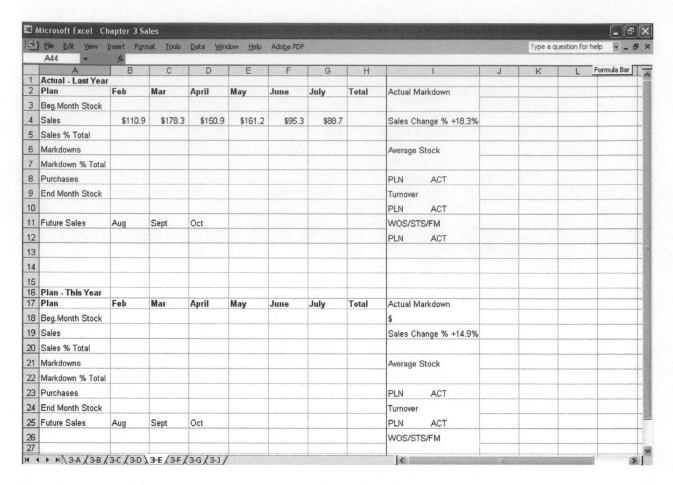

The spreadsheet shows:

	A	B	C	D	E	F	G	H	I
1	**Actual - Last Year**								
2	**Plan**	**Feb**	**Mar**	**April**	**May**	**June**	**July**	**Total**	Actual Markdown
3	Beg.Month Stock								
4	Sales	$110.9	$178.3	$150.9	$161.2	$95.3	$88.7		Sales Change % +18.3%
5	Sales % Total								
6	Markdowns								Average Stock
7	Markdown % Total								
8	Purchases								PLN ACT
9	End Month Stock								Turnover
10									PLN ACT
11	Future Sales	Aug	Sept	Oct					WOS/STS/FM
12									PLN ACT
13									
14									
15									
16	**Plan - This Year**								
17	**Plan**	**Feb**	**Mar**	**April**	**May**	**June**	**July**	**Total**	Actual Markdown
18	Beg.Month Stock								$
19	Sales								Sales Change % +14.9%
20	Sales % Total								
21	Markdowns								Average Stock
22	Markdown % Total								
23	Purchases								PLN ACT
24	End Month Stock								Turnover
25	Future Sales	Aug	Sept	Oct					PLN ACT
26									WOS/STS/FM
27									

EXCEL SPREADSHEET 3-E Application: Sales with holiday shift.

CREATE IT IN EXCEL!

Throughout this text, each chapter will conclude with a single plan that will be built upon using each step as it is learned. The practice plan will be a jewelry department and will be noted by the chapter number followed by the letter *J*. For example, this chapter will be 3J. To gain comfort using Excel, the following instructions will provide a step-by-step setup that can be used for the J plan and for all worksheets in this text.

Begin by creating an Excel grid worksheet that will become your template.

Open Excel and save the file to a mobile media storage device.

Save the file as Jewelry Sample Plan.

Once the spreadsheet is set up, copy and paste the template to as many tabs as needed.

There are many possible ways of organizing Excel spreadsheets. For the purposes of this class, it is recommended that you create new files for each chapter and name them by the chapter name—Chapter 3, Chapter 4, and so on. Each tab within the worksheet can be named based on the worksheet number, such as 3-1, 3-2, etc.

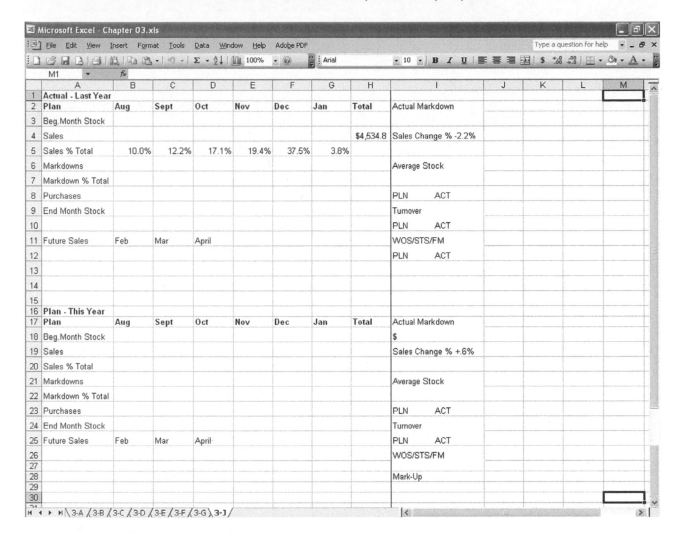

EXCEL SPREADSHEET 3-J Homework: Sales.

ENTERING SALES FORMULAS FOR LAST YEAR WHEN MONTHLY SALES ARE KNOWN

Using the sample plan J, complete the Excel spreadsheet as follows:

To enter sales formulas when monthly sales are known and percentages are unknown, follow these steps:

1. Manually enter the sales in each month on the Sales line.

2. Sum across the Sales line, ending with the total.

3. B4:H4 click Σ (AutoSum).

4. Using the total sales plan, enter the formula to calculate the percentage of sales by month.

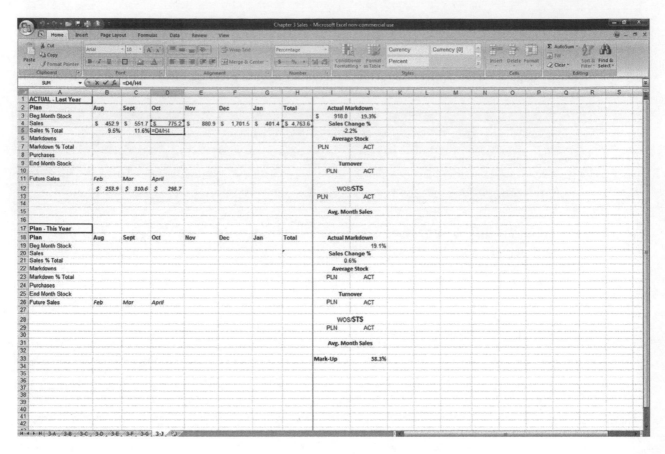

FIGURE 3.2 Sales % to Total.

5. Place your cursor in the cell for the first month sales percentage line.

   Cursor in B5: = B4/H4 *enter*

   Cursor in C5: = C4/H4 *enter*

   Cursor in D5: = D4/H4 *enter*

   a. Continue until each month has been entered.

   b. Sum across to ensure that the entries total 100 percent.

ENTERING SALES FORMULAS TO CALCULATE THIS YEAR

1. Place your cursor in the total season sales this year (cell H19) and enter the following formula:

   Cell H20: =H4+(H4*0.6%) *enter*

2. Enter the formula for calculating sales for each month. Place your cursor in cell B20.

   Cursor in B20: =H20*B21 *enter*

   Cursor in C20: =H20*C21 *enter*

   Cursor in D20: =H20*D21 *enter*

   Continue until each month has been entered.

   Note: Once the formula is entered, you may need to click on the % button and convert to the appropriate decimal placement.

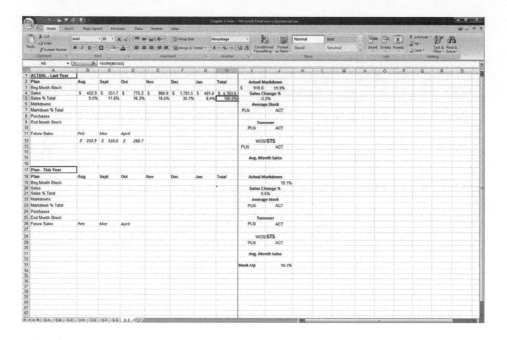

FIGURE 3.3 Sales % by Month = 100% Total.

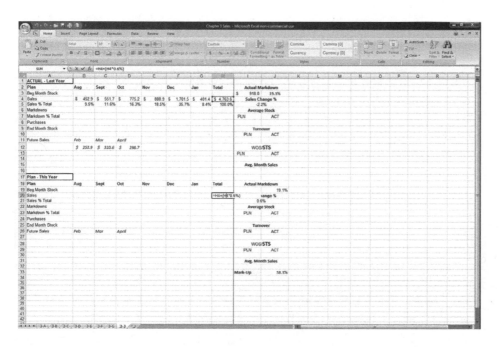

FIGURE 3.4 Sales % Change Total Season.

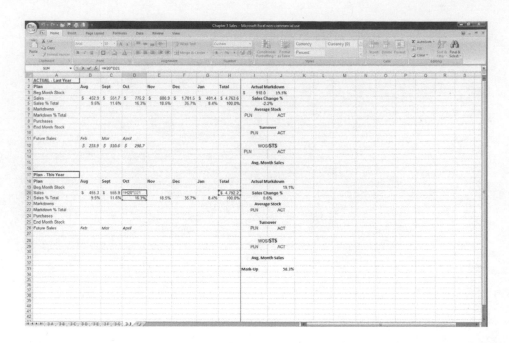

FIGURE 3.5 Sales Multiplied by Month %.

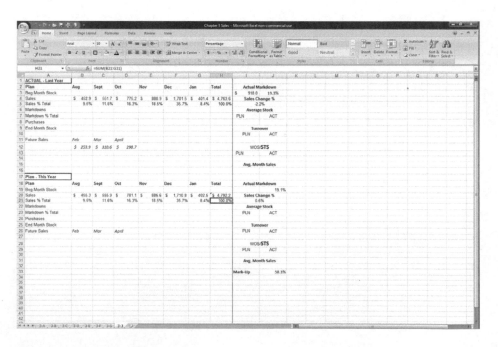

FIGURE 3.6 Total Season Sales.

A BUYER'S LIFE

TERMINOLOGY

4-5-4 or 4-4-5: Refers to the fiscal calendar. The year is broken down into complete weeks, Sunday through Saturday. The numbers refer to the number of weeks in the given month.

% change: The percentage change from one season (spring to spring) or month (May to May) to the next.

% total: The percentage that one month represents to the total season.

bottom up: A planning process that operates in the opposite direction of the top-down approach whereby the plan begins with the buyer and works up to the CEO.

holiday/event shift: The shift in business when a holiday or major storewide event moves from one fiscal month into another.

sales: An amount reflecting the retail price that consumers pay for the merchandise they receive.

sales total: The total sales for a period of time. For the purposes of this text it is usually all six months of a season.

six-month plan: Refers to the process and variables of business planning for a period of time, usually January through June or July through December.

top down: A planning process that begins with the chief executive officer (CEO) or board of directors.

trend: A tendency displayed in the areas of fashion, lifestyle, or statistics.

FORMULAS

Total Sales $ = $ Month 1 + $ Month 2 + $ Month 3 + $ Month 4 + $ Month 5 + $ Month 6

e.g., $396.4 (Spring) = $38.2 (J) + $46.7 (F) + $55.8 (M) + $82.9 (A) + $122.6 (M) + 50.2 (J)

Sales Change % = This Year $ Sales ÷ Last Year $ Sales

e.g., + 6.3% (106.3%) = $396.4 ÷ $372.9

−9.1% (90.9%) = 396.4 ÷ 435.9

This Year $ Sales Plan = Last Year $ Sales + % Change Plan

e.g., $396.4 = $372.9 + 6.3%

Month Sales % Total = $ Month Sales ÷ $ Total Sales

e.g., 9.6% = $38.2 ÷ $396.4

Month $ Sales = Total Sales $ × Month Sales % Total

e.g., $55.8 = $396.4 × 14.0%

4

MARKDOWNS

Retail pricing strategies will always involve some form of **markdown.** The reasons for this vary, and they can be due to many factors. In general, markdowns are the result of slow sales performance. This could be the result of **poor planning or timing**, lack of understanding **customer preferences**, changes in **trend cycles, seasonality,** weather, **economic factors,** or **regional trends or events.** Some of these factors can be minimized, but it is virtually impossible for the buyer to make product selections that have optimal sales performance 100 percent of the time. Depending on the reason for slow-selling products, buyers will make decisions on how best to eliminate the unproductive inventory while maintaining financial objectives.

This chapter considers the various types of markdowns that can be implemented and discusses how they are projected into the six-month plan. Some buyers will use a top-down process; others use the bottom-up process. Generally, large retail structures use the top-down method and smaller retailers use bottom-up. Regardless of which process is in place, buyers need to understand and analyze all markdown types. With an understanding of markdown types, causes, and solutions, the buyer can begin to formulate a cohesive plan for the six-month season.

SLOW SELLERS

The first and most formidable markdown category is **slow-seller** markdowns, or **aging markdowns.** These markdowns are reactive in nature because they are in response to business trends not predicted by the buyer. Often these are the largest portion of buyer markdowns, particularly in end-of-season selling months. Slow seller **permanent markdowns** are generally in-season products, while aging markdowns tend to be late-season or even out-of-season products that have aged. A reasonable time frame for slow-seller apparel products is no longer than six weeks with dismal sales results.

Some basic products, such as housewares, may remain in inventory for six months or longer without being considered slow sellers. The reason for this is that the product has little or no change. The difference between apparel and housewares may seem dramatic—and, in fact, it is. Regardless of the product, buyers need to have a keen sense of all inventories and their subsequent age. Slow-seller markdowns can be broken down into further categories as described in the following sections.

PROMOTIONAL MARKDOWNS AT POINT-OF-SALE

A second form of markdown is known as a **promotional markdown**. These markdowns can take multiple forms and tend to have a POS format. The most common form of permanent markdown occurs when specific products are put on sale at specific times of the year. Unlike slow-selling POS markdowns, promotional markdowns occur regularly and are often planned in partnership with vendor suppliers. Markdowns in partnership are achieved through a balance of building relationships and **vendor negotiation** (this topic is covered in Chapter 13).

Increasing pre-season awareness and reliance on annual events also are considered promotional markdowns. Some examples of promotional markdowns include storewide anniversary events, storewide credit card holder events, white sales, or back-to-school sales. The primary difference between a slow-seller POS markdown and a promotional markdown is that slow-seller POS markdowns vary in their offerings. Promotional markdowns, however, are typically presented annually, and the inventory is specifically purchased for the promotional event. One might consider this approach to be a proactive, business-driving markdown.

Point-of-sale (POS) markdowns are temporary price reductions taken at the cash register upon checkout (the point of sale). This form of markdown is often used to give an early or midseason boost to sales. Examples can usually be seen on holiday weekend sales such as Memorial Day or Veterans Day. POS markdowns generally range from 25 to 40 percent off. POS markdowns are also used for planned promotions when merchandise was purchased at a special price and the subsequent savings is passed along to the consumer. These special purchase types of markdowns are also intended for special events.

POS markdowns, though effective, are used for only a short period of time—usually 1 to 5 days—with a specific start and end date. Some POS markdowns can run as long as 14 days; those markdowns are discussed later in this chapter.

Through the use of technology and the Internet, two new forms of POS markdowns have emerged. Using sophisticated POS technology, buyers are able to implement localized markdown strategies that boost sales and profit. Localized markdowns were piloted in the early 2000s and have grown over the years. Buyers are able to markdown specific products in one location but not another or take deeper markdown reductions in one location versus another. It is possible to have two stores a mile apart and offer the same merchandise but at differing prices. This strategy allows the buyer to sell at prices the consumer is willing to pay by location.

Internet markdowns are another means to increase sales of slow-selling inventory. Such sales can take two forms. One uses technology through the Internet to entice buyers to add on to their purchase. For example, when purchasing a basic crew neck T-shirt in one color, the customer might receive a prompt that if they buy two or three they will receive a discount. This technology in the Internet is targeted at discounting overstocked colors or sizes and can benefit both retailer and consumer. Another form is known as a private, or member, sale event. These sale events are offered to registered consumers and may last for as little as 4 hours or as long as 36 hours. Such events might include specific merchandise on sale, promotional products with purchase, or shipping incentives. Each of these strategies is aimed at leveraging technology to boost profit and sales.

Permanent Markdowns or Clearance Markdowns

Permanent markdowns are long-term markdowns. Retailers use this form of markdown when POS markdowns are no longer effective. Some say taking this type of markdown is like throwing a rock off a cliff—once it is marked down, it must continue on a markdown cycle until the inventory is 100 percent sold out. Permanent markdowns generally follow a **markdown cadence**, such as going from 25 percent to 40 percent to 75 percent off; or from 40 percent to 75 percent off. Following a specific markdown cadence varies by product and by retailer. The idea is to sell the most amount of inventory at the first markdown price.

Some products or particularly slow-selling products do not **sell through** (that is, sell out) until they are at a very low price. Sell-through is the percentage of inventory sold over a specified period of time. If 200 units of a product arrive in store on September 5, and 78 units are sold in two weeks, the sell-through is 39 percent. This sell through would be considered strong. Product with slower sell-throughs tend to be those with great size variability or products having excessive inventory based on demand. When customer demand is low, the buyer takes action by initiating a markdown to stimulate sales. Sometimes customers react to such products at the first markdown, while other times they wait for a lower price rather than feeling an urgency to buy now. While some products require one markdown, others may require two or three markdowns in the cycle to achieve the acceptable sell-through. Products that sell through with one markdown tend to be un-sized items, typically begin with lower inventory levels, or rarely go on sale. When customers see these items on sale, they react quickly. They feel an urgency to buy because they realize the products will go quickly and they want to take advantage of this sale opportunity.

OTHER MARKDOWNS

There are additional forms of markdowns to be addressed. These markdowns have less impact, but they must be planned for within the buyer's monthly and seasonal planning process. These markdowns include **employee discount, shortage, damaged and defective inventory**, and **competitive price matching**.

For large corporate retailers, these price-reduction impacts may be planned for within their own financial planning programs or as line items. Another mechanism for capturing these types of markdowns is through internal accounting practices. Regardless of how miscellaneous markdowns are accounted for, the buyer is responsible for understanding each type and for working them into the season plan. For small retail operations, it is important to plan for these markdowns within the overall markdown category, as doing so will affect overall performance. For example, if theft is high and inventory shortages are increasing, the impact on sales will be profound. If inventory is depleted by theft, and the buyer has not accounted for the possibility of that theft, inventory will be reduced and sales will suffer. By planning and budgeting for these inventory reductions each month, the buyer will have a more accurate accounting of inventory available for sale.

Once the markdown categories have been identified, the buyer can begin to plan for future markdowns. Historical data and anticipation of future needs are both necessary factors in proper allocation of markdown dollars. Beginning with historical data is an ideal starting point. Analyzing the actual results from the prior year and/or season gives the buyer a starting point that will indicate plans for the current season. The buyer adjusts these numbers based on any non-statistical information available. For example, a boutique owner may have a new employee who tends to buy more than most employees, the employee discount rate will increase. Conversely, if historical data suggests large amounts of competitive markdowns from one competitor, and that competitor has changed its strategy or is no longer a competitor, markdowns will be reduced.

A general framework for projecting markdowns begins with percentage or dollar calculations. These calculations should be viewed from last year and be modified for this year. Large-store buyers will typically apply these values as percentages; small, single-store buyers are more likely to use dollars. Complete the simple framework for reviewing markdowns. Calculating markdowns by type can change from year to year. To gain a better understanding of how markdowns are spent, the buyer can review each markdown type either by percentage or dollar amount. The following exercise includes last year actual markdowns and projections for this year markdowns. Calculate the percentages for this year.

EXERCISE 4.1

1. Calculate the total markdowns for this year.
2. Calculate the percentage by type for this year.

Month: _____

TYPE	Last Year $	Last Year %	This Year $	This Year %
POS	$12.2	24.0%	$12.5	
Permanent	$25.6	50.4%	$18.5	
Promotional	$4.3	8.5%	$8.5	
Employee discount	$2.6	5.1%	$2.6	
Shortage	$4.1	8.1%	$4.1	
Damaged/defective	$1.5	2.9%	$1.5	
Competition	$.5	1%	$1.0	
TOTAL	$50.8	100%		

DISCUSSION

How does this year's total compare to last year's? What would cause these markdown dollars to change in this plan? What would this plan look like if 15 percent less of the total markdown dollars were available?

Once the buyer has carefully reviewed the monthly detail, he or she is ready to begin developing the total monthly plan. The monthly plan is formulated by applying percentages that are based on sales. Because markdowns are directly linked to sales, they are planned as a percentage of sales, thus ensuring profitability. If sales increase, markdowns can increase. When prior year profit margins are lower than necessary, buyers may need to decrease markdown plans, which will result in higher profits. Following the same logic, if sales decrease, markdowns must follow suit. As with promotional markdowns, another method of reducing **markdown liabilities** is through vendor markdown assistance. While this strategy can be beneficial, negotiation strategies must be carefully planned to anticipate both risks and benefits for the continued health of the business.

Calculate the markdown percentage by month.

Month	Markdown $	Markdown % Total
Aug	$15.8	
Sept	$18.3	
Oct	$16.9	
Nov	$22.2	
Dec	$90.3	
Jan	$22.3	
TOTAL		

DISCUSSION

1. What markdowns types are likely being used in August? Why?

2. Project a possible scenario for December and January using all markdown types.

3. If December markdowns were reduced to $30.5, what type of business might this be?

APPLICATION

In this section, you will (1) develop a six-month markdown plan and (2) create a markdown plan. Markdowns follow a similar process as sales, which were calculated in Chapter 3.

CALCULATING A SIX-MONTH PLAN

Excel Spreadsheet 4-A presents last year sales and markdown dollars as well as this year markdown dollars. See Appendix B for full-size versions of all Excel Spreadsheets, which can be pulled from the book and worked on separately.

1. Follow the step-by-step markdown process:

2. Use the process of projecting sales from Chapter 3. Based on the information given, complete the last year and this year sales total, monthly sales, monthly percent to total, and percent change in last year sales.

3. Calculate markdowns.

   a. Last year percentage markdowns by month: Calculate the percent to total markdowns that each month represents to the total season's markdowns.

Feb:	$8.3 ÷ $92.3 = 9.0%
Mar:	$15.2 ÷ $92.3 = 16.5%
April:	$9.6 ÷ $92.3 = 10.4%
May:	$28.3 ÷ $92.3 = 30.7%
June:	$18.4 ÷ $92.3 = 19.9%
July:	$12.5 ÷ $92.3 = 13.5%

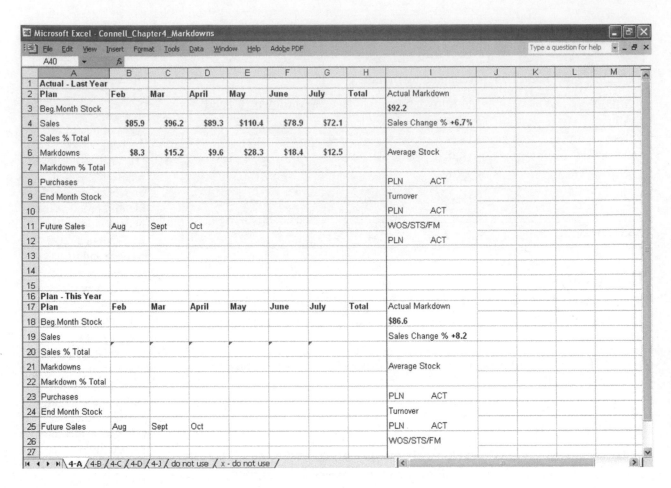

EXCEL SPREADSHEET 4-A Application: Markdowns LY, $ Known.

4. Check your work:
   a. Add the percentages: 9.0% + 16.5% + 10.4% + 30.7% + 19.9% + 13.5% = 100%.
   b. Now apply the percentages to Plan—This Year.
   c. Total season markdown dollars = $86.6.

5. Apply the monthly markdown percentages to the total markdown dollars, and enter the monthly markdowns.

   Feb: $86.6 × 9.0% = $7.8
   Mar: $86.6 × 16.5% = $14.3
   April: $86.6 × 10.4% = $9.0
   May: $86.6 × 30.7% = $26.6
   June: $86.6 × 19.9% = $17.3
   July: $86.6 × 13.5% = $11.7

6. Add the total markdowns: $7.8 + $14.3 + $9.0 + $26.6 + $17.3 + $11.7 = $86.6.

7. Calculate the season total markdowns percentage to total: $86.6 / $576.5 = 15.0%.

Your Turn

In class: Excel Spreadsheets 4-B and 4-C.

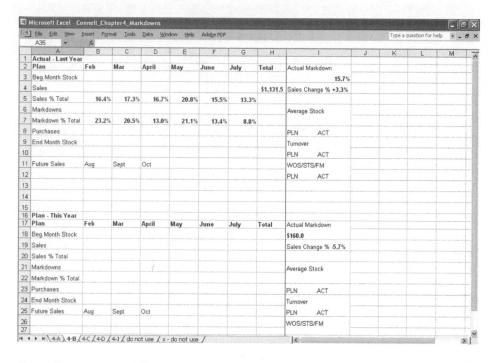

EXCEL SPREADSHEET 4-B Application: Markdowns LY, % Known.

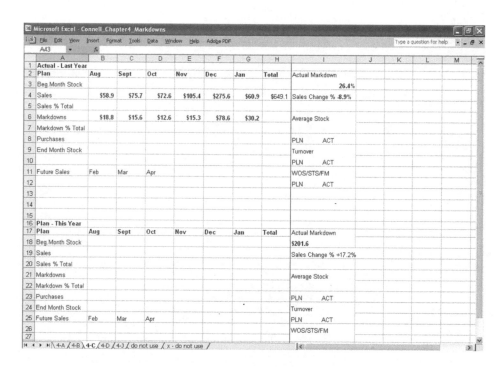

EXCEL SPREADSHEET 4-C Application: Markdowns LY, $ Known.

Complete Excel Spreadsheets 4-D and 4-E for homework.

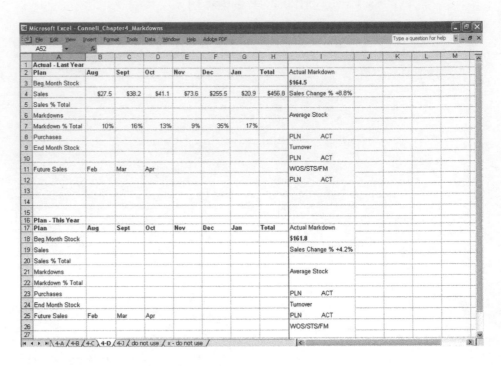

EXCEL SPREADSHEET 4-D Homework: Markdowns.

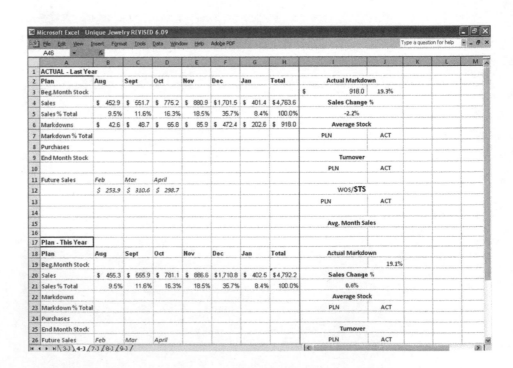

EXCEL SPREADSHEET 4-E Homework: Markdowns.

A BUYER'S LIFE

COMPLETE MARKDOWNS FOR THE JEWELRY DEPARTMENT EXAMPLE

Add the markdown process to the jewelry department sample problem.

In Chapter 3 you created a sales plan for a jewelry department. Using Excel Spreadsheet 4-E, apply the markdown concept to the plan from Chapter 3.

CREATE IT IN EXCEL!

Follow the template created in Chapter 3. There are two options for saving your file. Your file may be either saved as Chapter 4 Markdowns, or you can save it as a new tab, Chapter 4. This will allow you to keep each step separate and avoid confusion as the plan builds. At the end of the planning process, you will have a complete plan.

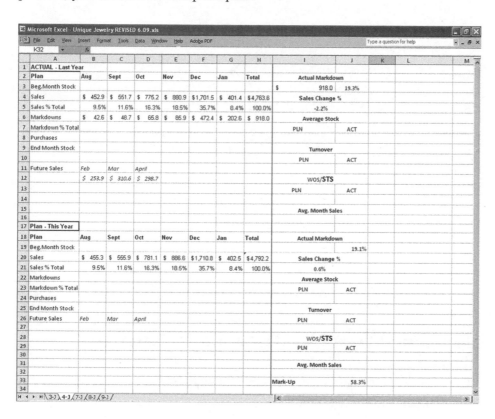

EXCEL SPREADSHEET 4-J.

ENTERING MARKDOWN FORMULAS FOR LAST YEAR WHEN MONTHLY MARKDOWNS ARE KNOWN

Using the sample plan 4-J, complete the Excel spreadsheet as follows:

To enter sales formulas when monthly markdowns are known and percentages are unknown, follow these steps:

1. Manually enter the markdowns in each month on the Markdown $ line.

2. Sum across the Markdown $ line, ending with the total.

3. B6:H6 click Σ

4. Using the total Markdown $, enter the formula to calculate the percentage of markdowns by month.

5. Place your cursor in the cell for the first markdown percentage month line.

    Cursor in B7: = B6/H6 *enter*

    Cursor in C7: = C6/H6 *enter*

    Cursor in D7: = D6/H6 *enter*

    a. Continue until each month has been entered.

    b. Sum across to ensure that the entries total 100 percent.

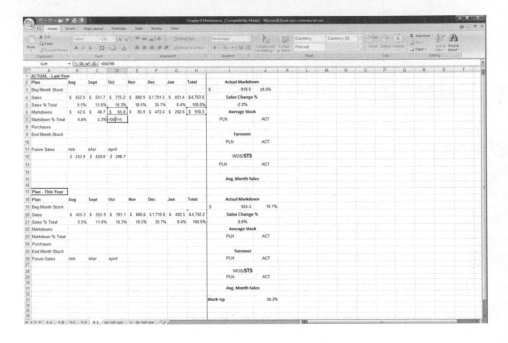

FIGURE 4.1 Calculating Markdowns Monthly % to Total.

ENTERING MARKDOWN FORMULAS TO CALCULATE THIS YEAR

1. Place your cursor in the total season markdown $ this year (cell H21) and enter the following formula:

    =(H20*J19) *enter*

2. Enter the formula for calculating markdowns for each month. Place your cursor in cell B21.

    Cursor in B22: =J19*D7 *enter*

    Cursor in C22: =J19*C7 *enter*

    Cursor in D22: =J19*D7 *enter*

    Continue until each month has been entered.

    Continue by calculating the markdown percentage total for each month as was done earlier.

A BUYER'S LIFE

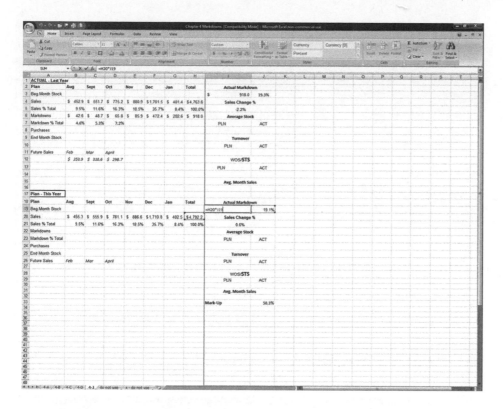

FIGURE 4.2 Calculating Total Markdown $ LY.

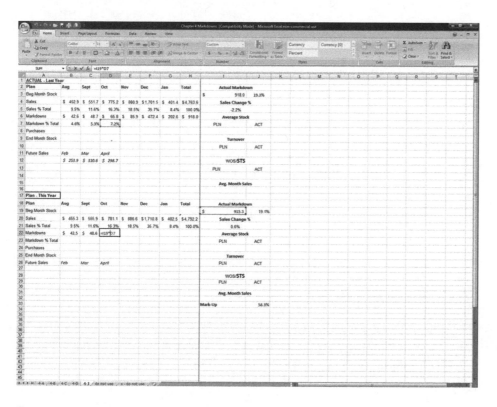

FIGURE 4.3 Calculating Markdowns Monthly $ TY.

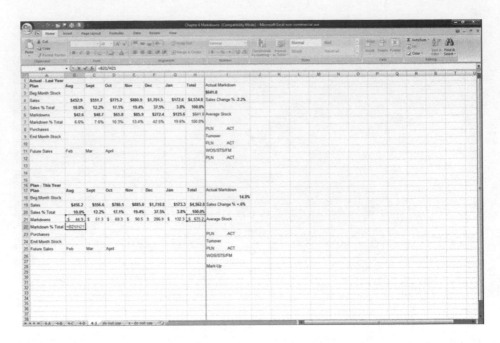

FIGURE 4.4 Applying Percentage.

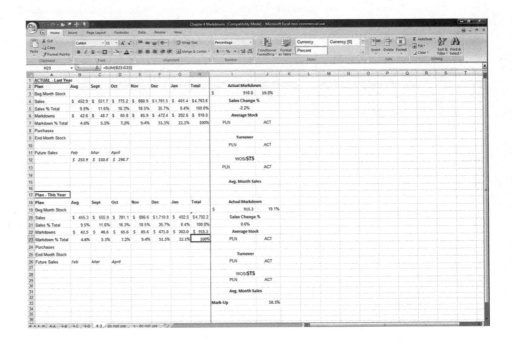

FIGURE 4.5 Adjusting Decimal.

Note: Once the formula is entered, you may need to click on the % key and convert to the appropriate decimal placement.

A BUYER'S LIFE

TERMINOLOGY

aging inventory: A product that is usually three months or older and is no longer viable.

competitive price matching: The reduction of price, usually through a point-of-sale markdown, to meet a competitor price.

customer preference: What customers want, when they want it, and at what price they want it.

damaged and defective: The reduction of inventory dollars based on product that can no longer be sold and is either physically given away to charity or destroyed.

economic factors: Issues of the overall economy such as unemployment and inflation that affect a consumer's confidence related to purchases they make.

employee discount: A reduction in price taken for employee purchases.

markdown: any reduction of the original retail price.

markdown cadence: The rate at which markdowns are implemented and the relationship to sell-through.

markdown liabilities: The total of inventory categories not meeting sales expectations; in the broadest terms, all inventory is a liability.

permanent markdown: Markdowns that are permanently reduced and will incur further reductions until the product is gone.

poor planning/timing: May be related to delayed shipment, goods being ordered too late, or goods being ordered too early; one cause of markdowns.

POS markdown: Point-of-sale markdowns; temporary reductions in price, taken at the cash register during checkout, that will return to regular full price after a specified number of days.

promotional markdown: A price reduction processed as a POS markdown but categorized as a consistent markdown by year, month, or season.

regional trends or events: Specific events such as weather, or the politics within a city or region, that affect product and pricing.

seasonality: Factor describing the trend that some products that have a limited season for selling, particularly products intended for use in cold or hot weather.

sell-through: Amount of product or inventory sold, expressed as a percentage sold through from the original amount received.

shortage: The manually calculated reduction of inventory dollars based on anticipated theft or paperwork errors. Upon completion of a physical inventory, usually once per year, shortage dollars are permanently removed from stock dollars.

slow seller: A product that is not meeting sell-through expectations. This product is typically in the inventory for up to 3 months without significant sell-through.

trend cycles: The product life-cycle stage based on customer preferences.

vendor negotiation: Working with vendors and suppliers either preseason, midseason, or postseason to strategize financial partnerships that may include assisting with the costs of marking down inventory.

FORMULAS

Total Markdown $ = $ Month 1 + $ Month 2 + $ Month 3 + $ Month 4 + $ Month 5 + $ Month 6

e.g., $92.3 (spring) = $12.5 (J) + $15.8 (F) + $27.3 (M) + $15.9 (A) + $10.6 (M) + $10.2 (J)

Monthly Markdown % Total = $ Markdown Month ÷ $ Markdown Total Season

e.g., 13.5% = $12.5 (J) ÷ $92.3 (Spring)

Season Markdown % Total = $ Markdown Total Season ÷ $ Sales Total Season

e.g., 16.0% = $92. ÷ $576.3

5

STOCK LEVELS: CAPACITY, STABILITY, AND PROFIT = AVERAGE STOCK

All retail business planning begins with projected retail sales. Buyers cannot begin to plan inventory until retail sales are established. This concept may seem elementary, yet buyers can fall into alternative methods that negate careful financial planning. While defining the differences between electronic booked inventory and physical inventory, this chapter discusses the many variables affecting inventory levels and cautions buyers against alternative methods relying on instinct rather than analytical data.

WHAT IS INVENTORY?

Consumers view inventory as the products they see on the selling floor in a retail environment. Buyers have a different view, one that is more widely encompassing. For the buyer, **inventory** is any dollar amount **booked** to the financial budget. Booked inventory is the dollar amount that has been charged, usually electronically, to the buyer's budget or account. For example, think of consumers who write checks from a checking account. They write the check and note it in their transaction register, but the check is not booked until it is registered with the consumer's bank. Likewise, a buyer may purchase inventory at market, but the inventory is not booked until the vendor processes the invoice and transmits the invoice to the retailer.

Moving on from the broad definition of *inventory*, there are specific timing issues of inventory to be considered. Some inventory is invisible, although most inventory is visible in the retail store.

INVISIBLE INVENTORY

Invisible inventory is not physically present but has been booked into the budget. Categories of invisible inventory involve timing and include the following:

- Electronic inventory
- Shortage inventory (physical and paperwork)
- Repair inventory
- Transfer inventory

ELECTRONIC INVENTORY

Electronic inventory refers to the dollar value of inventory that is in transit or not physically present in the retail store. Electronic inventory is prevalent in large-store environments but may be nonexistent in small, single-unit environments.

Since the advent of **electronic data interchange (EDI)**, vendor computer systems and retailer computer systems have the ability to exchange information without physical interaction. Typically, retailers pay the freight costs of goods and thus take ownership of the goods when they leave the vendor. For this reason, the inventory is charged or booked to the retailer's inventory once it leaves the vendor's door. This is done via EDI. Therefore, a buyer's dollar amount of inventory reflects electronic inventory that may not be physically present but is in transit from the vendor. Again, this practice is commonplace among large retailers but much less likely with small, single-unit, independent store owners. As technology improves and becomes more cost effective, it is conceivable that independent retailers will have EDI capabilities in the near future.

SHORTAGE INVENTORY

Chapter 4 discussed various methods to account for shortage. In this chapter shortage is reinforced as invisible inventory. **Shortage inventory** can take the form of shortage due to theft, paperwork, or human error. Inventory shortage is reconciled each time the physical inventory is counted. This is usually once or twice per year. Immediately following the physical inventory count, buyers can consider stock levels to be relatively accurate. However, with each week that passes, the stock levels become less accurate, and they are at their greatest level of inaccuracy just before the next physical inventory count.

It is often said that inventory shortage is one-third external theft, one-third internal theft, and one-third paperwork—meaning that two-thirds of inventory shortage is due to theft. Keeping a close eye on physical inventory and preventing situations that foster theft will reduce physical inventory shortage. Shortage inventory cannot be eliminated, but it can be deterred through policies and procedures. Paperwork and human error inventory shortages are generally preventable. Simple errors in calculations, data entry, and miscounts all contribute to paperwork and human error.

The use of technology has, in some cases, reduced paperwork error, but it has increased in other cases, thus resulting in a need to continue monitoring such errors. In conjunction with EDI systems, **Universal Product Codes (UPCs)** have improved inventory shortages via a quick swipe of a bar code. This technology has greatly reduced the element of human error—that is, of course, unless the UPC code is incorrect or will not scan. Employees who must manually enter information are more likely to be incorrect and result in shortage.

REPAIR INVENTORY

A third form of invisible inventory is **repair inventory**, which is booked and owned but may be out for repair. Sometimes inventory may need a minor repair, such as strengthening a seam or fixing a zipper, or even minor cleaning. Retail decision makers decide the cost versus benefit of classifying the item as damaged and not selling it or initiating a minor repair so the item can be sold at the full retail selling price. Large retailers may have in-house repair departments; smaller retailers may need to send inventory out for professional repair.

TRANSFER INVENTORY

The fourth and final form of invisible inventory is **transfer inventory**, which is product transferred between stores. High transportation costs have made this practice less common; however, it is still relevant. To maximize full-price selling activity, inventory may be moved between stores. When transfer inventory leaves one store en route to another, it is not physically in either store; however, it must be financially owned. Generally the inventory is financially owned by the sending store until it arrives at the receiving store. Once the inventory is received, its ownership is then transferred to the receiving store. Note this transfer of ownership is different from inventory that is being shipped from a vendor. Transfer inventory is owned by the retail store with accountability for ownership between locations within the retailer. Store policies vary with regard to when the actual ownership is booked into inventory.

VISIBLE INVENTORY

Visible inventory is any inventory that can be seen or touched within the retail store. Categories of visible inventory are much greater and easier to comprehend. Visible inventory categories include the following:

- Floor inventory
- Back-stock inventory
- Warehouse inventory
- Inventory on hold
- Damaged and defective inventory

Floor Inventory

Floor inventory, as the name implies, is any product that is physically on the selling floor. **Back-stock inventory** includes any product that is within the selling store but is not directly accessible to the customer. Any inventory being housed in a back stockroom is likely to be damaged, stolen, or forgotten. The challenges of meeting financial objectives, coupled with the high costs associated with real estate, are leading retailers to maximize their selling square footage. This goal has necessitated increasingly creative strategies for back-stocking excess colors and sizes. Store planning and visual merchandising have developed fixture displays that are both visually appealing and maximize storage.

Warehouse Inventory

Warehouse inventory typically consists of household goods, such as bridal registry items and other products, that are shipped directly to the customer. This type of visible inventory may not be physically in the retail store, but it is generally present at an alternative location and is available for sale. Warehouse inventory may be shipped either from a large distribution center or direct from the vendor.

Inventory on Hold

Inventory on hold refers to any item that has not been sold but was placed on hold for a potential customer. Many retailers have eliminated this costly service to customers. Analysis has shown that the vast majority of customers do not return to purchase the product. This results in lost sales to subsequent customers, who cannot locate a size or color because it is on hold for another customer.

Damaged and Defective Inventory

Damaged and defective inventory is any product that is physically and financially owned inventory but is unsalable. This form of inventory often sits in corners, drawers, and boxes within stockrooms or management offices. Because the inventory is not salable, it falls out of view and is often forgotten. For the buyer, this inventory remains within the total financial inventory, but it is unproductive due to its damaged or defective status.

When inventory is found to be defective, managers are responsible for notifying buyers or vendors immediately. If the product can be returned to the vendor or repaired, taking timely action is critical. On the other hand, inventory damaged by either store employees or customers is the responsibility of the store. Damaged inventory may be donated to charity or destroyed. Either method of disposition will result in reducing inventory both physically and financially. Removing damaged inventory from the store and from the financial budget makes available additional dollars for replacement products. When buyers and stores hold unproductive, damaged, or defective inventory for long periods of time, they are using precious dollars that would otherwise be spent on productive inventory.

INVENTORY PLANNING

With a full understanding of what constitutes inventory, the buyer can begin to consider how inventory is planned. A thorough analysis of the market is the first step in planning inventory. This may be done through two common marketing tools: SWOT analysis and PEST analysis. But first, this section considers alternative methods of inventory planning that are less analytical and may result in excessive inventory.

As mentioned at the start of this chapter, inventory planning revolves around sales planning. Buyers who stray from realistic sales projections must be aware of the risks involved. Inventory planning that relies on intuition, physical space allocation or constraints, fixture capacity, or following the competition is unrealistic. Small-store owners that lack the expertise or technological tools for more careful planning sometimes take this approach.

Intuitive practices are acceptable for individual purchasing decisions, but they should not be used to determine total inventory levels. Physical space allocation can also cause buyers trouble. Planning inventory based on the space available results in either too much or too little inventory. When space is excessive, buyers can find creative visual merchandising solutions that take advantage of space but have limited inventory expenditure. Conversely, when space is constrained, buyers may not purchase enough inventory to maximize a strong sales trend. Careful inventory flow management is essential to increase sales potential through regular and small inventory shipments. As with physical space issues, relying on fixture capacity can be misleading. Again, creative strategies or regular, small shipments can alleviate fixture capacity challenges (read more about fixture capacity later in this chapter).

Last, following the competition can also result in too much or too little inventory. Monitoring the competition is an important aspect of overall decision making. Buyers who periodically analyze their competitor's inventory positions will have a better understanding of both sales and inventory. Rather than merely looking at inventory, an appropriate analysis will highlight sales strengths and weaknesses.

SWOT Analysis

SWOT analysis refers to the process of calculating the strengths, weaknesses, opportunities, and threats existing in the market. Strengths and weaknesses are associated with internal factors; opportunities and threats signify external factors.

PEST Analysis

A further review is in the **PEST analysis**, which encompasses the political, environmental, social, and technological aspects of the market. During periods of economic turmoil or significant change, taking the time to identify PEST factors is prudent. Issues prevalent in a PEST analysis are external; however, they are important because the buyer has little or no control over these factors. Navigating through such times is possible only when a buyer acknowledges the issues and faces them with cautious decision making.

Other Types of Analysis

Another step in the inventory planning process is to identify any other business factors pertinent to the buyer's area of responsibility. These factors may be identified through SWOT or PEST analysis but are often related only to that buyer's area of business. Planning tools for such factors include trend curve or product life-cycle analysis and product market analysis.

Trend curve analysis identifies specific upside product opportunities in the areas of testing through post-peak. However, it also addresses the downside of the curve in products at the peak and outgoing stages. Trend curve, or product life-cycle analysis, is further addressed in Chapter 6.

A **product market analysis** can pinpoint specific issues within the product category. These might include vendor or product changes as well as product ratios. Product ratios could include top to bottom ratios, earring to necklace ratios, or shampoo to conditioner ratios. Any products that are related and often sold in tandem may be reviewed as a ratio and should be planned accordingly. These issues could also be addressed within SWOT or PEST analysis; however, a product market analysis offers a third type of review to help identify further challenges and opportunities.

APPLICATION

Creating an Excel spreadsheet such as the one in Excel Spreadsheet 5-A provides a tool for a thoughtful review of both increases and decreases in sales. Applying percentages and/or dollars will directly inform the decision making for sales and subsequently for inventory levels.

Your Turn

Select a product category, and conduct various forms of research to identify business increases and decreases for that category. Visit stores and search the Internet for business-related stories, consumer spending reports, retailer annual reports, etc. Complete Excel Spreadsheet 5-B. See Appendix B for full-size versions of all Excel Spreadsheets, which can be pulled from the book and worked on separately.

Capacity: Minimum and Maximum Models

Once the total financial planning is analyzed, the buyer will begin to look at lower levels of planning, which would include inventory fixture capacity. Relying solely on inventory dollars may not account for acceptable presentation of inventory. Thus, buyers sometimes need to manipulate inventory through capacity models. Capacity involves determining the minimum or maximum amount of inventory to be housed. **Minimum capacity** inventory levels are sought during slow selling periods, such as post-holiday or summer months. Conversely, **maximum capacity** inventory results in peak inventory levels during holidays or special selling periods.

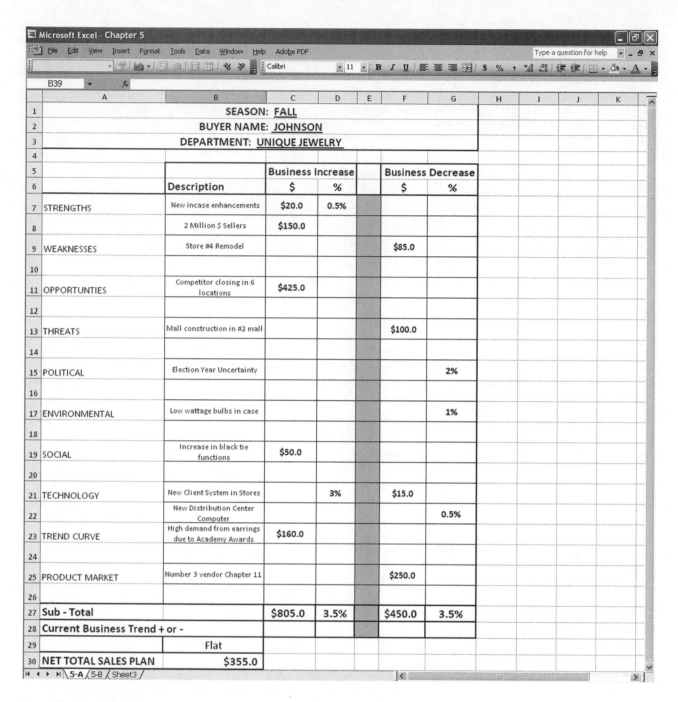

Microsoft Excel - Chapter 5

B39

	A	B	C	D	E	F	G
1	SEASON: **FALL**						
2	BUYER NAME: **JOHNSON**						
3	DEPARTMENT: **UNIQUE JEWELRY**						
4							
5			**Business Increase**			**Business Decrease**	
6		**Description**	**$**	**%**		**$**	**%**
7	STRENGTHS	New incase enhancements	$20.0	0.5%			
8		2 Million $ Sellers	$150.0				
9	WEAKNESSES	Store #4 Remodel				$85.0	
10							
11	OPPORTUNTIES	Competitor closing in 6 locations	$425.0				
12							
13	THREATS	Mall construction in #2 mall				$100.0	
14							
15	POLITICAL	Election Year Uncertainty					2%
16							
17	ENVIRONMENTAL	Low wattage bulbs in case					1%
18							
19	SOCIAL	Increase in black tie functions	$50.0				
20							
21	TECHNOLOGY	New Client System in Stores		3%		$15.0	
22		New Distribution Center Computer					0.5%
23	TREND CURVE	High demand from earrings due to Academy Awards	$160.0				
24							
25	PRODUCT MARKET	Number 3 vendor Chapter 11				$250.0	
26							
27	Sub - Total		$805.0	3.5%		$450.0	3.5%
28	Current Business Trend + or -						
29		Flat					
30	NET TOTAL SALES PLAN	$355.0					

5-A / 5-B / Sheet3

EXCEL SPREADSHEET 5-A.

Consider the costume jewelry department example. One four-sided earring spinner display can accommodate four earrings per row, and the spinner has eight rows per side. (These assumptions are calculated after measuring the size of the earring card in inches and the size of the spinner.) Based on this information, the maximum capacity is 128 earrings per spinner. During peak holiday selling periods such as Mother's Day, the spinner should house a full inventory capacity of 128 pairs of earrings. In looking at the spinner, the buyer

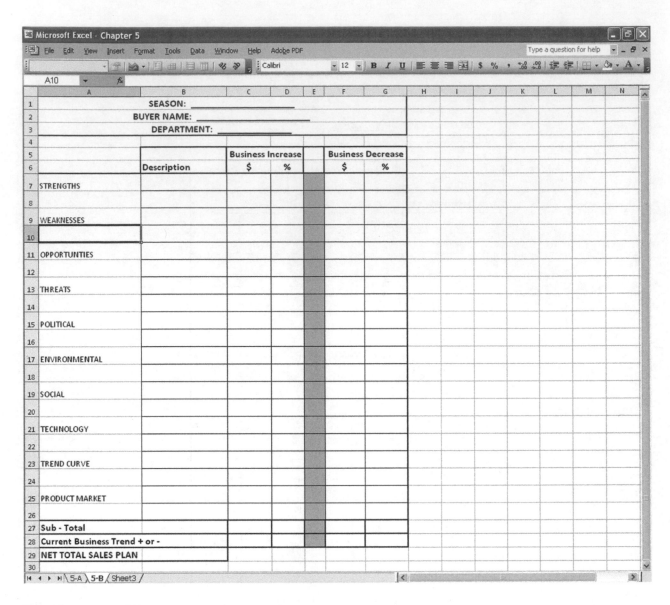

EXCEL SPREADSHEET 5-B.

needs to determine the minimum capacity. If the buyer reduces the earrings per row to three, the minimum capacity becomes 96 pairs of earrings. A reduction to three pairs per row can be accomplished by sliding the earrings to the center of the fixture and leaving equal open space on each end. This reduces the amount of inventory and maintains consistency that is visually appealing. Based on an average retail selling price of $48, the inventory is as follows:

Maximum Capacity:

4 per row × 8 rows × 4 sides = 128 earrings @ $48 each = $6144

Minimum Capacity:

3 per row × 8 rows × 4 sides = 96 earrings @ $48 each = $4608

Inventory reduction is equal to 32 earrings per spinner at $1536, or 25%. The earrings are reduced by $1536, which is also 25 percent, reflecting the dollar reduction and percentage reduction. Consider the impact this reduction can have when applied to dozens of earring spinners per store in hundreds of stores. For the large retailer, it could mean significant inventory reduction. For the small, single-unit retailer, it could be the difference between placing one reorder for a hot-selling item or one new order to test a new product.

AVERAGE INVENTORY AND/OR AVERAGE STOCK

For both large and small retailers, every inventory dollar is significant and must be carefully managed. This means that with a detailed analysis of sales projections, buyers can systematically plan inventory dollars. To begin planning inventory dollars, buyers will calculate **average inventory** or average stock. This is the average amount of inventory spread over a six-month season. The average takes into account both maximum and minimum inventory periods. Buyers need to keep in mind that the average encompasses all types of inventory—invisible and visible as well as productive or unproductive. The calculation for average stock is expressed as a mathematical average.

Creating a stable inventory flow that mirrors sales flow will maximize profitability by reducing markdowns. Additionally, with careful planning, the right inventory will be provided at the right time and in the right place.

Average stock is calculated as follows:

Average Stock =
Each Month BOM (Beginning of Month) + Last Month EOM (End of Month) =
Total Stock ÷ 7

January BOM:	$110.4
Feb. BOM:	$131.8
Mar. BOM:	$135.6
April BOM:	$148.2
May BOM:	$175.1
June BOM:	$140.7
June EOM:	$125.9
TOTAL:	$967.7 ÷ 7 = $138.2

PRACTICE PROBLEMS

1. If total stock over a six-month season is $598.3, what is average stock?

2. If average stock is $1342.6, what is total stock for a six-month season?

3. Stock levels for spring are as follows. Calculate the average stock for the season.

   Jan. BOM: $58.9
   Feb. BOM: $76.3

Mar. BOM:	$87.2
April BOM:	$68.9
May BOM:	$71.3
June BOM:	$101.7
June EOM:	$77.3

TERMINOLOGY

Average inventory and/or **average stock:** The average amount of inventory dollars or units spread over a specified period of time (usually six months).

back-stock inventory: Any product that is physically in the store yet located in a stockroom or other area that is not accessible to the customer.

booked: The result of an accounting process that charges any dollar amount to the financial budget. *Booked* could refer to sales, inventory, markdowns, or any other business phase that affects the financial budget.

damaged and defective inventory: Product that is physically and financially owned by the retailer but is unsalable.

electronic data interchange (EDI): A virtual, paperless exchange of information between vendor and retailer.

electronic inventory: Inventory that has left the vendor but is still in transit to the retail store. This inventory may be with the freight carrier, in a distribution center, or simply on a truck waiting to be unloaded at the store.

floor inventory: Any product physically on the selling floor and accessible to customers.

inventory: Any physical product or invisible product expressed as a dollar amount and booked into the financial budget.

inventory on hold: Items that are on hold for customers but have not yet been paid for by the customer.

invisible inventory: Inventory that is not physically present or visible but has been booked into the budget. Examples include electronic inventory, shortage inventory, repair inventory, and transfer inventory.

maximum capacity: The maximum amount of inventory units that can be housed within a fixture and within a physical floor space allocation without obstructing traffic patterns or overflowing product fixture limitations.

minimum capacity: The minimum amount of inventory units that can be housed within a fixture and within a physical floor space allocation. Minimum capacity is the smallest amount of inventory possible without deterring sales.

PEST analysis: Identification of external environmental factors including political, environmental, social, and technological influences.

repair inventory: Inventory that is booked and owned but may be out of the store for repair.

product market analysis: A process used to pinpoint specific issues within the product category.

shortage inventory: A shortage that is determined from theft or paperwork error but remains booked to inventory even if the inventory does not exist. Shortage inventory is projected on a regular basis and is updated for accuracy following a physical inventory count.

SWOT analysis: Identification of the business's internal strengths and weaknesses as well as the external opportunities and threats.

transfer inventory: Inventory that is transferred between store locations. The sending store is booked for the inventory until it is fully received by the receiving store. Transfer of dollar ownership in the accounting process occurs either at the sender or receiver but may be physically invisible while in transit. Store policy varies as to when the dollar transfer of ownership occurs yet the overall retail store owns the inventory.

trend curve or product life-cycle analysis: The process of mapping products or categories into the life-cycle spectrum. The analysis includes testing, incoming, pre-peak, peak, post-peak, decline, and outgoing stages.

Universal Product Code (UPC): Bar code identification system that allows product data to be scanned rather than entered manually.

visible inventory: Any inventory that can be seen or touched within the retail store.

warehouse inventory: Typically household or hard-line products that are stored at a secondary location but are readily available to ship direct to customers.

FORMULAS

Average Stock =

Each Month BOM (Beginning of Month) + Last Month EOM (End of Month) =

Total Stock ÷ 7

e.g., $135.4 (J) + $152.9 (F) + $160.6 (M) + $165.2 (A) + $197.2 (M) + $147.3 (J) + $131.2 (J) = $1,089.8 (TS) ÷ 7 = $155.7 (AS)

6

INVENTORY TURNOVER

Managing inventory turnover is directly related to profit margins. When inventory sells quickly at the full retail price, profit levels are high, but buyers may miss business because inventory sells too quickly. Total demand is unknown when inventory is sold out. This scenario often finds the buyer wondering what could have been sold if more inventory were available. Conversely, when inventory builds up and sells at a slow pace, buyers take action by initiating markdown strategies, as they will fuel sales. However, due to the reduction in price, profit levels will decline. Therefore, buyers must project inventory turnover to achieve optimal results—not selling too quickly, leading to **stock-outs**, and not selling too slowly, leading to excessive markdowns.

Inventory turnover is the number of times the inventory is turned over within a given, period such as month, quarter, season, or year. For simplicity, consider this example: during a six-month period, if a small store owns 100 sweaters, sells 100 sweaters, and brings into inventory 100 more sweaters, the inventory has turned over one time. This example is expressed in units, but the same holds true for dollars.

RATES OF INVENTORY TURNOVER

How quickly inventory is turned over depends on the product category. The major determining factor relates to shelf life. **Shelf life** refers to the length of

time the product can remain on the shelf without reducing its value. Three general categories of inventory demonstrate low, medium, and high rates of inventory turnover. Basic products tend to have low turnover, classic fashion products tend to have medium turnover, and high-fashion or perishable items tend to have high turnover rates.

Low Inventory Turnover

Basic products that rarely change have **low inventory turnover**. Examples include paper towels, white socks, or Levi's 505 jeans. These products could be considered needs versus wants. Maintaining reasonable levels of inventory at all times does cost inventory dollars; however, the retail selling price for these items is not hindered over time. These items are not time sensitive or fashion sensitive. Retaining a reasonable amount of inventory in these items ensures an in-stock status at all times. Consumers often purchase these products in multiple quantities, therefore maintaining adequate stock levels can increase sales results.

Medium Inventory Turnover

Classic fashion products strive for **medium** or **mid-level inventory turnover**. The idea of a classic fashion product may sound like an oxymoron, but it actually is not. Products classified as medium turnover can include items that change color or undergo seasonal style modifications. Some examples are men's clothing and fine jewelry. Styling of men's suits generally evolves over time. Colors and fabrics may change, and lapels may widen or narrow, but dramatic changes take time—more than one season. Women's jewelry is similar. Although fine and high-end jewelers want women to buy more jewelry, they tend to design collections that flow or relate to past collections. A jewelry designer might introduce five collections per year, but those collections will evolve and overlap to reduce the need for end-of-month or end-of-season markdowns.

High Inventory Turnover

High inventory turnover products are the third category. Perishable items exhibit the highest levels of turnover. Milk is an excellent example. Grocers carefully place milk cartons in the cooler so that the cartons about to expire are in the front and those with a longer expiration date are toward the back. The same is true for cosmetics. The shelf life of cosmetics can be longer for dry products but shorter for liquid and cream products. Moisturizing creams can begin to separate in the bottle. This makes them less effective and certainly less attractive for purchase at the full retail price. High-fashion products also fall into the high-turnover category.

Retail stores such as H&M, Zara, and others base their entire business strategy on high turnover. These retailers look for the most up-to-the-minute

SEARCH THE NET

▲ Visit the following websites:

www.target.com

www.hm.com

www.potterybarn.com

Randomly select some products, and determine how you would plan inventory turnover for them. Begin by placing them into a low, medium, or high turnover category. Explain your rationale and how you would convince your divisional merchandise manager to support your position.

fashions, produce them within weeks, and deliver them to stores for immediate sale. Inventory levels for these products are carefully analyzed and planned to move quickly. This means smaller quantities are available, and they are sharply priced. Sharply priced is low or well priced. Customers buy it now because it is at a good price and they don't want to miss the opportunity. The result? These items are hot, and consumers tend to buy them now.

PRODUCT LIFE CYCLE

Another aspect of inventory turnover relates to the **product life cycle** (also known as the trend curve). Products can be classified into specific categories of the product life cycle. Classification into the product life cycle is necessary for the buyer to make decisions about sales results and estimate how long the product is valid and at what price. Individual products or categories of products can fall into one of the following phases: testing, incoming, pre-peak, peak, post-peak, decline, or outgoing (Note: the names of these phases correspond to common marketing terms but are presented in a typical language for buyers as they refer to actions the buyer is taking within the product life cycle.)

TESTING PHASE

The **testing phase** is the initial phase of a product. Buyers should set aside a specified inventory dollar amount for testing new inventory. The testing phase generally involves a small amount of inventory that is strategically placed in test locations. Buyers can get a valid test by placing the inventory in limited locations with a variety of volume levels and geographic locations. For example, urban stores tend to sell new items more quickly. Consumers in these locations may travel or be more aware of trends; they are referred to as early adopters, or people interested in trying something new. A test in this type of store generates a significantly different test than one in a rural or suburban store. Pricing at this level is at the full retail price. It is commonplace for DMMs (Divisional Merchandise Managers) and GMMs (General Merchandise Managers) to periodically ask a buyer what products are testing and what the results are. This can provide valuable insight for the company as a whole.

INCOMING PHASE

The **incoming phase** immediately follows the testing phase. When a product tests well and shows a strong sales result, buyers will then purchase the product for more stores and/or reorder it for the testing stores. Products in the incoming phase are still relatively new but are gaining popularity. Pricing at this level is also at the full retail price.

PRE-PEAK PHASE

The **pre-peak phase** involves an even greater level of distribution. Usually, the product is carried in all locations and may also be offered by a variety of manufacturers. Product at this level is generally widely accepted and known. Pricing at this level may be seen at multiple price points, but pre-peak product is still offered at full retail price.

PEAK PHASE

The **peak phase** is the highest level of productivity but also the most tenuous level. The length of time product remains within the peak phase may be months or weeks. Buyers carefully monitor selling results to project how long the peak phase will last. Products in the peak phase are widely distributed and at many price points. Pricing at the peak phase is scattered; most product is at the full retail price but is often found on sale for special POS short-term events.

POST-PEAK PHASE

During the **post-peak phase**, products remain at high volume and wide distribution, but they are often seen on sale or at many prices. Retailers who stocked product in the early stages of testing are typically out of the product at this time and have moved on to new test products.

DECLINE PHASE

Products in the **decline phase** may still be widely available, but inventory is no longer being replenished. Buyers who are cautious at the peak phase will find themselves with a limited amount of decline inventory and in a desirable position to sell what is left at a minimal markdown. Products in the decline phase are regularly promoted at a markdown price.

OUTGOING PHASE

The **outgoing phase** is the final phase of the product life cycle. This phase is characterized by permanent markdowns at all levels. The goal for buyers in this phase is to liquidate the inventory to zero. See Figure 6.1 for a visual diagram of the product life cycle.

APPLICATION

By considering the internal and external factors affecting inventory turnover, the buyer is better equipped to plan and forecast the coming season. After determining average inventory and sales, the buyer can calculate inventory turnover. The formula for inventory turnover is as follows:

Average Stock =
Each Month BOM (Beginning of Month) + Last Month EOM (End of Month) =
Total Stock ÷ 7

Aug. BOM: $176.5
Sept. BOM: $196.2

Attribute	TESTING	INCOMING	PRE-PEAK	PEAK	POST-PEAK	DECLINE	OUTGOING
AVAILABILITY	Limited, possibly only available in certain areas	Limited supply	It's everywhere!	Everyone has it and it's in large supply	Everyone has it and it's in large supply	Large supply with decreasing demand	Ready to unload
COMPETITION	Not likely, you could be first	Moving beyond specialty stores	Specialty, Department Stores, Chain Stores.	Specialty stores are backing away	Specialty and leader "A" level stores are backing away	Promotional Stores	Discounter clearance houses
PRICE	Not a factor, customer willing to pay for excitement	Regular price	Regular price with some promotional activity	Balance between regular and promotional with promo on the increase	Primarily promotional	Price points and enticing discounts	Deep discounts
MARKET WATCH	Seen in trend bulletins	Media darling, seen through a variety of media	"Must Have" in all stores	Household name	n/a	n/a	n/a
KEY QUESTION	Does my assortment need something new?	How can I position this product to sell more?	Am I maximizing unit sales and profitability?	How long can this item last?	What's next?	How long before I can get out of this?	n/a
ACT!	Constantly test newness, re-test if necessary. It's possible to be too early.	Monitor sales, add color or price point based on results.	Call out in visual and signage "own" the business in your market.	Be carful to balance assortment.	Sell it as long as profitable but be cautious not to be left with too much	Maximize any remaining sales opportunity with caution!	Run!

FIGURE 6.1. Product Life Cycle.

EXERCISE 6.1

Visit the same websites listed earlier in the chapter. Select 10–15 different items from different locations in the websites. Choose five from new arrivals, five from clearance or sale, and five from any other location. Determine the phase of each item in the product life cycle. What criteria did you use to make your choices?

Hint: Review price, size availability, color availability, and range. Some sites will highlight what is a new arrival, and it's up to you to decide if it is a new testing item or just a new delivery.

EXERCISE 6.2

Select one product category (e.g., tanks, jeans, pillows). Review only that category within the product life cycle. As the buyer, how would you predict future products in that category? What aspects of the product have salability in today's environment? Consider changes to color, style, embellishment, price, brands, or designers.

Oct. BOM:	$196.9
Nov. BOM:	$169.0
Dec. BOM:	$145.6
Jan. BOM:	$89.0
Jan. EOM:	$70.4
TOTAL:	$1043.6 ÷ 7 = $149.1

Turnover = Total Sales ÷ Average Stock
Total Sales $667.1 ÷ $149.1 = 4.47

PRACTICE PROBLEMS

1. If total stock is $598.3 and turnover is 3.2, what are sales?

2. If turnover is 2.67 and sales are $2078.2, what is average stock?

3. If sales are $45.9 and average stock is $25.6, what is turnover?

4. If average stock is $719.4 and sales are $1617.2, what is turnover?

5. If turnover is 3.45 and average stock is $120.4, what are sales?

6. If sales are $12,090.0 and turnover is 1.88, what is average stock? Total stock?

Your Turn

Complete Excel Spreadsheets 6-A, 6-B, and 6-C. Calculate average stock and turnover. See Appendix B for full-size versions of all Excel Spreadsheets, which can be pulled from the book and worked on separately.

	A	B	C	D	E	F	G	H	I	J	K	L	M
1	Actual - Last Year												
2	Plan	Feb	Mar	April	May	June	July	Total	Actual Markdown				
3	Beg.Month Stock	325.4	330.9	335.7	398.6	297.4	278.3						
4	Sales	178.6	185.2	187.1	211.4	165.3	155.2		Sales Change % +5.3				
5	Markdowns	18.2	25.6	22.1	72.3	40.1	15.7		Average Stock				
6	Purchases								PLN ACT				
7	End Month Stock						272.4		Turnover				
8									PLN ACT				
9	Future Sales	Aug	Sept	Oct					WOS/STS/FM				
10									PLN ACT				
11													
12													
13													
14	Plan - This Year												
15	Plan	Feb	Mar	April	May	June	July	Total	Actual Markdown				
16	Beg.Month Stock								$ 17.7%				
17	Sales								Sales Change % (5.3)				
18	Markdowns								Average Stock				
19	Purchases								PLN ACT				
20	End Month Stock								Turnover				
21	Future Sales	Aug	Sept	Oct					PLN 3.25 ACT				
22									WOS/STS				
23													
24									Mark-Up				
25													
26													
27													
28													
29													
30													

EXCEL SPREADSHEET 6-A.

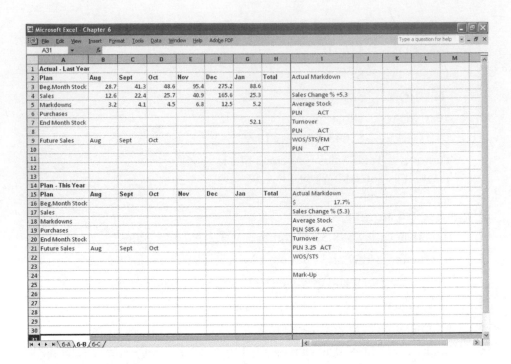

EXCEL SPREADSHEET 6-B.

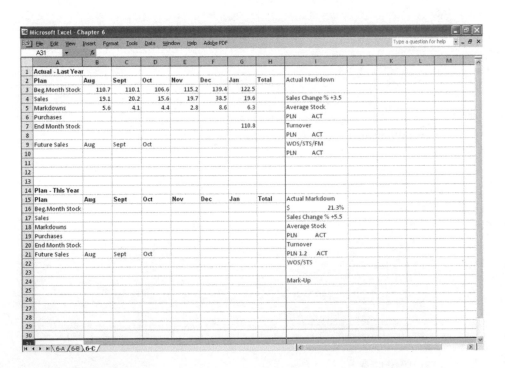

EXCEL SPREADSHEET 6-C.

A BUYER'S LIFE

TERMINOLOGY

decline phase: The phase during which products may still be widely available, but inventory is no longer being replenished and products are consistently on sale.

high inventory turnover: Inventory that moves in and out of inventory quickly. This category typically includes high-fashion or highly perishable products with a limited shelf life.

incoming phase: The phase during which products are still relatively new but gaining popularity. Such products are sold at full retail price.

inventory turnover: The number of times, within a specified period (usually a six-month season) per season, that inventory is bought, sold, and replaced.

low inventory turnover: Inventory that has an unlimited or long shelf life. These products do not change rapidly, and their price remains constant.

medium inventory turnover: Inventory that has a limited shelf life, usually seasonal. These products do not change frequently and may be sold at full retail price for most of a season.

outgoing phase: The final phase of the product life cycle, characterized by permanent markdowns at all levels with a goal to liquidate the inventory to zero.

peak phase: The phase during which products are widely distributed and at many price points.

post-peak phase: The phase during which products have higher volume and wide distribution but are often seen on sale.

pre-peak phase: The phase during which product is carried in all locations, and may also be seen from a variety of manufacturers or price points, but is generally still sold at full retail price.

product life cycle analysis: The process of mapping products or categories into the life-cycle spectrum. The analysis includes testing, incoming, pre-peak, peak, post-peak, decline, and outgoing phases. Also known as trend curve analysis.

shelf life: The amount of time a product can remain in inventory or on the shelf until it can no longer be sold at full value.

stock-outs: Inventory that sells too quickly and is unavailable.

testing phase: The phase during which a generally small amount of inventory is strategically placed in test locations and sold at full retail price.

FORMULAS

$\sum$ Average Stock =

Each Month BOM (Beginning of Month) + Last Month EOM (End of Month) =

Total Stock ÷ 7

e.g., \$135.4 (J) + \$152.9 (F) + \$160.6 (M) + \$165.2 (A) + \$197.2 (M) + \$147.3 (J) + \$131.2 (J) = \$1089.8 (TS) ÷ 7 = \$155.7 (AS)

Turnover = Total Sales ÷ Average Stock

e.g., Total Sales \$310.2 ÷ \$155.7 = 1.99

7

STOCK-TO-SALES RATIO METHOD OF INVENTORY

To achieve optimal profit results, buyers must link average inventory levels, turnover, and sales to actual inventory stock levels for a specified period. Buyers use specific methods to determine how much inventory to hold in stock. This text identifies two methods for determining inventory: the stock-to-sales method and the weeks-of-supply method (discussed in Chapter 8).

The **stock-to-sales (STS) method** projects stock levels on a monthly basis and determines how much inventory must be available at the start of each month to reach sales projections. The **weeks-of-supply method** operates by calculating lead time variability. Using this method, the buyer must balance inventory stock levels to avoid excess inventory and, conversely, a shortage of inventory.

FACTORS THAT AFFECT PROFIT LEVELS

Excess inventory can lead to several factors that eventually erode profit levels as a result of additional and unplanned markdowns. These factors include the following:

- Too much inventory, coupled with low sales, eventually increases markdowns.
- Excessive back-stock inventory hinders locating sizes, colors, or styles.

- Back-stock inventory is easily lost, damaged, or stolen.
- Customer service levels suffer when customers are overwhelmed by abundant choices.
- Cluttered sales floor layouts threaten visual appeal.

TOO MUCH INVENTORY

When customer demand is lower than projected sales, the results are that inventory rises, sales fall, and markdowns ultimately increase. The only way to bring in additional new inventory to boost sales is to reduce the current stock level. To reduce slow-selling inventory and stimulate sales, buyers are forced to initiate unplanned markdowns.

EXCESSIVE BACK-STOCK INVENTORY

Excessive back-stock inventory makes locating size, color, or style difficult and eventually leads to a loss of sales. When stockrooms are overflowing with inventory, sales team members become overwhelmed when looking for specific items. The time a team member takes away from the sales floor making him or her less productive; team members thus become unwilling to search for stock in a stockroom. They often choose to sell what is readily available rather than searching for inventory.

This situation also holds true for inventory that may be excessive in one store and low in another. Many department stores offer free shipping for out-of-stock items to be shipped from another location. Although this policy addresses the retailer's overall inventory, again it takes time away from selling. Commissioned sales team members may not see the benefit and either not offer the service or fail to look for the inventory, whether it is in the building or at another location. To overcome this challenge, retailers with a strong Internet presence have installed computers in the store or enabled smartphone users to allow customers to look up the item and place the order themselves directly from the store.

LOST, DAMAGED, OR STOLEN INVENTORY

When inventory is out of sight and located in a stockroom, it is easily lost, damaged, or stolen. As more inventories arrive in the store, older back-stock inventory can be relocated to less accessible parts of a stockroom. That inventory is eventually forgotten until the retailer takes a physical inventory or someone decides to organize and clean the stockroom.

Damage to inventory is also prevalent when products are stored on top shelves, in elevated hanging areas, or on bottom shelves. This inventory can become soiled from the daily air flow and dust often found in a stockroom. Also, when hanging areas are too full, product is likely to fall from the rack and become soiled or damaged on the stockroom floor.

Last, a full stockroom is the perfect location for theft. With an abundance of inventory, managers and buyers lose track of what is or is not in the stockroom. Inventory can easily be stolen.

TOO MANY CHOICES

Customer service levels suffer when customers are overwhelmed by choices. Time is one of the most significant obstacles for consumers. They want to come into a store, locate a product with ease, make their purchase, and be on their way. If sales floors and fixtures are crowded and overwhelming, shoppers may not take the time to search for the item. Customers have many choices today and can decide to visit a competitor—or, with a few clicks, they can shop online in a no hassle, time-sensitive environment.

POOR VISUAL APPEAL

Visual appeal is essential to attracting customers and drawing them in to buy. Overstock threatens visual appeal with cluttered sales floor layouts and overflowing fixtures. Buyers cannot develop or achieve clear and concise merchandising objectives when sales floors contain too much inventory. Additionally, overcrowding hampers physical floor rotation for new inventory. Regular changes in visual platforms, windows, and key focal areas attract customers to the store or selling space. Without regular rotation of new and exciting inventory, customers grow bored and move to stores offering fresh, enticing inventory.

EXCESSIVE STOCK LEVELS

Besides the preceding factors contributing to increased markdowns, excessive stock levels also prevent buyers from making additional purchases. These purchases can include reordering best sellers, placing new orders of introductory product, replenishing basic inventory, and obtaining new test product. Holding too much of the wrong inventory prevents buyers from purchasing additional best-selling or new inventory. Stock levels are linked directly to the rate of inventory turnover. Slow turnover results in reduced profits.

EXERCISE 7.1

Select from the following types of stores, and visit their websites: two department stores, two specialty stores, two boutique stores, or two discount stores. Where possible, also visit these same two brick-and-mortar stores. Then answer these questions (Note: Without knowledge of the actual buying plan, this exercise may not reveal the cause or effect of a real inventory problem, but it does give some indication of how to look at inventory with a critical eye.):

1. What inventory appears to be overstocked for each store website or store you visited? Based on the inventory you identified, why do you think it could be overstocked?

2. What is the correlation between these stores and the current sales trend for a particular product category?

3. Review the issues of inventory overstock. What are the challenges for Internet buyers versus brick-and-mortar buyers? How does each buyer (Internet and brick-and-mortar) overcome these challenges?

APPLYING THE STS RATIO METHOD OF INVENTORY

The STS ratio operates on the premise of a direct ratio or relationship between sales for a given month and the amount of inventory needed at the start of that month. Sales and stock are planned as a mirror image. For example, if sales in August are planned at $154.0, a ratio is applied to the sales amount; the stock to begin August is then determined and obtained at the appropriate level. In months of high sales or steadily increasing sales, such as during major holidays, the stock ratio might be higher than in months when stock is decreasing or entering a slow period.

Manual calculations of the STS ratio will give buyers a broad understanding of how to determine appropriate inventory levels. However, buyers should note that many statistical computer programs can quickly and accurately calculate inventory and thus simplify the planning process. When the office computer is not at hand, understanding the manual method enhances knowledge and prepares buyers for decision making and quick vendor negotiations.

The process for calculating the STS ratio is as follows:

Average Stock ÷ Sales = Stock-to-Sales Ratio
$458.3 ÷ $212.7 = 2.15:1

This ratio can be utilized by week, month, quarter, season, or year. For the purposes of the six-month plan, we will consider the season ratio and apply it to each month. It should be noted that by using computer software or simply more advanced planning methods, the STS usually varies by month. The purpose of this chapter is to understand the basic concept and how to calculate and apply a six-month plan.

PRACTICE PROBLEMS

1. What is the STS ratio if sales are $28.8 and average stock is $67.3?

2. What are the sales if average stock is $1,091.2 and the STS ratio is 3.9:1?

3. What is the average stock if sales are $4,698.2 and the STS ratio is 2.33:1?

4. What is the STS ratio if sales are $658.7 and average stock is $887.2?

5. What is the average stock if sales are $112.7 and the STS ratio is 4.2:1?

6. What are the sales if the average stock is $2,376.9 and the STS ratio is 2.87:1?

APPLICATION

By using the STS ratio method of inventory, buyers can determine monthly inventory stock levels based on their relationship to monthly sales.

CALCULATING THE STS RATIO IN A SIX-MONTH PLAN

Using Excel Spreadsheet 7-A, plan *last year* BOM (beginning of month) stock using the STS ratio. See Appendix B for full-size versions of all Excel Spreadsheets, which can be pulled from the book and worked on separately.

Calculate Last Year Actual for Sales and Markdowns

Follow the step-by-step process:

1. Using turnover, calculate the planned average stock:

   Total Sales ÷ Turnover = Average Stock
   $564.4 ÷ 4.12 = $137.0

2. Calculate average monthly sales:

   Total Sales ÷ 6 = Average Monthly Sales
   $564.4 ÷ 6 = $94.0

3. Calculate the STS ratio:

   Average Stock ÷ Average Monthly Sales
   $137.0 ÷ $94.0 = 1.46:1

4. Apply the STS ratio to the monthly sales to determine the BOM inventory:

Month	Sales		STS		BOM Inventory
Aug	$87.0	×	1.46	=	$127.0
Sept	$124.9	×	1.46	=	$182.4
Oct	$110.3	×	1.46	=	$161.0
Nov	$88.6	×	1.46	=	$129.4
Dec	$105.3	×	1.46	=	$153.7
Jan	$48.3	×	1.46	=	$70.5
Feb	$52.1	×	1.46	=	$76.1*

   *Note: Jan. EOM = Feb. BOM.

5. Enter the BOMs into the six-month plan (Excel Spreadsheet 7-A).

6. Total the six-month season BOMs:

   $127.0 + $182.4 + $161.0 + $129.4 + $153.7 + $70.5 = $823.9

7. Apply the BOMs to the EOMs—the stock level at the beginning of each month is equivalent to the previous month's ending stock.

8. Total the six-month season EOMs:

   $182.4 + $161.0 + $129.4 + $153.7 + $70.5 + $66.0 = $763.0

9. Calculate the actual average stock:

   Total BOMs + Last Month EOM ÷ 7 = Actual Average Stock
   $823.0 + $76.1 ÷ 7 = $128.6

10. Calculate the actual turnover:

    Total Sales ÷ Actual Average Stock = Actual Turnover
    $564.4 ÷ $128.6 = $4.39

11. Calculate the actual STS ratio:

Actual Average Stock ÷ Average Monthly Sales = Actual STS Ratio
$128.6 ÷ $94.0 = $1.37

CONTINUE CALCULATING THE STS RATIO FOR THE SIX-MONTH PLAN

Using Excel Spreadsheet 7-A, plan *this year* BOM stock using the STS ratio.

Calculate Last Year Actual for Sales and Markdowns
Follow the step-by-step process:

1. Using turnover, calculate the planned average stock:

Total Sales ÷ Turnover = Average Stock
$667.1 ÷ 3.98 = $167.6

2. Calculate average monthly sales:

Total Sales ÷ 6 = Average Monthly Sales
$667.1 ÷ 6 = $111.2

3. Calculate the STS ratio:

Average Stock ÷ Average Monthly Sales
$167.6 ÷ 111.2 = 1.51:1

4. Apply the STS ratio to the monthly sales to determine the beginning of month (BOM) inventory:

Month	Sales		STS		BOM Inventory
Aug	$102.7	×	1.51	=	$155.1
Sept	$147.4	×	1.51	=	$222.6
Oct	$130.1	×	1.51	=	$196.5
Nov	$104.7	×	1.51	=	$158.1
Dec	$124.7	×	1.51	=	$188.3
Jan	$57.5	×	1.51	=	$86.8
Feb	$53.4	×	1.51	=	$80.6*

*Note: Jan. EOM = Feb. BOM.

5. Enter the BOMs into the six-month plan (Excel Spreadsheet 7-A).

6. Total the six-month season BOMs:

$155.1 + $222.6 + $196.5 + $161.1 + $188.3 + $83.8 = $1007.4

7. Apply the BOMs to the EOMs—the stock level at the beginning of each month is equivalent to the previous month's ending stock.

8. Total the six-month season EOMs:

$222.6 + $196.5 + $161.1 + $188.3 + $83.8 + $80.6 = $932.9

9. Calculate the actual average stock:

Total BOMs + Last Month EOM ÷ 7 = Actual Average Stock
$1,007.4 + $80.6 ÷ 7 = $155.4

10. Calculate the actual turnover:

Total Sales ÷ Actual Average Stock = Actual Turnover
$667.1 ÷ $155.4 = 4.25

11. Calculate the actual STS ratio:

Actual Average Stock ÷ Average Monthly Sales = Actual STS Ratio
$155.1 ÷ $110.7 = 1.40

	Microsoft Excel - Chapter 7												
	File Edit View Insert Format Tools Data Window Help Adobe PDF								Type a question for help				
	A31		fx										
	A	B	C	D	E	F	G	H	I	J	K	L	M
1	Actual - Last Year												
2	Plan	Aug	Sept	Oct	Nov	Dec	Jan	Total	Actual Markdown				
3	Beg.Month Stock												
4	Sales	87.0	124.9	110.3	88.6	105.3	48.3	564.4	Sales Change %				
5	Markdowns	10.2	15.3	12.9	11.5	31.8	17.2	98.9	Average Stock				
6	Purchases								PLN ACT				
7	End Month Stock								Turnover				
8									PLN 4.12 ACT				
9	Future Sales	Feb	Mar	Apr					WOS/STS				
10		52.1	68.9	72.3					PLN ACT				
11									Avg. Monthly Sales				
12													
13													
14	Plan - This Year												
15	Plan							Total	Actual Markdown				
16	Beg.Month Stock								$130.1				
17	Sales								Sales Change +18.2%				
18	Markdowns								Average Stock				
19	Purchases								PLN ACT				
20	End Month Stock								Turnover				
21	Future Sales	Feb	Mar	Apr					PLN 3.98 ACT				
22									WOS/STS				
23									PLN ACT				
24									Avg. Monthly Sales				
25													
26									Mark-Up				
27													
28													
29													
30													

H ◀ ▶ H \ 7-A / 7-B / 7-C / 7-D / 7-E /

EXCEL SPREADSHEET 7-A.

Your Turn

Complete Excel Spreadsheets 7-B and 7-C.

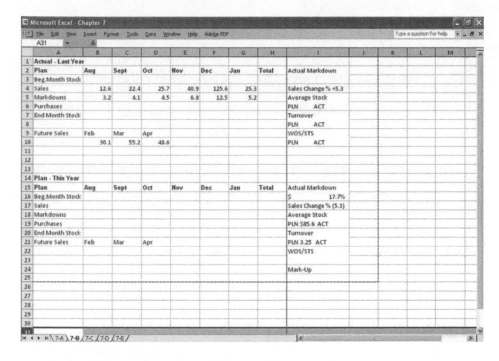

EXCEL SPREADSHEET 7-B.

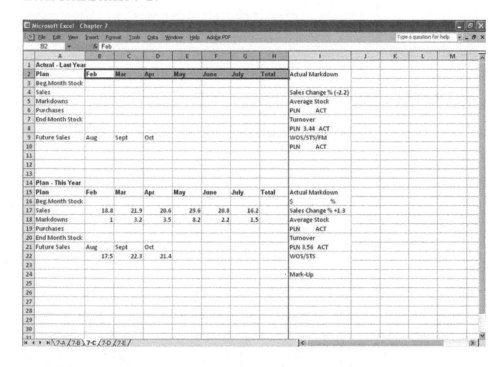

EXCEL SPREADSHEET 7-C. This year markdown % 15.3 %

COMPLETE THE STS METHOD OF INVENTORY FOR THE JEWELRY DEPARTMENT EXAMPLE

Add the STS method of inventory to the jewelry department sample problem.

Thus far you have created sales and markdown plans for the jewelry department. Using Excel Spreadsheet 7-J, apply the STS concept to the plan.

Complete Excel Spreadsheets 7-D and 7-E for homework.

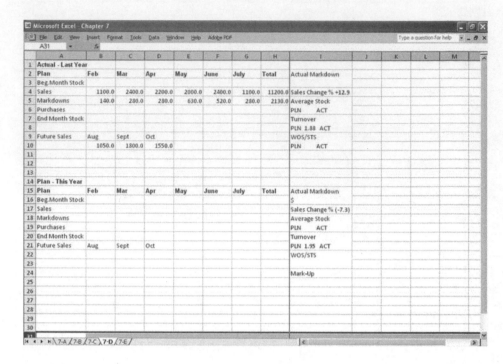

EXCEL SPREADSHEET 7‑D. This year markdown % 18.3%

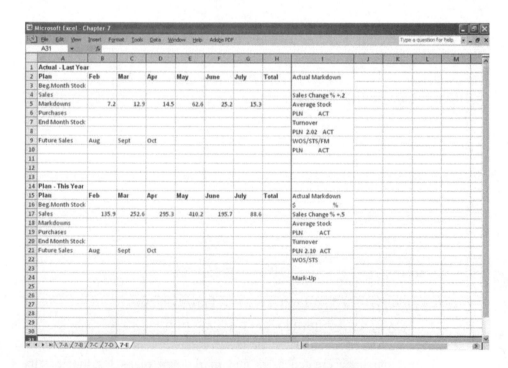

EXCEL SPREADSHEET 7‑E. Assume TY markdown % same as LY %

CREATE IT IN EXCEL!

Follow the template created in Chapter 4. There are two options for saving your file. Your file may be either saved as "Chapter 7 STS Method of Inventory," or you can save it as a new tab, Chapter 7, in a single Buyer's Life file. This will allow you to keep each step separate and avoid confusion as the plan builds. At the end of the planning process, you will have a complete plan.

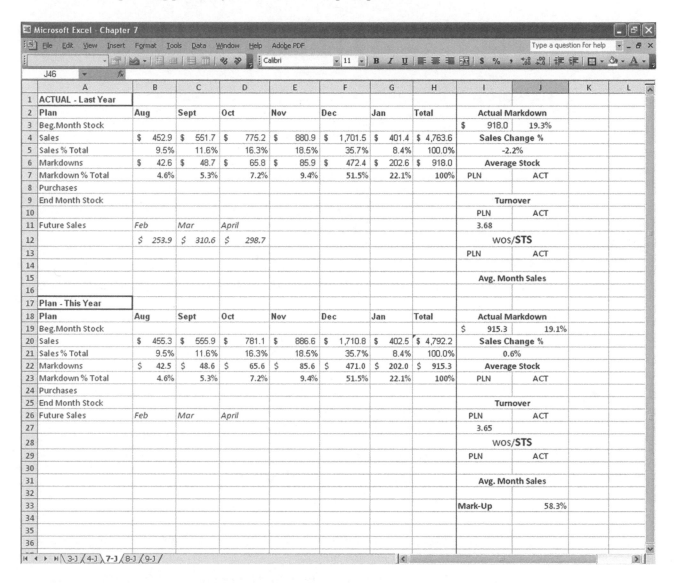

EXCEL SPREADSHEET 7-J.

1. Using turnover, calculate the last year planned average stock:

   Total LY Sales ÷ LY Turnover = LY Average Stock

   Place your cursor under average stock Cell I8 and enter the following:

   Cell I8: =H4/3.68 *enter*

   (See Figure 7.1)

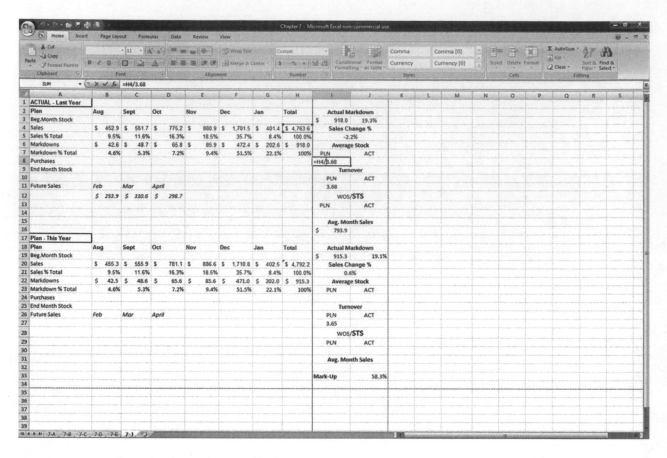

FIGURE 7.1 LY Planned Average Stock.

2. Calculate average monthly sales:

   Total LY Sales ÷ 6 = Average Monthly Sales
   Cell I16: = H4/6 *enter*

3. Calculate the STS ratio:

   Average Stock ÷ Average Monthly Sales
   Cell I14: = I8/I16 *enter*
   (See Figure 7.2)

4. Apply the STS ratio to the monthly sales to determine the beginning of month (BOM) inventory:

   Month Sales × STS Ratio = BOM Inventory
   To enter August, place cursor in Cell B3

   Cell B3: =B4*1.63 *enter*
   To enter September, place cursor in Cell C3

   Cell C3: =C4*1.63 *enter*
   Continue entering each BOM
   (See Figure 7.3)

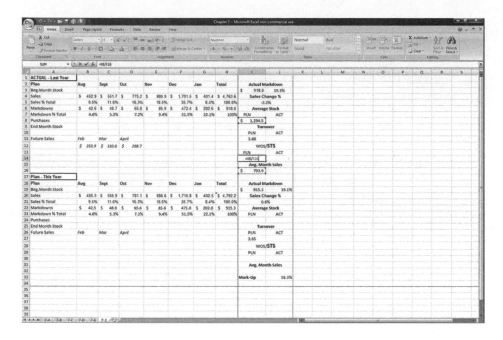

FIGURE 7.2 Average Monthly Sales, Stock to Sales Ratio.

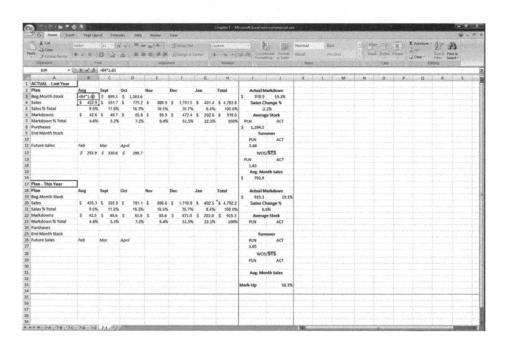

FIGURE 7.3 BOM Calculation.

Note: Jan. EOM = Feb. BOM. Use future sales for February to calculate the Jan. EOM.

5. Apply the BOMs to the EOMs—the stock level at the beginning of each month is equivalent to the previous month's ending stock. This can be done by manually entering each EOM or by copy and pasting the BOM into the EOM cell.
(See Figure 7.4)

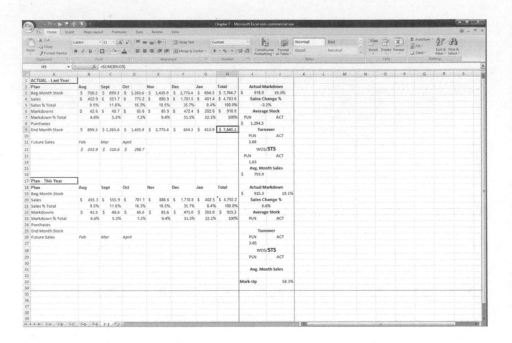

FIGURE 7.4 Apply BOM to EOM.

6. Calculate the actual average stock:

Total BOMs + Last Month EOM ÷ 7 = Actual Average Stock
(See Figure 7.5)

7. Calculate the actual turnover:

Total Sales ÷ Actual Average Stock = Actual Turnover
(See Figure 7.6)

8. Calculate the actual STS ratio:

Actual Average Stock ÷ Average Monthly Sales = Actual STS Ratio
(See Figure 7.7)

CONTINUE CALCULATING THE STS RATIO FOR THE SIX-MONTH PLAN

Using Excel Spreadsheet 7-J, plan *this year's* BOM stock using the STS ratio. (See Figure 7.8).

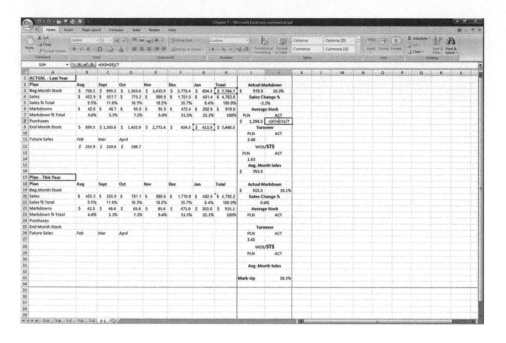

FIGURE 7.5 Calculate Average Stock.

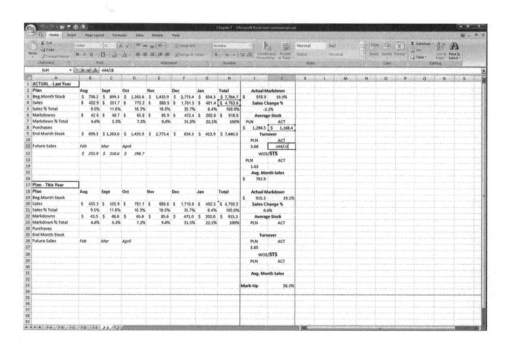

FIGURE 7.6 Calculate Actual Turnover.

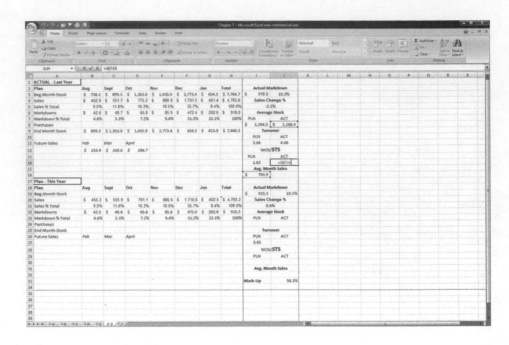

FIGURE 7.7 Calculate Actual Average Stock.

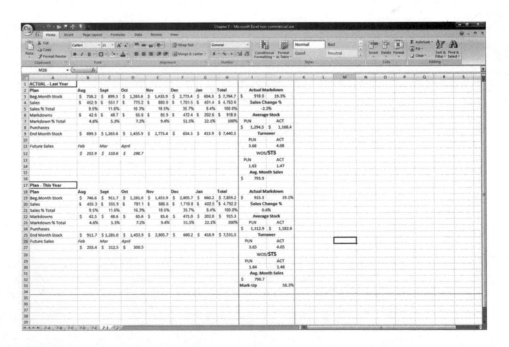

FIGURE 7.8 Calculate Actual Total Season STS Ratio.

TERMINOLOGY

stock-to-sales (STS) method of inventory: The calculation of inventory levels planned as a ratio to planned sales.

weeks-of-supply method of inventory: The calculation of monthly inventory needs based on planned sales for a specified number of weeks. This method more accurately accounts for variability in new inventory and sales fluctuation.

FORMULAS

Average Monthly Sales = Total Sales ÷ 6

e.g., $96.2 = 576.9 ÷ 6

STS Ratio = Average Stock ÷ Average Monthly Sales

e.g., 2.02 : 1 = $872.4 ÷ $429.2

Average Monthly Sales = Average Stock ÷ STS Ratio

e.g., $429.2 = $872.4 ÷ 2.03

Average Stock = Sales × STS Ratio

e.g., $872.4 = $429.2 × 2.03

8

Weeks-of-Supply Method of Inventory

Calculating inventory based on the stock-to-sales (STS) ratio method applies inventory stock levels as a ratio to monthly sales. The idea is to plan one month's inventory level in accordance with that same month's sales plan. The **weeks-of-supply (WOS) method of inventory** is also forward planning, but it considers a specific period of weeks rather than a month alone. The WOS method also operates under the premise that if product demand were to remain constant and no additional inventory were to arrive, the product would be completely sold out in the specified weeks of supply. As with the STS method, the WOS method can be planned using month, quarter, season, or year. Again, for the purposes of understanding the concept, we will use WOS at a seasonal level.

BENEFITS OF THE WOS METHOD

Using the WOS method can better account for variability in sales planning as well as variability in product delivery lead times. Like the STS method, the WOS method plans inventory based on future demand and plans for optimal inventory levels. This approach helps buyers avoid excess inventory and control markdowns. The WOS method also aids the buyer during the planning process and the in-season forecasting process by offering these benefits:

- Greater decision making for high-turnover businesses, such as in quickly changing fashion products
- Fluidity in merchandise arrivals, which are spread over several weeks rather than in one or two concentrated weeks

WHEN ARE CUSTOMERS LIKELY TO BUY A PRODUCT?

Depending on the product category, buyers need to determine customer acceptability time frames. For example, swimwear has a relatively short acceptance period. Particularly in northern climates, the swimwear season begins no earlier than Memorial Day and ends on or before Labor Day. This short selling season leaves little room for error. New swimwear is carefully planned for a specific arrival time. For every day after that arrival time, sales are lost and markdowns will result.

In addition to the actual usability of the swimwear, consumers are sensitive to price. Products with high turnover also require distinct pricing strategies that mirror consumer acceptance. The start of the short swimwear season attracts some consumers at the front end of the product life cycle. These consumers want the newest swimwear styles first, and they are willing to pay full retail price. Other consumers are willing to pay full retail price because they are difficult to fit or wear sizes that are often minimally stocked. The WOS method allows buyers to plan for the early selling period and maximize sales at full retail price. This selling period might be planned for as little as four weeks of supply.

In this example, swimwear buyers would subsequently also plan for the height of the season, analyzing the breadth and depth of product assortment and calculating price. Another type of consumer shops based on immediate need. These consumers lag behind the early-adopter consumers and look for swimwear when it is warm or when they need it for vacation. This period is usually during the height of the season, but it can also occur when buyers need to start clearing out inventory because the season end is in sight. Providing a range of style and size assortments at various prices attracts the immediate-need consumer and reduces inventory. The time frame for this inventory might be four to six weeks, but it overlaps the initial early delivery.

Delivery periods for the WOS method tend to flow more constantly than for the STS method. The STS method assumes large shipments in the month before the sales plan. This concept is also referred to as **front loading**. Front loading delivers all of the swimwear in April so that it is ready for the Memorial Day selling period in May. The WOS method provides inventory on a weekly basis. In theory, the constant flow of inventory replenishes inventory as it sells; this idea is also known as inventory out, inventory in (or vice versa). Achieving a constant flow of inventory increases inventory turnover and gives the buyer greater decision-making control. A constant flow also helps to maintain an interesting product assortment for the consumer. Retailers with constant newness find that consumers shop their stores more regularly in anticipation of new arrivals.

KNOWING WHEN TO BUY—AND HOW MUCH

For buyers, knowing when to buy—and how much—can seem like trying to read a crystal ball. The WOS method controls such buying decisions by assigning specific consumer acceptance periods for each product category. When the buyer is ordering inventory for short selling periods, reaction time or reorder time is improved.

High-fashion businesses are often led by the entertainment industry. When a movie causes a new trend to emerge, buyers must quickly react—but not overreact. The WOS method allows them to plan inventory and sales for a short time frame, from two weeks to as long as three months. The WOS method pinpoints when to get in the business and when to get out. By carefully analyzing actual sales compared to planned sales, the buyer knows when to initiate markdowns if sales are lagging or to place a quick reorder if sales are excelling.

Another benefit of the WOS method is its ability to account for variability. External forces—unforeseen weather conditions, economic turmoil, or the sudden rise of a local sports team—can all impact sales plans. Internal forces, such as warehouse backups, can also play a role in sales results. Fluctuations in delivery allow the buyer to make important decisions about current demand and determine whether to accept a late shipment, cancel an order, or request earlier deliveries.

APPLYING THE WOS METHOD OF INVENTORY

Applying the WOS method requires a high level of planning for each week. Manually calculating inventory for a six-month season is more time-consuming and cumbersome than with the STS method. The exercises in this chapter will help you gain a broad understanding of WOS for the season. Many sophisticated computer programs are available for buyers who use the WOS method. Such programs can calculate highly precise weeks of supply inventories and produce a result within seconds of buyer input.

A retail accounting calendar is necessary to plan the WOS method. Such calendars are referred to as 4-5-4 or 4-4-5 calendars. Retail accounting calendars differ from traditional calendars in that each week begins on Sunday and ends on Saturday, whereas a traditional calendar begins with the date regardless of the day of the week. Traditional calendars always begin with January as the first month of the year. Accounting calendars do not necessarily begin in January; rather, they begin at the start of the organization's fiscal year. In the example below, the fiscal year begins with February. Each month accommodates either a 4- or 5-week month. Refer to the following retail accounting calendar to determine the number of weeks by month.

	S	M	T	W	T	F	S
FEB	30	31	1	2	3	4	5
	6	7	8	9	10	11	12
	13	14	15	16	17	18	19
	20	21	22	23	24	25	26

	S	M	T	W	T	F	S
MAY		1	2	3	4	5	6	7
	8	9	10	11	12	13	14
	15	16	17	18	19	20	21
	22	23	24	25	26	27	28

	S	M	T	W	T	F	S
AUG	31	1	2	3	4	5	6
	7	8	9	10	11	12	13
	14	15	16	17	18	19	20
	21	22	23	24	25	26	27

	S	M	T	W	T	F	S
NOV	30	31	1	2	3	4	5
	6	7	8	9	10	11	12
	13	14	15	16	17	18	19
	20	21	22	23	24	25	26

	S	M	T	W	T	F	S
MAR	27	28	1	2	3	4	5
	6	7	8	9	10	11	12
	13	14	15	16	17	18	19
	20	21	22	23	24	25	26
	27	28	29	30	31	1	2

	S	M	T	W	T	F	S
JUN	29	30	31	1	2	3	4
	5	6	7	8	9	10	11
	12	13	14	15	16	17	18
	19	20	21	22	23	24	25
	26	27	28	29	30	1	2

	S	M	T	W	T	F	S
SEP	28	29	30	31	1	2	3
	4	5	6	7	8	9	10
	11	12	13	14	15	16	17
	18	19	20	21	22	23	24
	25	26	27	28	29	30	1

	S	M	T	W	T	F	S
DEC	27	28	29	30	1	2	3
	4	5	6	7	8	9	10
	11	12	13	14	15	16	17
	18	19	20	21	22	23	24
	25	26	27	28	29	30	31

	S	M	T	W	T	F	S
APR	3	4	5	6	7	8	9
	10	11	12	13	14	15	16
	17	18	19	20	21	22	23
	24	25	26	27	28	29	30

	S	M	T	W	T	F	S
JUL	3	4	5	6	7	8	9
	10	11	12	13	14	15	16
	17	18	19	20	21	22	23
	24	25	26	27	28	29	30

	S	M	T	W	T	F	S
OCT	2	3	4	5	6	7	8
	9	10	11	12	13	14	15
	16	17	18	19	20	21	22
	23	24	25	26	27	28	29

	S	M	T	W	T	F	S
JAN	1	2	3	4	5	6	7
	8	9	10	11	12	13	14
	15	16	17	18	19	20	21
	22	23	24	25	26	27	28

http://www.calendarsquick.com

FIGURE 8.1 4-5-4 Retail Accounting Calendar. (*www.calendarsquick.com/printables/pages/images/large/4-5-4_retail_accounting_calendar_yearly_L.png*)

The process of determining weeks of supply is as follows:

1. Calculate average weekly sales:

    Monthly Sales ÷ Number of Weeks in a Month = Average Weekly Sales

    $52.9 (February) ÷ 4 (# of weeks in February) = 13.225*

*Note that the average weekly sales are not rounded; this is to ensure accuracy and precision.

Calculate weeks of supply as follows:

2. Calculate the weeks of supply:

    26 ÷ Turnover = Weeks of Supply*

*Note that 26 refers to the number of weeks in a six-month season. Calculate quarterly calculations by using 13 weeks and the corresponding quarterly turnover.

If inventory turnover is 3.28, weeks of supply is determined using the number of weeks in the season divided by the inventory turnover.

26 ÷ 3.28 = 7.93 Weeks of Supply

PRACTICE PROBLEMS

1. Calculate average monthly sales for each month:

Month	Total Sales	Average Weekly Sales
Jan.	$28.9	
Feb.	$35.6	
March	$52.9	
April	$38.7	
May	$69.9	
June	$32.5	

2. If inventory turnover is 3.62, what is weeks of supply (WOS)?

3. If WOS in the jewelry department is 13.21, what is turnover?

4. Based on the following average weekly sales, calculate monthly sales:

Month	Average Weekly Sales	Monthly Sales
Aug.	$8.362	
Sept.	$10.587	
Oct.	$14.51	
Nov.	$10.05	
Dec.	$19.475	
Jan.	$9.12	

5. Calculate the WOS for the following businesses:

Business	Turnover	WOS
Designer Handbags	2.62	
Winter Coats	6.23	
Jeans	4.56	

6. If the WOS is increased, what is the impact on turnover?

7. In a top-down planning process, the Accessories divisional merchandise manager (DMM) must arrive at a total division turnover of 3.58. How would the DMM proportion each business to achieve that plan? Identify possible turnover and WOS for each business category.

   Hosiery
   Scarves
   Cold Weather Accessories
   Hair Accessories
   Designer Handbags
   Private Label Handbags
   Small Leather Goods
   Designer Jewelry
   Fashion Jewelry
   Millinery

8. Suppose that global warming is showing signs of increasingly mild winters. The cold weather accessory buyer experienced a turnover of 4.63 last year. The DMM feels that the buyer should decrease WOS by 1.7 weeks this year. What was the WOS last year, and how would the buyer plan turnover and WOS this year?

9. A single-unit fashion boutique owner is planning business for the next season. Last year the boutique sales were $565.0 for the fall season. The owner estimates that average inventory was $1017.0. Calculate inventory turnover and WOS for last year.

   If the boutique owner wants to reduce inventory, what advice would you give and why?

APPLICATION

Buyers using the WOS method of inventory will determine monthly inventory stock levels by using specific weeks of supply. The application explained in this chapter is a simplified process using monthly beginning of month (BOM) planning. Many sophisticated computer programs can process the WOS method of inventory quickly and more precisely with monthly WOS variability. Using the manual calculations in this chapter will enable the buyer to determine WOS and make purchasing decisions when computer software is not available.

CALCULATING THE WOS METHOD IN A SIX-MONTH PLAN

Using Spreadsheet 8-A, plan *last year* BOM stock using the WOS method of inventory.

Calculate Last Year Actual for Sales and Markdowns

Follow the step-by-step process:

1. Using turnover, calculate the planned WOS:

   26 ÷ Turnover = Weeks of Supply
   26 ÷ 4.12 = 6.31 Planned Weeks of Supply

2. Calculate Average Weekly Sales By Month:

Month	Sales ÷ # of Weeks	Average Weekly Sales
Aug.	87.0 ÷ 4	= 21.75
Sept.	124.9 ÷ 5	= 24.98
Oct.	110.3 ÷ 4	= 27.575
Nov.	88.6 ÷ 4	= 22.15
Dec.	105.3 ÷ 5	= 21.06
Jan.	48.3 ÷ 4	= 12.075
Feb.	45.2 ÷ 4	= 11.3
March	28.6 ÷ 5	= 5.72
April	18.2 ÷ 4	= 4.55

3. Using the WOS method of inventory, calculate the BOM stocks:

AUGUST				
# Wks Needed	Month	# Wks Used	×	Avg. Wkly. Sales
6.31	August: 4	4		$87.0
2.31	September: 2.31	2.31	×	$24.98 = $57.70
AUGUST BOM				**$144.7**

SEPTEMBER				
# Wks Needed	Month	# Wks Used	×	Avg. Wkly. Sales
6.31	September: 5	5		$124.9
1.31	October: 1.31	1.31	×	$27.575 = $36.12
SEPTEMBER BOM				**$161.0**

OCTOBER				
# Wks Needed	Month	# Wks Used	×	Avg. Wkly. Sales
6.31	October:	4		$110.3
2.31	November: 2.31	2.31	×	$22.15 = $51.17
OCTOBER BOM				**$161.5**

NOVEMBER				
# Wks Needed	Month	# Wks Used	×	Avg. Wkly. Sales
6.31	November:	4		$88.6
2.31	December: 2.31	2.31	×	$21.06 = $48.65
NOVEMBER BOM				**$137.3**

DECEMBER				
# Wks Needed	Month	# Wks Used	×	Avg. Wkly. Sales
6.31	December:	5		$105.3
1.31	January: 1.31	1.31	×	$12.075 = $15.82
DECEMBER BOM				**$121.1**

JANUARY				
# Wks Needed	Month	# Wks Used	×	Avg. Wkly. Sales
6.31	January:	4		$48.3
2.31	February: 2.31	2.31	×	$11.3 = $26.103
JANUARY BOM				**$74.4**

FEBRUARY				
# Wks Needed	Month	# Wks Used	×	Avg. Wkly. Sales
6.31	February:	4		$45.2
2.31	March: 2.31	2.31	×	$5.72 = $13.21
FEBRUARY BOM				**$58.4**

4. Enter each month BOM into the Excel Spreadsheet 8-A plan:

Aug.	$144.7
Sept.	$161.0
Oct.	$161.5
Nov.	$137.3
Dec.	$122.8
Jan.	$63.9
Jan. EOM	$66.6

5. Total the six-month BOMs:

$144.7 + $161.0 + $161.5 + $137.3 + $122.8 + $63.9 = $791.2

6. Apply the BOMs to the EOMs: The stock level at the beginning of each month is equivalent to the previous month's ending stock.

7. Total the six-month season EOMs:

$161.0 + $161.5 + $137.3 + $122.8 + $63.9 + $66.6 = $713.1

8. Calculate the actual average stock:

   Total BOMs + Last Month EOM ÷ 7 = Actual Average Stock
   $791.2 + $66.6 ÷ 7 = $122.5

9. Calculate the actual turnover:

   Total Sales ÷ Actual Average Stock = Actual Turnover
   $564.4 ÷ $122.5 = 4.61

10. Calculate the actual WOS:

    26 ÷ Actual Turnover = Actual Weeks of Supply
    26 ÷ 4.61 = 5.64

Calculate This Year's Plan for Sales and Markdowns

Follow the step-by-step process:

1. Using turnover, calculate the planned WOS:

   26 ÷ Turnover = Weeks of Supply
   26 ÷ 3.98 = 6.53 Planned Weeks of Supply

2. Calculate average weekly sales by month:

Month	Sales ÷ # of Weeks	Average Weekly Sales
Aug.	102.7 ÷ 4	= 25.675
Sept.	147.4 ÷ 5	= 29.48
Oct.	130.1 ÷ 4	= 32.525
Nov.	106.7 ÷ 4	= 26.675
Dec.	124.7 ÷ 5	= 24.94
Jan.	55.5 ÷ 4	= 13.875
Feb.	53.4 ÷ 4	= 13.35
March	33.8 ÷ 5	= 6.76
April	21.5 ÷ 4	= 5.375

3. Using the WOS method of inventory, calculate the BOM stocks:

AUGUST				
# Wks Needed	Month	# Wks Used	×	Avg. Wkly. Sales
6.53	August: 4	4		$102.7
2.53	September: 2.53	2.53	×	$29.48 = $74.58
AUGUST BOM				**$177.3**

SEPTEMBER				
# Wks Needed	Month	# Wks Used	×	Avg. Wkly. Sales
6.53	September: 5	5		$147.4
1.53	October: 1.53	1.53	×	$32.525 = $49.76
SEPTEMBER BOM				**$197.2**

OCTOBER				
# Wks Needed	Month	# Wks Used	×	Avg. Wkly. Sales
6.53	October:	4		$130.1
2.53	November: 2.53	2.53	×	$26.675 = $67.49
OCTOBER BOM				**$197.6**

NOVEMBER				
# Wks Needed	Month	# Wks Used	×	Avg. Wkly. Sales
6.53	November:	4		$106.7
2.53	December: 2.53	2.53	×	$24.94 = $63.98
NOVEMBER BOM				**$170.7**

DECEMBER				
# Wks Needed	Month	# Wks Used	×	Avg. Wkly. Sales
6.53	December:	5		$124.7
1.53	January: 1.53	1.53	×	$13.875 = $21.23
DECEMBER BOM				**$145.9**

JANUARY				
# Wks Needed	Month	# Wks Used	×	Avg. Wkly. Sales
6.53	January:	4		$55.5
2.53	February: 2.53	2.53	×	$13.35 = $33.78
JANUARY BOM				**$89.3**

FEBRUARY				
# Wks Needed	Month	# Wks Used	×	Avg. Wkly. Sales
6.53	February:	4		$53.4
2.53	March: 2.53	2.53	×	$6.76 = $17.10
FEBRUARY BOM				**$70.5**

4. Enter each month's BOM into the Excel Spreadsheet 8-A plan:

Aug.	$177.3
Sept.	$197.2
Oct.	$197.6
Nov.	$170.7
Dec.	$145.9
Jan.	$89.3
Jan. EOM	$70.5

5. Total the six-month BOMs:

   $177.3 + $197.2 + $197.6 + $170.7 + $145.9 + $89.3 = $978.0

6. Apply the BOMs to the EOMs: The stock level at the beginning of each month is equivalent to the previous month's ending stock.

7. Total the six-month season EOMs:

   $197.2 + $197.6 + $170.7 + $145.9 + $89.3 + $70.5 = $871.2

8. Calculate the actual average stock:

   Total BOMs + Last Month EOM ÷ 7 = Actual Average Stock
   $978.0 + $70.5 ÷ 7 = $149.8

9. Calculate the actual turnover:

   Total Sales ÷ Actual Average Stock = Actual Turnover
   $667.1 ÷ $149.8 = 4.45

10. Calculate the actual WOS:

26 ÷ Actual Turnover = Actual Weeks of Supply
26 ÷ 4.45 = 5.84

	A	B	C	D	E	F	G	H	I	J	K	L	M
1	Actual - Last Year												
2	Plan	Aug	Sept	Oct	Nov	Dec	Jan	Total	Actual Markdown				
3	Beg.Month Stock												
4	Sales								Sales Change %				
5	Markdowns	10.2	15.3	12.9	11.5	31.8	17.2		Average Stock				
6	Purchases								PLN ACT				
7	End Month Stock								Turnover				
8									PLN 4.12 ACT				
9	Future Sales	Feb	Mar	Apr					WOS/STS				
10									PLN ACT				
11													
12													
13													
14	Plan - This Year												
15	Plan							Total	Actual Markdown				
16	Beg.Month Stock								$130.1				
17	Sales	102.7	147.4	130.1	106.7	124.7	55.5		Sales Change +18.2%				
18	Markdowns								Average Stock				
19	Purchases								PLN ACT				
20	End Month Stock								Turnover				
21	Future Sales	Feb	Mar	Apr					PLN 3.98 ACT				
22			53.4	33.8	21.5				WOS/STS				
23													
24									Mark-Up				
25													
26													
27													
28													
29													

Sheet tabs: 8-A / 8-B / 8-C / 8-D / 8-E / STS.WOS Comparison

EXCEL SPREADSHEET 8-A.

STOCK TO SALES AND WEEKS OF SUPPLY STS/WOS COMPARISON

Review the comparison spreadsheet. Note that the sales actual and plan are the same for each plan. Using the STS method or the WOS method results in two different BOM stock levels for each month.

What is the primary difference in the flow of inventory?

How will changing inventory arrivals affect profitability?

Identify what businesses would benefit from STS? From WOS?

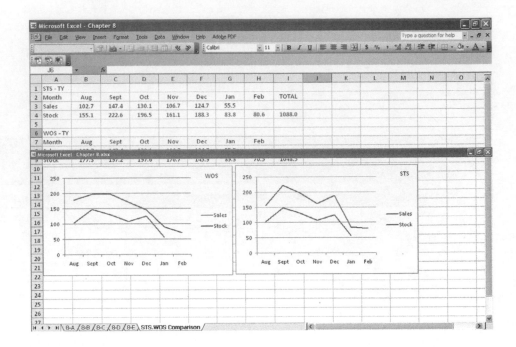

FIGURE 8.2 STS. WOS Comparison.

Your Turn

Complete Excel Spreadsheets 8-B and 8-C.

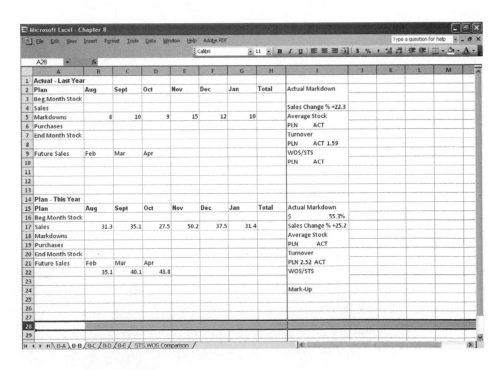

EXCEL SPREADSHEET 8-B.

A BUYER'S LIFE

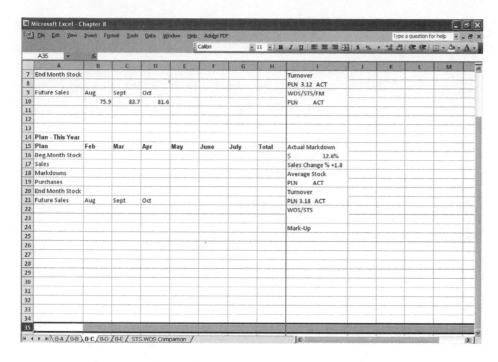

	A	B	C	D	E	F	G	H	I	J	K	L	M
7	End Month Stock								Turnover				
8									PLN 3.12 ACT				
9	Future Sales	Aug	Sept	Oct					WOS/STS/FM				
10		75.9	83.7	81.6					PLN ACT				
11													
12													
13													
14	Plan - This Year												
15	Plan	Feb	Mar	Apr	May	June	July	Total	Actual Markdown				
16	Beg.Month Stock								$ 12.6%				
17	Sales								Sales Change % +1.8				
18	Markdowns								Average Stock				
19	Purchases								PLN ACT				
20	End Month Stock								Turnover				
21	Future Sales	Aug	Sept	Oct					PLN 3.18 ACT				
22									WOS/STS				
23													
24									Mark-Up				
25													
26													
27													
28													
29													
30													
31													
32													
33													
34													
35													

EXCEL SPREADSHEET 8-C.

Complete Excel Spreadsheets 8-D and 8-E for homework.

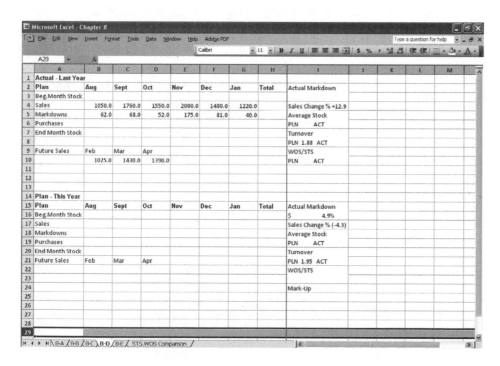

	A	B	C	D	E	F	G	H	I	J	K	L	M
1	Actual - Last Year												
2	Plan	Aug	Sept	Oct	Nov	Dec	Jan	Total	Actual Markdown				
3	Beg.Month Stock												
4	Sales	1050.0	1760.0	1550.0	2000.0	1480.0	1220.0		Sales Change % +12.9				
5	Markdowns	62.0	68.0	52.0	175.0	81.0	40.0		Average Stock				
6	Purchases								PLN ACT				
7	End Month Stock								Turnover				
8									PLN 1.88 ACT				
9	Future Sales	Feb	Mar	Apr					WOS/STS				
10		1025.0	1430.0	1390.0					PLN ACT				
11													
12													
13													
14	Plan - This Year												
15	Plan	Aug	Sept	Oct	Nov	Dec	Jan	Total	Actual Markdown				
16	Beg.Month Stock								$ 4.9%				
17	Sales								Sales Change % (-4.3)				
18	Markdowns								Average Stock				
19	Purchases								PLN ACT				
20	End Month Stock								Turnover				
21	Future Sales	Feb	Mar	Apr					PLN 1.95 ACT				
22									WOS/STS				
23													
24									Mark-Up				
25													
26													
27													
28													
29													

EXCEL SPREADSHEET 8-D.

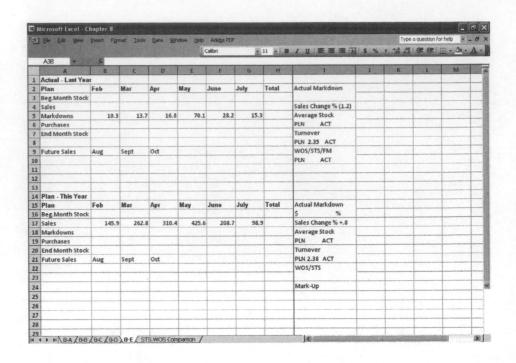

Excel Spreadsheet 8-E.

	A	B	C	D	E	F	G	H	I
1	Actual - Last Year								
2	Plan	Feb	Mar	Apr	May	June	July	Total	Actual Markdown
3	Beg.Month Stock								
4	Sales								Sales Change % (1.2)
5	Markdowns	10.3	13.7	16.8	70.1	28.2	15.3		Average Stock
6	Purchases								PLN ACT
7	End Month Stock								Turnover
8									PLN 2.35 ACT
9	Future Sales	Aug	Sept	Oct					WOS/STS/FM
10									PLN ACT
11									
12									
13									
14	Plan - This Year								
15	Plan	Feb	Mar	Apr	May	June	July	Total	Actual Markdown
16	Beg.Month Stock								$ %
17	Sales	145.9	262.8	310.4	425.6	208.7	98.9		Sales Change % +.8
18	Markdowns								Average Stock
19	Purchases								PLN ACT
20	End Month Stock								Turnover
21	Future Sales	Aug	Sept	Oct					PLN 2.38 ACT
22									WOS/STS
23									
24									Mark-Up
25									
26									
27									
28									
29									

CREATE IT IN EXCEL!

Setting up the WOS method in an Excel spreadsheet is a lengthy process but can ultimately save significant time over the long course. As mentioned earlier in the text, many retailers have in-house computer programs that will produce a WOS plan in seconds. In the meantime, utilization of this Excel spreadsheet will aid the small boutique owner and enhance Excel proficiency.

CALCULATING THE WOS METHOD IN A SIX-MONTH PLAN

Using Excel Spreadsheet 8-J, plan *last year's* BOM stock using the WOS method of inventory.

Calculate Last Year Actual for Sales and Markdowns
Follow the step-by-step process to plan WOS:

1. Using turnover, calculate the planned WOS:

    26 ÷ Turnover = Weeks of Supply
    26 ÷ 4.12 = 6.31 Planned Weeks of Supply
    Cell I1: = 26/I22 *enter*

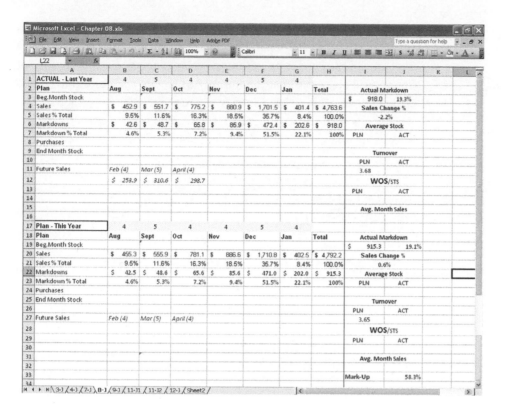

EXCEL SPREADSHEET 8-J.

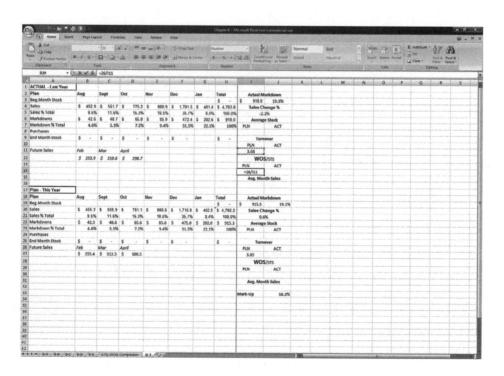

FIGURE 8.3 Calculate Planned WOS.

2. Calculate average weekly sales by month:
This can be done on a separate sheet of paper or it can be entered into this same Excel sheet by adding rows or placing it at the bottom of the worksheet. Note that the number of weeks by month have been added above each month for easy reference.
On line 14 create a new reference for average weekly sales by month. Create the title in cell A14, and enter the formula by month as follows:

<u>Month Sales ÷ # of Weeks</u> = <u>Average Weekly Sales</u>
<u>Aug. Cell B14: =B4/B1</u>
<u>Sept. Cell C14: =C4/C1</u>
<u>Oct. Cell D14: =D4/D1</u>

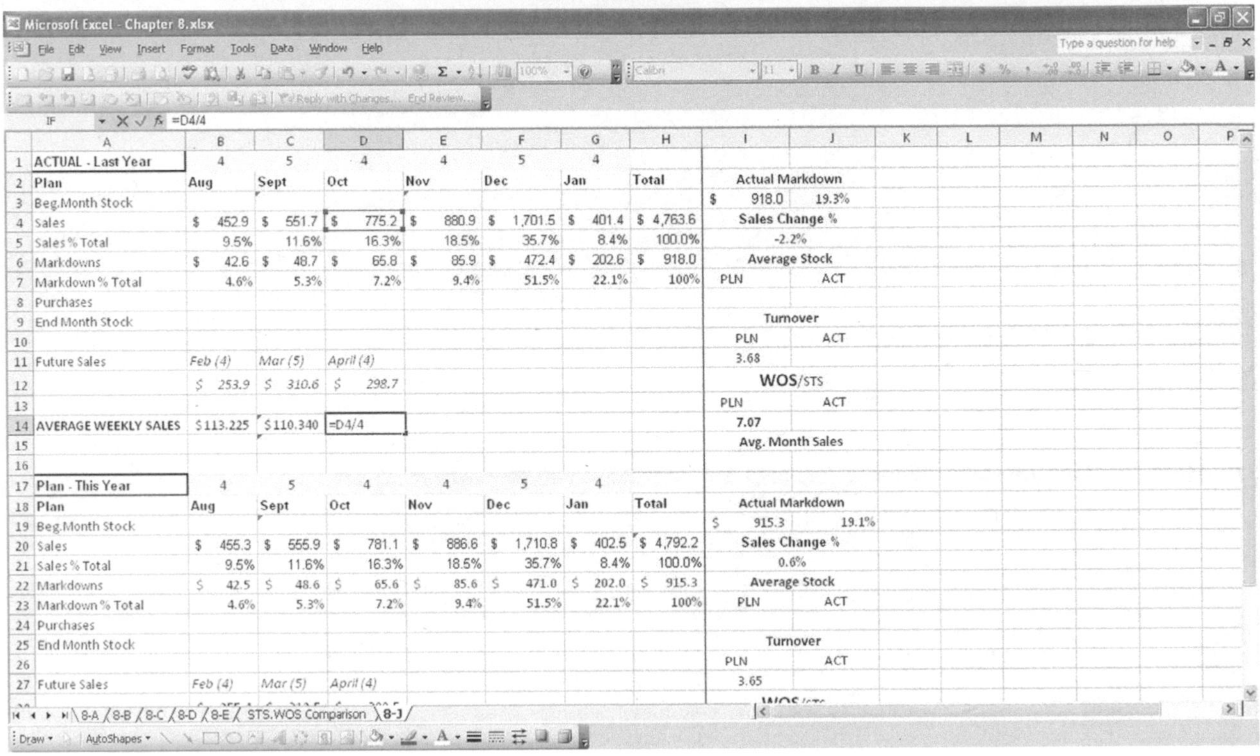
Microsoft Excel - Chapter 8.xlsx

IF =D4/4

	A	B	C	D	E	F	G	H	I	J
1	ACTUAL - Last Year	4	5	4	4	5	4			
2	Plan	Aug	Sept	Oct	Nov	Dec	Jan	Total	Actual Markdown	
3	Beg.Month Stock								$ 918.0	19.3%
4	Sales	$ 452.9	$ 551.7	$ 775.2	$ 880.9	$ 1,701.5	$ 401.4	$ 4,763.6	Sales Change %	
5	Sales % Total	9.5%	11.6%	16.3%	18.5%	35.7%	8.4%	100.0%	-2.2%	
6	Markdowns	$ 42.6	$ 48.7	$ 65.8	$ 85.9	$ 472.4	$ 202.6	$ 918.0	Average Stock	
7	Markdown % Total	4.6%	5.3%	7.2%	9.4%	51.5%	22.1%	100%	PLN	ACT
8	Purchases									
9	End Month Stock								Turnover	
10									PLN	ACT
11	Future Sales	Feb (4)	Mar (5)	April (4)					3.68	
12		$ 253.9	$ 310.6	$ 298.7					WOS/STS	
13									PLN	ACT
14	AVERAGE WEEKLY SALES	$113.225	$110.340	=D4/4					7.07	
15									Avg. Month Sales	
16										
17	Plan - This Year	4	5	4	4	5	4			
18	Plan	Aug	Sept	Oct	Nov	Dec	Jan	Total	Actual Markdown	
19	Beg.Month Stock								$ 915.3	19.1%
20	Sales	$ 455.3	$ 555.9	$ 781.1	$ 886.6	$ 1,710.8	$ 402.5	$ 4,792.2	Sales Change %	
21	Sales % Total	9.5%	11.6%	16.3%	18.5%	35.7%	8.4%	100.0%	0.6%	
22	Markdowns	$ 42.5	$ 48.6	$ 65.6	$ 85.6	$ 471.0	$ 202.0	$ 915.3	Average Stock	
23	Markdown % Total	4.6%	5.3%	7.2%	9.4%	51.5%	22.1%	100%	PLN	ACT
24	Purchases									
25	End Month Stock								Turnover	
26									PLN	ACT
27	Future Sales	Feb (4)	Mar (5)	April (4)					3.65	

8-A / 8-B / 8-C / 8-D / 8-E / STS.WOS Comparison / 8-J

FIGURE 8.4 Calculating Average Weekly Sales.

3. Using the WOS method of inventory, calculate the BOM stocks:

AUGUST				
<u># Wks Needed</u>	<u>Month</u>	<u># Wks Used</u>	<u>×</u>	<u>Avg. Wkly. Sales</u>
7.07	August: 4	4		$452.9
3.07	September: 3.07	3.07	×	<u>$110.340 = $338.7</u>
AUGUST BOM				**$791.6**

Enter August BOM in cell B3 as follows:
Cell B3: =B4+(3.07*C14)

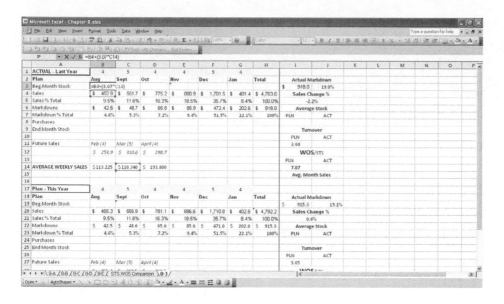

FIGURE 8.5 Calculate August BOM.

SEPTEMBER				
# Wks Needed	Month	# Wks Used	×	Avg. Wkly. Sales
7.07	September: 5	5		$551.7
2.07	October: 2.07	2.07	×	$193.80 = $401.17
SEPTEMBER BOM				**$952.9**

Enter September BOM in cell C3 as follows:
    Cell C3: =C4+(2.07*D14)

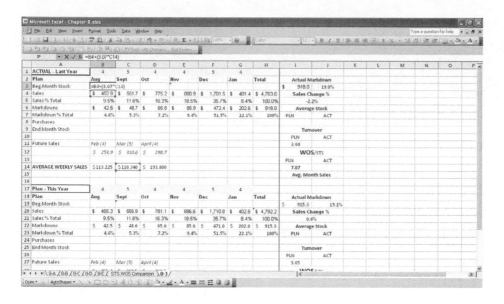

FIGURE 8.6 Calculate September BOM.

OCTOBER				
# Wks Needed	Month	# Wks Used	×	Avg. Wkly. Sales
7.07	October:	4		$775.2
3.07	November: 3.07	3.07	×	$220.225 = $676.09
OCTOBER BOM				**$1451.3**

Enter October BOM in cell D3 as follows:

Cell D3: =D4+(3.07*E14)

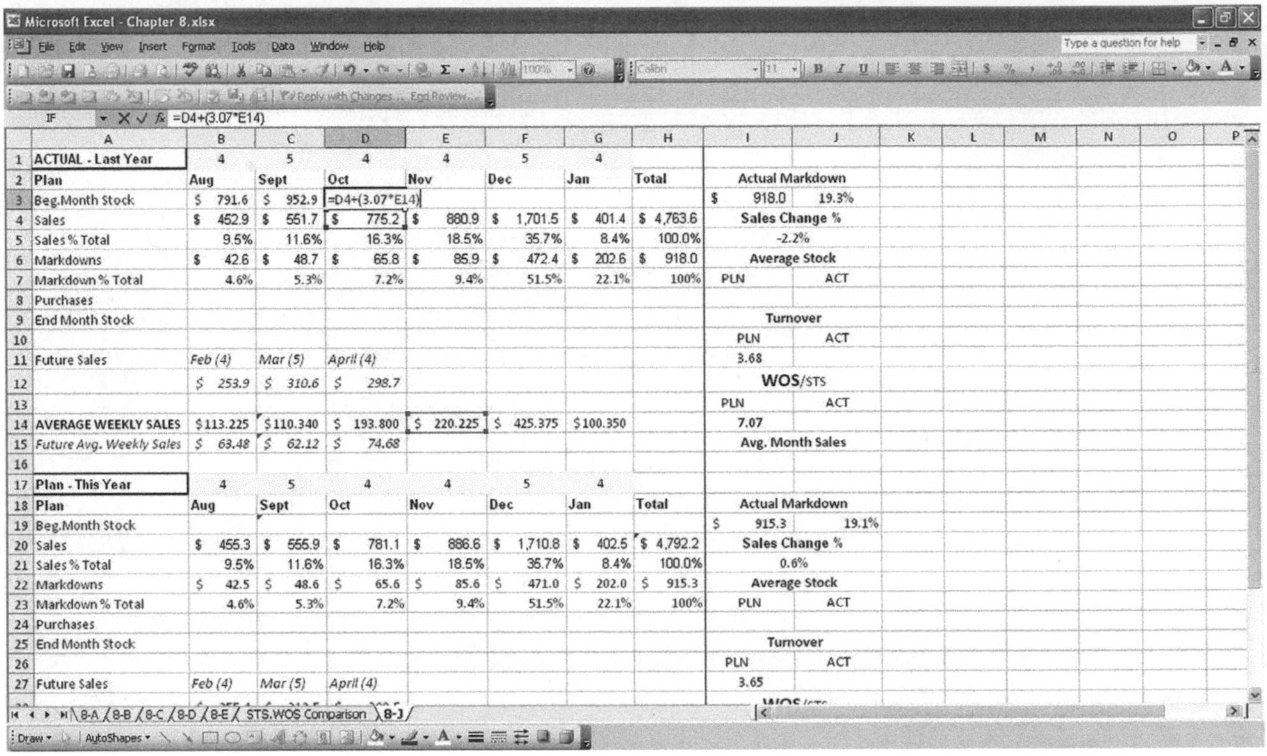

Microsoft Excel - Chapter 8.xlsx

IF =D4+(3.07*E14)

	A	B	C	D	E	F	G	H	I	J
1	ACTUAL - Last Year	4	5	4	4	5	4			
2	Plan	Aug	Sept	Oct	Nov	Dec	Jan	Total	Actual Markdown	
3	Beg.Month Stock	$ 791.6	$ 952.9	=D4+(3.07*E14)					$ 918.0	19.3%
4	Sales	$ 452.9	$ 551.7	$ 775.2	$ 880.9	$ 1,701.5	$ 401.4	$ 4,763.6	Sales Change %	
5	Sales % Total	9.5%	11.6%	16.3%	18.5%	35.7%	8.4%	100.0%	-2.2%	
6	Markdowns	$ 42.6	$ 48.7	$ 65.8	$ 85.9	$ 472.4	$ 202.6	$ 918.0	Average Stock	
7	Markdown % Total	4.6%	5.3%	7.2%	9.4%	51.5%	22.1%	100%	PLN	ACT
8	Purchases									
9	End Month Stock								Turnover	
10									PLN	ACT
11	Future Sales	*Feb (4)*	*Mar (5)*	*April (4)*					3.68	
12		*$ 253.9*	*$ 310.6*	*$ 298.7*					WOS/STS	
13									PLN	ACT
14	AVERAGE WEEKLY SALES	$113.225	$110.340	$ 193.800	$ 220.225	$ 425.375	$100.350		7.07	
15	*Future Avg. Weekly Sales*	*$ 63.48*	*$ 62.12*	*$ 74.68*					Avg. Month Sales	
16										
17	Plan - This Year	4	5	4	4	5	4			
18	Plan	Aug	Sept	Oct	Nov	Dec	Jan	Total	Actual Markdown	
19	Beg.Month Stock								$ 915.3	19.1%
20	Sales	$ 455.3	$ 555.9	$ 781.1	$ 886.6	$ 1,710.8	$ 402.5	$ 4,792.2	Sales Change %	
21	Sales % Total	9.5%	11.6%	16.3%	18.5%	35.7%	8.4%	100.0%	0.6%	
22	Markdowns	$ 42.5	$ 48.6	$ 65.6	$ 85.6	$ 471.0	$ 202.0	$ 915.3	Average Stock	
23	Markdown % Total	4.6%	5.3%	7.2%	9.4%	51.5%	22.1%	100%	PLN	ACT
24	Purchases									
25	End Month Stock								Turnover	
26									PLN	ACT
27	Future Sales	*Feb (4)*	*Mar (5)*	*April (4)*					3.65	

8-A / 8-B / 8-C / 8-D / 8-E / STS.WOS Comparison / 8-J

FIGURE 8.7 Calculate October BOM.

4. Continue entering each BOM for November, December, and January and the EOM for January by using the future months sales.
5. Total the six-month BOMs.
6. Apply the BOMs to the EOMs: The stock level at the beginning of each month is equivalent to the previous month's ending stock.
7. Total the six-month season EOMs.

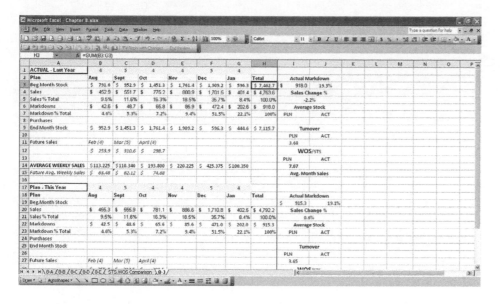

FIGURE 8.8 Total LY BOMs.

8. Calculate the actual average stock:

Total BOMs + Last Month EOM ÷ 7 = Actual Average Stock

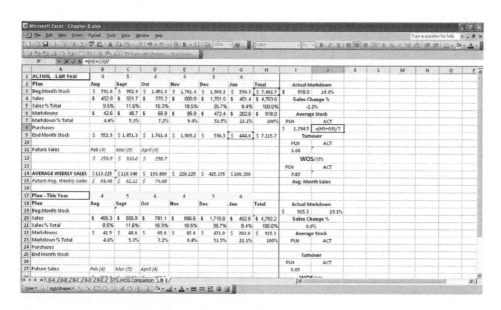

FIGURE 8.9 Calculate Actual Average Stock.

9. Calculate the actual turnover:

Total Sales ÷ Actual Average Stock = Actual Turnover

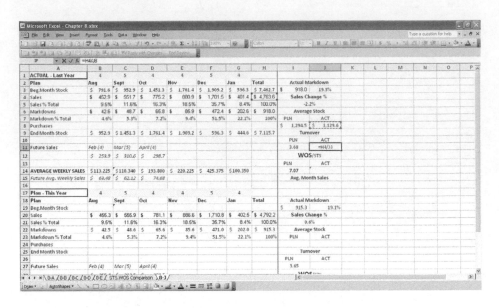

FIGURE 8.10 Calculate Actual Turnover.

10. Calculate the actual WOS:

26 ÷ Actual Turnover = Actual Weeks of Supply

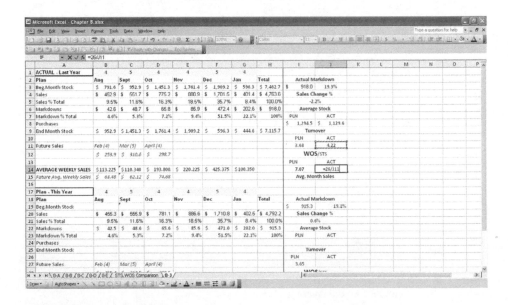

FIGURE 8.11 Calculate Actual WOS.

Continue the Process for This Year Plan

FIGURE 8.12 Completed WOS Plan.

TERMINOLOGY

front loading: Delivering most of the inventory at the start of a season or month.

weeks-of-supply (WOS) method of inventory: The calculation of monthly inventory needs based on planned sales for a specified number of weeks. This method more accurately accounts for variability in new inventory and sales fluctuations.

FORMULAS

Monthly Average Sales = Total Month Sales ÷ # of Weeks in Month

e.g., $64.2 = $256.9 ÷ 4

Weeks of Supply = 26 ÷ Turnover

e.g., 7.14 = 26 ÷ 3.64

9

PLANNING PURCHASE RECEIPTS

Planning purchase receipts is the final step in the six-month merchandising plan. The buyer calculates this final step only after establishing sales, markdowns, and stock levels.

ESTABLISH THE PLAN COMPONENTS

As discussed in Chapter 3, sales are the most critical component of the six-month plan. Determining a sales plan that is realistic yet challenging is at the core of all other planning activities.

Buyers determine markdowns (see Chapter 4) based on several factors, including projecting a reasonable amount for unsold inventory. When sales exceed planned levels, markdowns usually decrease. However, when sales fall short of planned levels, markdowns inevitably increase.

Planned inventory stock levels are directly correlated with sales and markdowns. Buyers face the constant challenge of carefully balancing stock and sales because these components directly affect profitability. After planning the sales, markdowns, BOMs, and EOMs, the buyer can easily calculate monthly purchase receipts.

CALCULATE THE MONTHLY PURCHASE RECEIPTS

Purchase receipts are essentially the amount of inventory needed each month to maintain BOM stock levels. After calculating the dollar amount of stock, the buyer computes the BOM for a given month, subtracts the outgoing sales and markdown reductions of inventory, and then computes the difference between the remaining inventory dollar amount and what is necessary to begin the next month.

The basic calculation of purchase receipts is essential in setting purchase boundaries for buyers. Staying within the purchase plan can be challenging—it requires thoughtful planning and discipline. In a sense, purchase plans are similar to a personal budget. After paying all of the bills and accounting for expenses, one can decide how to spend the money that remains.

Identifying the actual monthly purchase dollars available is first planned at the total department level. In Chapters 7 and 8, the stock-to-sales (STS) ratio method of inventory and the weeks-of-supply (WOS) method of inventory were calculated to determine BOM stock levels. In this chapter, the purchase dollars are subsequently calculated. By comparing each method of inventory and analyzing the flow of purchase receipts, you will further understand each method and learn to identify the preferred method for specific businesses. Although this is the final step in creating the six-month plan, the buyer is not quite ready to head to market and make actual purchases. This six-month plan serves as a baseline for the total department plan, which should be further broken down by classification and be manipulated to meet the needs of the business. The result of this could resemble a top-down plan and then a bottom-up plan, all within the buyership. Planning and reviewing the business in this manner ensures internal checks and balances so that the buyer is able to review the business from every angle based on a snapshot of a moment in time.

APPLICATION

This application uses the STS and WOS methods of inventory to compare inventory and purchase receipts for each planning method. By using the calculations in this chapter, buyers can manually calculate total purchase receipts by month. The receipts can then be broken down into categories for deciding on actual purchases. Although it is important to stay within the guidelines of this plan, it can be carefully manipulated to meet the needs of an individual business. Manual shifting of inventory is cumbersome because it involves recalculating totals; however, this task can be easily accomplished using specialized computer programs.

CALCULATING PLANNED RECEIPTS IN A SIX-MONTH PLAN

Calculating the planned receipts in a six-month plan is dependent on establishing sales, markdowns, and BOM and EOM stock levels. Once complete, the purchase plan is calculated using a two-step process.

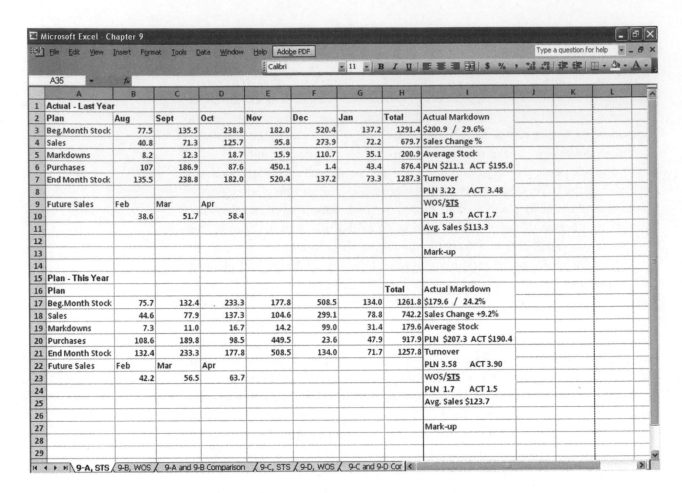

	A	B	C	D	E	F	G	H	I	J	K	L
1	Actual - Last Year											
2	Plan	Aug	Sept	Oct	Nov	Dec	Jan	Total	Actual Markdown			
3	Beg.Month Stock	77.5	135.5	238.8	182.0	520.4	137.2	1291.4	$200.9 / 29.6%			
4	Sales	40.8	71.3	125.7	95.8	273.9	72.2	679.7	Sales Change %			
5	Markdowns	8.2	12.3	18.7	15.9	110.7	35.1	200.9	Average Stock			
6	Purchases	107	186.9	87.6	450.1	1.4	43.4	876.4	PLN $211.1 ACT $195.0			
7	End Month Stock	135.5	238.8	182.0	520.4	137.2	73.3	1287.3	Turnover			
8									PLN 3.22 ACT 3.48			
9	Future Sales	Feb	Mar	Apr					WOS/STS			
10		38.6	51.7	58.4					PLN 1.9 ACT 1.7			
11									Avg. Sales $113.3			
12												
13									Mark-up			
14												
15	Plan - This Year											
16	Plan							Total	Actual Markdown			
17	Beg.Month Stock	75.7	132.4	233.3	177.8	508.5	134.0	1261.8	$179.6 / 24.2%			
18	Sales	44.6	77.9	137.3	104.6	299.1	78.8	742.2	Sales Change +9.2%			
19	Markdowns	7.3	11.0	16.7	14.2	99.0	31.4	179.6	Average Stock			
20	Purchases	108.6	189.8	98.5	449.5	23.6	47.9	917.9	PLN $207.3 ACT $190.4			
21	End Month Stock	132.4	233.3	177.8	508.5	134.0	71.7	1257.8	Turnover			
22	Future Sales	Feb	Mar	Apr					PLN 3.58 ACT 3.90			
23		42.2	56.5	63.7					WOS/STS			
24									PLN 1.7 ACT 1.5			
25									Avg. Sales $123.7			
26												
27									Mark-up			
28												
29												

9-A, STS / 9-B, WOS / 9-A and 9-B Comparison / 9-C, STS / 9-D, WOS / 9-C and 9-D Cor

EXCEL SPREADSHEET 9-A.

Use the STS method of inventory

Using Excel Spreadsheet 9-A, complete the plan using the STS method of inventory. See Appendix B for full-size versions of all Excel Spreadsheets, which can be pulled from the book and worked on separately. Calculate last year's actual and this year's plan for all steps except purchases.

Follow the step-by-step process to calculate planned receipts:

Step 1: Month BOM – Sales – Markdowns = Available Inventory

Step 2: Month EOM – Available Inventory = Purchases

1. Begin by calculating last year monthly purchases:

August LY

Step 1: $77.5 – $40.8 – $8.2 = $28.5

Step 2: $135.5 – $28.5 = $107.0, August purchases

September LY

Step 1: $135.5 - $71.3 - $12.3 = $51.9

Step 2: $238.8 - $51.9 = $186.9

October LY

Step 1: $238.8 - $125.7 - $18.7 = $94.4

Step 2: $182.0 - $94.4 = $87.6

November LY

Step 1: $182.0 - $95.8 - $15.9 = $70.3

Step 2: $520.4 - $70.3 = $450.1

December LY

Step 1: $520.4 - $273.9 - $110.7 = $135.8

Step 2: $137.2 - $135.8 = $1.4

January LY

Step 1: $137.2 - $72.2 - $35.1 = $29.9

Step 2: $73.3 - $29.9 = $43.4

Calculate LY actual average stock, turnover, and STS:

Average stock: $1291.4 + $73.3 ÷ 7 = $195.0

Turnover: $679.7 ÷ $195.0 = 3.49

Stock-to-sales ratio: $195.0 ÷ $113.3 = 1.72

2. Calculate this year monthly purchases:

August

Step 1: $75.7 - $44.6 - $7.3 = $23.8

Step 2: $132.4 - $23.8 = $108.6, August purchases

September

Step 1: $132.4 - $77.9 - $11.0 = $43.5

Step 2: $233.3 - $43.5 = $189.8

October

Step 1: $233.3 - $137.3 - $16.7 = $79.3

Step 2: $177.8 - $79.3 = $98.5

November

Step 1: $177.8 - $104.6 - $14.2 = $59.0

Step 2: $508.5 - $59.0 = $449.5

December

Step 1: $508.5 - $299.1 - $99.0 = $110.4

Step 2: $134.0 - $110.4 = $23.6

January

Step 1: $134.0 - $78.8 - $31.4 = $23.8

Step 2: $71.7 - $23.8 = $47.9

3. Calculate TY actual average stock, turnover, and STS:

Average stock: $1261.8 + $79.9 ÷ 7 = $190.4

Turnover: $742.2 ÷ $190.4 = 3.90

Stock-to-sales ratio: $190.4 ÷ $123.7 = 1.5

	A	B	C	D	E	F	G	H	I
1	Actual - Last Year	4	5	4	4	5	4		
2	Plan	Aug	Sept	Oct	Nov	Dec	Jan	Total	Actual Markdown
3	Beg.Month Stock	99.3	169.7	227.0	320.4	329.9	111.8	1258.1	$200.9 / 29.6%
4	Sales	40.8	71.3	125.7	95.8	273.9	72.2	679.7	Sales Change %
5	Markdowns	8.2	12.3	18.7	15.9	110.7	35.1	200.9	Average Stock
6	Purchases	119.4	140.9	237.8	121.2	166.5	76.5	862.3	PLN 211.1 ACT $191.3
7	End Month Stock	169.7	227.0	320.4	329.9	111.8	81.0	1239.8	Turnover
8									PLN 3.22 ACT 3.55
9	Future Sales	Feb	Mar	Apr					WOS/STS
10		38.6	51.7	58.4					PLN 8.1 ACT 7.3
11									Avg. Sales
12									
13									Mark-up
14									
15	Plan - This Year								
16	Plan							Total	Actual Markdown
17	Beg.Month Stock	96.0	141.1	223.6	302.0	344.4	113.6	1220.7	$179.6 / 24.2%
18	Sales	44.6	77.9	137.3	104.6	299.1	78.8	742.2	Sales Change +9.2%
19	Markdowns	7.3	11.0	16.7	14.2	99.0	31.4	179.6	Average Stock
20	Purchases	97	171.4	232.4	161.2	167.3	76.1	905.4	PLN $207.3 ACT $185.7
21	End Month Stock	141.1	223.6	302.0	344.4	113.6	79.5	1204.2	Turnover
22	Future Sales	Feb	Mar	Apr					PLN 3.58 ACT 4.0
23		42.2	56.5	63.7					WOS/STS
24									PLN 7.3 ACT 6.5
25									Avg. Sales $123.7
26									
27									Mark-up

Sheet tabs: 9-A, STS \ 9-B, WOS / 9-A and 9-B Comparison / 9-C, STS / 9-D, WOS / 9-C and 9-D Cor

EXCEL SPREADSHEET 9-B.

Use the WOS Method of Inventory

Using Excel Spreadsheet 9-B, complete the plan using the weeks-of-supply method of inventory. Calculate last year actual and this year plan for all steps except purchases.

Follow the step-by-step process:

Step 1: Month BOM – Sales – Markdowns = Available Inventory

Step 2: Month EOM – Available Inventory = Purchases

1. Calculate last year monthly purchases:

    August
    Step 1: $99.3 – $40.8 – $8.2 = $50.3
    Step 2: $169.7 – $50.3 = $119.4, August purchases
    September
    Step 1: $169.7 – $71.3 – $12.3 = $86.1
    Step 2: $227.0 – $86.1 = $140.9

October

Step 1: $227.0 – $125.7 – $18.7 = $82.6

Step 2: $320.4 – $82.6 = $237.8

November

Step 1: $320.4 – $95.8 – $15.9 = $208.7

Step 2: $329.9 – $208.7 = $121.2

December

Step 1: $329.9 – $273.9 – $110.7 = ($54.7)

Step 2: $111.8 + $54.7 = $166.5 (Note: In step 1 the calculation reveals that there is not enough inventory to support the sales and markdowns planned. Therefore, to achieve the BOM stock level of $111.8, the negative inventory of $54.7 is added to $111.8, which will provide receipts of $166.5.)

January

Step 1: $111.8 – $72.2 – $35.1 = $4.5

Step 2: $81.0 – $4.5 = $76.5

2. Calculate TY actual average stock, turnover, and WOS:

Average stock: $1258.1 + 81.0 ÷ 7 = $191.3

Turnover: $679.9 ÷ $191.3 = 3.55

Weeks of supply: 26 ÷ 3.55 = 7.3 WOS

3. Calculate this year monthly purchases:

August

Step 1: $96.0 – $44.6 – $7.3 = $44.1

Step 2: $141.1 – $44.1 = $97.0, August purchases

September

Step 1: $141.1 – $77.9 – $11.0 = $52.2

Step 2: $223.6 – $52.2 = $171.4

October

Step 1: $223.6 – $137.3 – $16.7 = $69.6

Step 2: $302.0 – $69.6 = $232.4

November

Step 1: $302.0 – $104.6 – $14.2 = $183.2

Step 2: $344.4 – $183.2 = $161.2

December

Step 1: $344.4 – $299.1 – $99.0 = ($53.7)

Step 2: $113.6 + $53.7 = $167.3

January

Step 1: $113.6 – $78.8 – $31.4 = $3.4

Step 2: $79.5 – $3.4 = $76.1

4. Calculate actual:

Average stock: $1,220.7 + $79.5 ÷ 7 = $185.7

Turnover: $742.2 ÷ $185.7 = 4.0

Weeks of supply: 26 ÷ 4.0 = 6.5 WOS

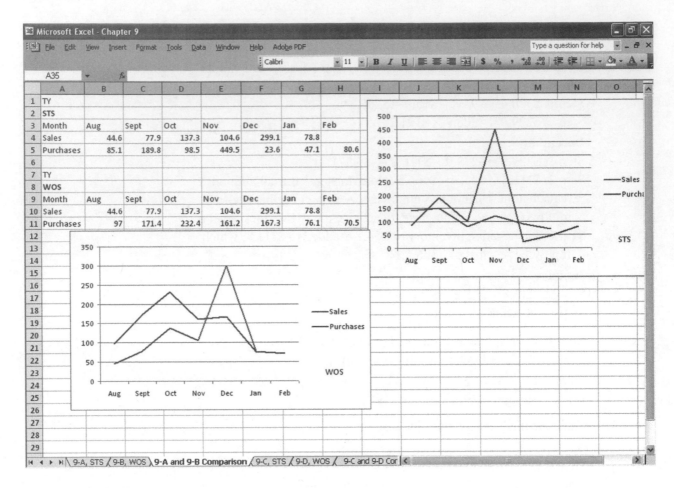

EXCEL SPREADSHEET 9-A AND 9-B COMPARISON.

EXERCISE

Compare the stock-to-sales ratio method with the weeks-of-supply method of inventory.

1. What is the difference between the two methods of inventory?

2. What types of businesses would benefit from each method?

3. Which method is a better use of cash flow? Why?

4. Explain the impact on turnover.

Your Turn

Complete Excel Spreadsheet 9-C using the STS method and Excel Spreadsheet 9-D using the WOS method.

Using Excel Spreadsheet 9-E, create two separate line graphs for each method. Compare the results.

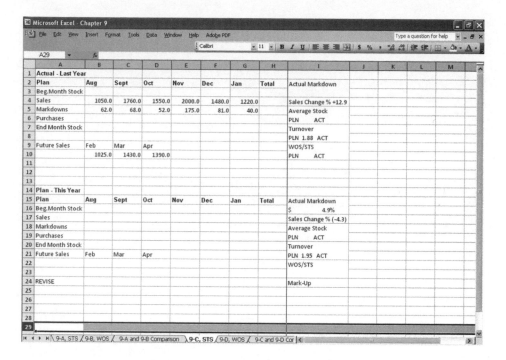

EXCEL SPREADSHEET 9-C.

	A	B	C	D	E	F	G	H	I
1	Actual - Last Year								
2	Plan	Aug	Sept	Oct	Nov	Dec	Jan	Total	Actual Markdown
3	Beg.Month Stock								
4	Sales	1050.0	1760.0	1550.0	2000.0	1480.0	1220.0		Sales Change % +12.9
5	Markdowns	62.0	68.0	52.0	175.0	81.0	40.0		Average Stock
6	Purchases								PLN ACT
7	End Month Stock								Turnover
8									PLN 1.88 ACT
9	Future Sales	Feb	Mar	Apr					WOS/STS
10		1025.0	1430.0	1390.0					PLN ACT
11									
12									
13									
14	Plan - This Year								
15	Plan	Aug	Sept	Oct	Nov	Dec	Jan	Total	Actual Markdown
16	Beg.Month Stock								$ 4.9%
17	Sales								Sales Change % (-4.3)
18	Markdowns								Average Stock
19	Purchases								PLN ACT
20	End Month Stock								Turnover
21	Future Sales	Feb	Mar	Apr					PLN 1.95 ACT
22									WOS/STS
23									
24	REVISE								Mark-Up
25									
26									
27									
28									
29									

Sheet tabs: 9-A, STS / 9-B, WOS / 9-A and 9-B Comparison / 9-C, STS / 9-D, WOS / 9-C and 9-D Cor

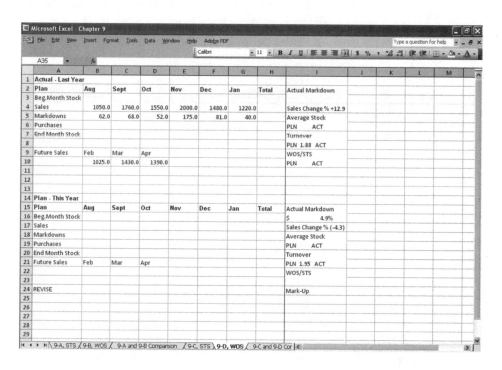

EXCEL SPREADSHEET 9-D.

	A	B	C	D	E	F	G	H	I
1	Actual - Last Year								
2	Plan	Aug	Sept	Oct	Nov	Dec	Jan	Total	Actual Markdown
3	Beg.Month Stock								
4	Sales	1050.0	1760.0	1550.0	2000.0	1480.0	1220.0		Sales Change % +12.9
5	Markdowns	62.0	68.0	52.0	175.0	81.0	40.0		Average Stock
6	Purchases								PLN ACT
7	End Month Stock								Turnover
8									PLN 1.88 ACT
9	Future Sales	Feb	Mar	Apr					WOS/STS
10		1025.0	1430.0	1390.0					PLN ACT
11									
12									
13									
14	Plan - This Year								
15	Plan	Aug	Sept	Oct	Nov	Dec	Jan	Total	Actual Markdown
16	Beg.Month Stock								$ 4.9%
17	Sales								Sales Change % (-4.3)
18	Markdowns								Average Stock
19	Purchases								PLN ACT
20	End Month Stock								Turnover
21	Future Sales	Feb	Mar	Apr					PLN 1.95 ACT
22									WOS/STS
23									
24	REVISE								Mark-Up
25									
26									
27									
28									
29									

Sheet tabs: 9-A, STS / 9-B, WOS / 9-A and 9-B Comparison / 9-C, STS / 9-D, WOS / 9-C and 9-D Cor

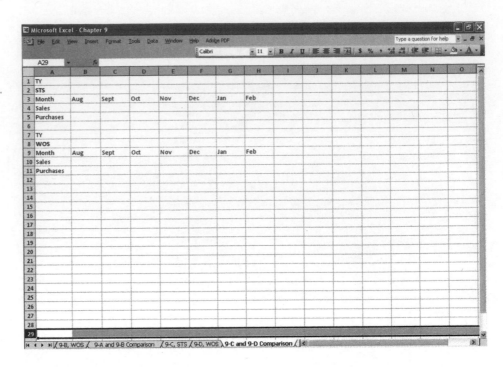

EXCEL SPREADSHEET 9-E.

CREATE IT IN EXCEL!

Using the existing jewelry plan from earlier chapters, a formula for calculating purchase receipts can now be integrated into the six-month plan. Begin with the STS plan from Chapter 7 and enter the appropriate formulas to calculate purchase receipts. The plan from Chapter 7 is shown below and is lacking on the purchase line.

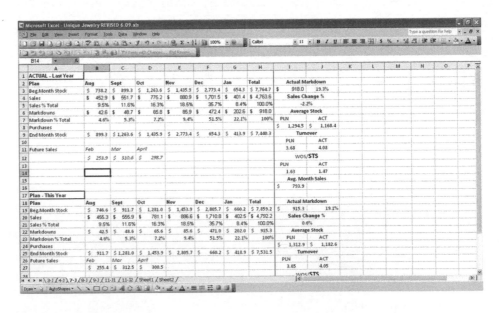

FIGURE 9.1 STS Plan.

Calculate August purchases by placing the cursor in cell B8 and enter as follows:

Cell B8: =C3–(B3–B4–B6) *enter*

September in cell C8

Cell C8: =D3–(C3–C4–C6) *enter*

October in cell D8

Cell D8: =E3–(D3–D4–D6) *enter*

(See Figure 9.2.)

Enter the remaining months of November, December, and January (see Figure 9.3).

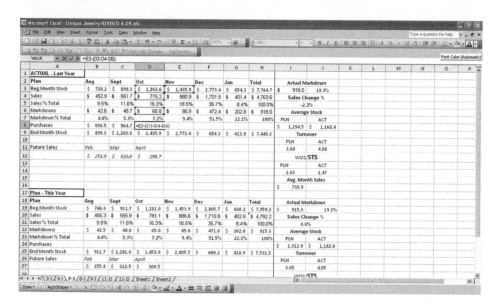

FIGURE 9.2 Calculate August thru October Purchases.

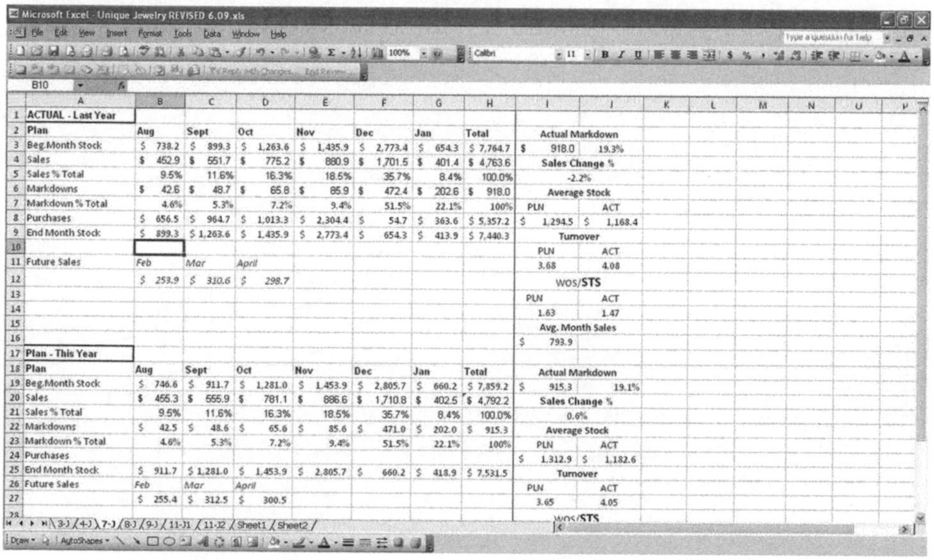

FIGURE 9.3 Calculate November thru January Purchases.

Complete the six-month plan by following the same process for this year plan as shown (see Figure 9.4).

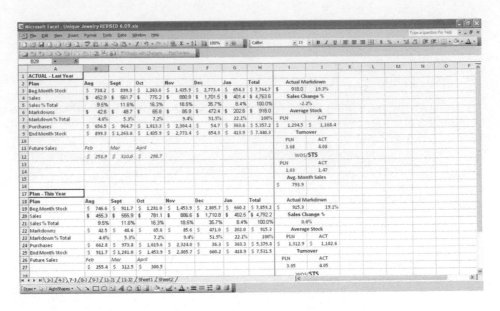

FIGURE 9.4 Calculate TY Purchases.

Now, follow the same process for the WOS plan from Chapter 8 and enter the appropriate formulas to calculate purchase receipts. The plan from Chapter 8 is shown below and again is missing the purchase line (see Figure 9.5).

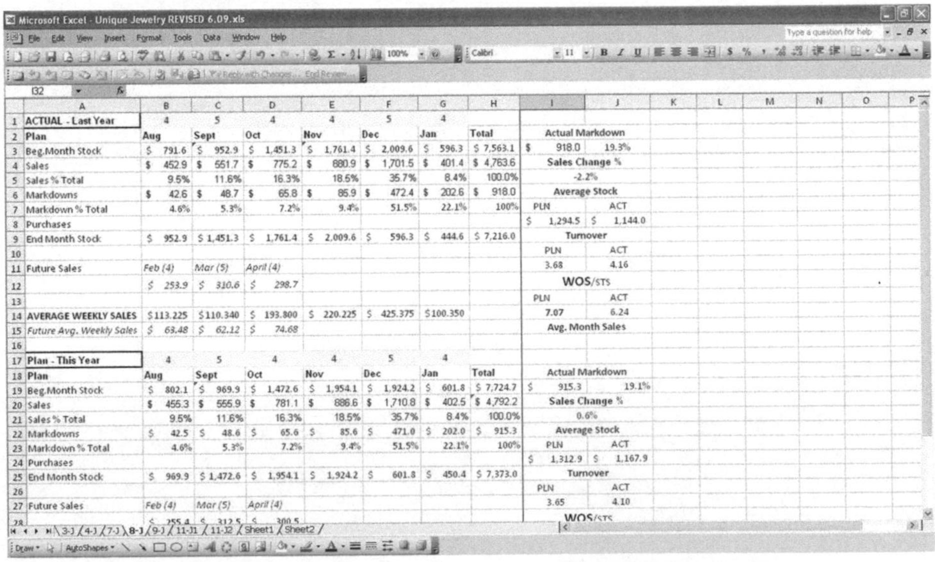

FIGURE 9.5 WOS Plan.

A BUYER'S LIFE

Calculate August purchases by placing the cursor in cell B8 and enter as follows:

Cell B8: =C3–(B3–B4–B6) *enter*

September in cell C8

Cell C8: =D3–(C3–C4–C6) *enter*

October in cell D8

Cell D8: =E3–(D3–D4–D6) *enter*

(See Figure 9.6)

Enter the remaining months of November, December, and January (see Figure 9.7).

Complete the six-month plan by following the same process for this year plan as shown (see Figure 9.8).

Compare sales and purchases for the STS method and the WOS method. Note the difference in the flow of inventory (see Figure 9.9).

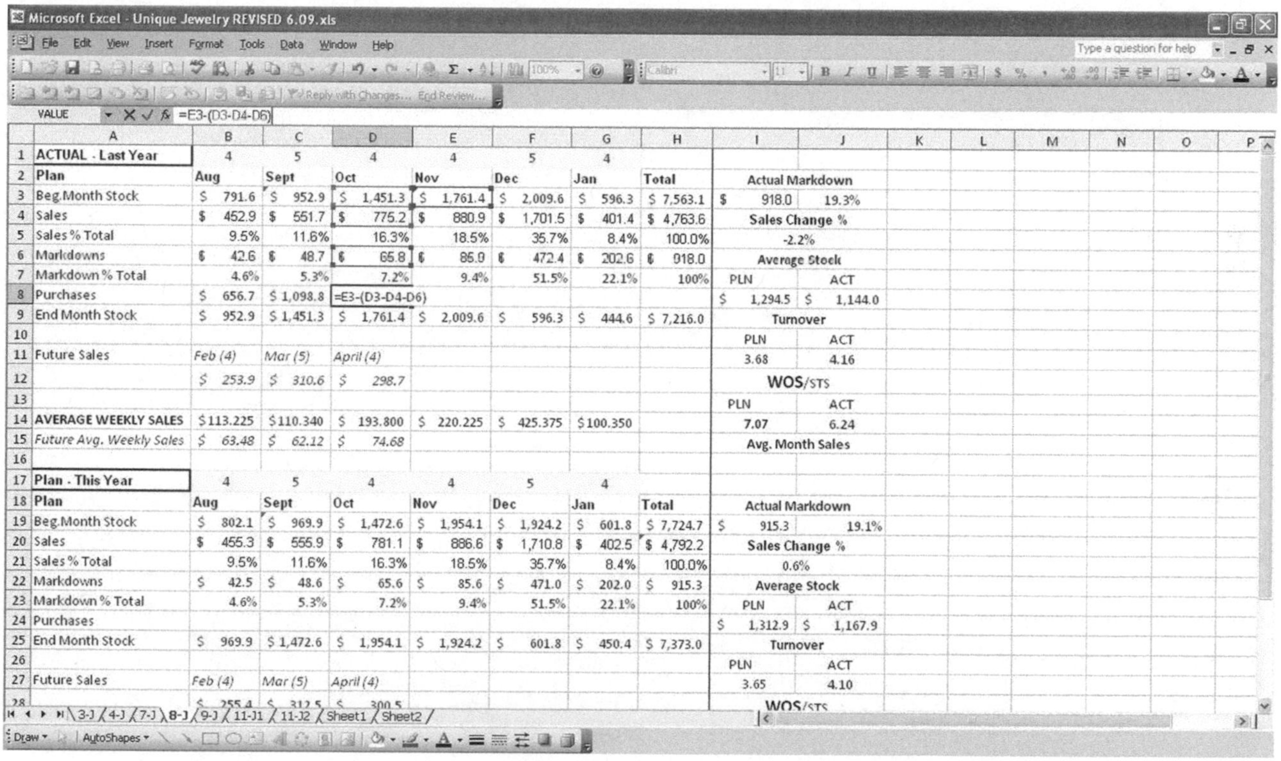

FIGURE 9.6 Calculate August thru October Purchases.

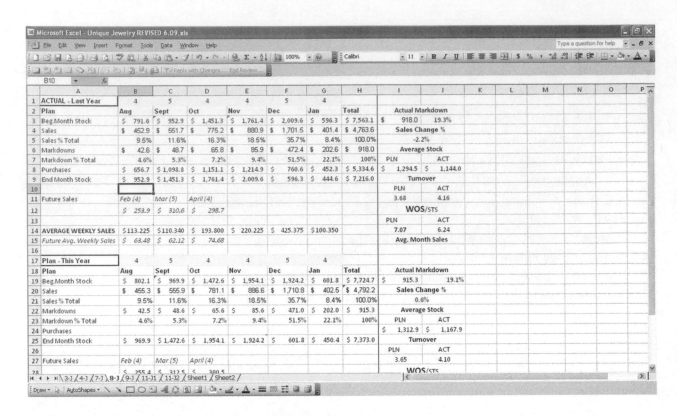

FIGURE 9.7 Calculate November thru January Purchases.

Plan	Aug	Sept	Oct	Nov	Dec	Jan	Total		
ACTUAL - Last Year	4	5	4	4	5	4			
Beg.Month Stock	$ 791.6	$ 952.9	$ 1,451.3	$ 1,761.4	$ 2,009.6	$ 596.3	$ 7,563.1	Actual Markdown $ 918.0	19.3%
Sales	$ 452.9	$ 551.7	$ 775.2	$ 880.9	$ 1,701.5	$ 401.4	$ 4,763.6	Sales Change %	
Sales % Total	9.5%	11.6%	16.3%	18.5%	35.7%	8.4%	100.0%	-2.2%	
Markdowns	$ 42.6	$ 48.7	$ 65.8	$ 85.9	$ 472.4	$ 202.6	$ 918.0	Average Stock	
Markdown % Total	4.6%	5.3%	7.2%	9.4%	51.5%	22.1%	100%	PLN / ACT	
Purchases	$ 656.7	$ 1,098.8	$ 1,151.1	$ 1,214.9	$ 760.6	$ 452.3	$ 5,334.6	$ 1,294.5	$ 1,144.0
End Month Stock	$ 952.9	$ 1,451.3	$ 1,761.4	$ 2,009.6	$ 596.3	$ 444.6	$ 7,216.0	Turnover	
								PLN / ACT	
Future Sales	Feb (4)	Mar (5)	April (4)					3.68	4.16
	$ 253.9	$ 310.6	$ 298.7					WOS/STS	
								PLN / ACT	
AVERAGE WEEKLY SALES	$ 113.225	$ 110.340	$ 193.800	$ 220.225	$ 425.375	$ 100.350		7.07	6.24
Future Avg. Weekly Sales	$ 63.48	$ 62.12	$ 74.68					Avg. Month Sales	
Plan - This Year	4	5	4	4	5	4			
Plan	Aug	Sept	Oct	Nov	Dec	Jan	Total		
Beg.Month Stock	$ 802.1	$ 969.9	$ 1,472.6	$ 1,954.1	$ 1,924.2	$ 601.8	$ 7,724.7	Actual Markdown $ 915.3	19.1%
Sales	$ 455.3	$ 555.9	$ 781.1	$ 886.6	$ 1,710.8	$ 402.5	$ 4,792.2	Sales Change %	
Sales % Total	9.5%	11.6%	16.3%	18.5%	35.7%	8.4%	100.0%	0.6%	
Markdowns	$ 42.5	$ 48.6	$ 65.6	$ 85.6	$ 471.0	$ 202.0	$ 915.3	Average Stock	
Markdown % Total	4.6%	5.3%	7.2%	9.4%	51.5%	22.1%	100%	PLN / ACT	
Purchases	$ 665.5	$ 1,107.2	$ 1,328.2	$ 942.3	$ 859.4	$ 453.2	$ 5,355.8	$ 1,312.9	$ 1,167.9
End Month Stock	$ 969.9	$ 1,472.6	$ 1,954.1	$ 1,924.2	$ 601.8	$ 450.4	$ 7,373.0	Turnover	
								PLN / ACT	
Future Sales	Feb (4)	Mar (5)	April (4)					3.65	4.10

FIGURE 9.8 Calculate TY Purchases.

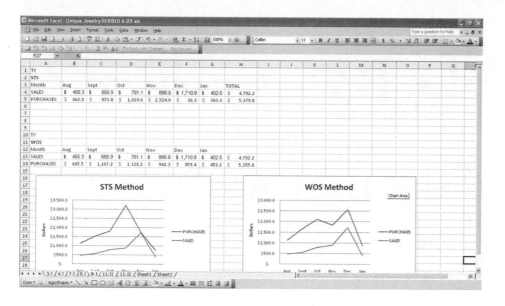

FIGURE 9.9 STS and WOS Purchase Comparison.

TERMINOLOGY

purchase receipts: The amount of inventory needed each month in order to maintain BOM stock levels.

FORMULAS

 Purchases

Step 1: Month BOM – Sales – Markdowns = Available Inventory

Step 2: Month EOM – Available Inventory = Purchases

e.g. Step 1: $598.4 (BOM) – $162.2 (Sales) – $34.7 (Markdowns) = $401.5 (Available Inventory)

Step 2: $552.7 (EOM) – $401.5 (Available Inventory) = $151.2 (Purchases)

10

PURCHASE AND PRICING STRATEGIES

Chapter 9 describes how to plan purchase receipts as total by month and as total for the specified season. The flow of inventory for the total season considers the high and low points of sales throughout the season. After completing a total purchase plan for each month, the buyer's next step is to identify how to allocate the monthly purchase dollars available, determine what to buy, and decide how to price the product at retail.

PURCHASE STRATEGIES

Monthly purchasing can be broken down into individual categories to ensure an adequate inventory for key product categories. By planning purchases ahead of the season, buyers set up a budget for inventory such as new products, reorders, and last-minute opportunities. Maintaining historical records of the prior year's purchase history can be helpful in planning purchases for the current year. Recording the details of purchases and sales helps buyers identify which products to repeat, what needs to change, and where there are new opportunities.

Every business has different parameters and needs, but a general guideline for allocating purchase receipts is as follows (allocations are listed in order

of importance, however, importance for items 4–6 could be widely varied by retailer):

1. Special orders
2. Basic replenishment
3. Promotional and advertised
4. Reorders
5. New receipts
6. Test inventory
7. Off-price specials
8. Reserve

These categories can be viewed as dollar or percentage allocations. Small fashion boutique owners might place most of the store's purchase money into new or test inventory. A large-discount-store buyer for basic socks or towels might budget most of its inventory for basic replenishment or reorders.

In another part of the spectrum, a bridal buyer's business is nearly all special orders. Special order business is unique because it typically involves inventory that is sold and either paid in full or is on hold with a deposit. This type of inventory has limited liability for the buyer and often falls into a separate category for planning.

SPECIAL ORDERS

Special orders are simply important for good customer service. When a buyer is able to place a special order on behalf of the customer, everyone can end up satisfied. But special orders should be offered with caution and usually include a no-return policy, especially when personalized. Most stores place a **special order** only when the customer has given written consent to order the items and has agreed to pay fully upon their arrival.

Many retailers place special orders in a separate classification so they can carefully track and monitor sales. This special classification has rapid turnover because little or no inventory is booked for a long period of time because the inventory is simultaneously in and out. No method is perfect, however; customers can, in some cases, return special order inventory. This situation is certainly not ideal, but every retailer has a specific policy and follows particular tracking methods. Special order inventory is common in areas such as bridal, jewelry, electronics, and made-to-order businesses like men's suiting.

BASIC REPLENISHMENT

Basic replenishment is a form of reorder. The primary difference between these two purchase strategies is that based on historical sales, basic replenishment quantities are highly predictable.

Replenishment inventory is often called the bread and butter of a business. These are dependable products with a consistent sales pattern, profit margin, and turnover. These products are also widely known for the customer. They know where to find the product, they know which retailer has their size and color available, and they know it is offered at a price they are willing to pay.

Basic replenishment depends on strong relationships between retail buyer and vendor. The vendor agrees to keep these specified products available for immediate shipment, usually each week. In turn, the vendor expects the buyer to place orders for these items and consistently forecast the future needs. Besides strong relationships and agreements, large retailers and large vendors have sophisticated replenishment programs that automatically generate EDI orders to vendors daily, weekly, or monthly.

PROMOTIONAL AND ADVERTISED

Promotional purchases include any product to be used for a sale or point-of-purchase event. Typical offerings might be special bedding ensembles that have been purchased for the annual white sale. These products may not be specifically advertised, but they are considered a valid offering for the sale event.

Advertised purchases vary from promotional in that they are not always offered at a sale price. Any product that is being advertised on television, the Internet, in catalogs, through inserts or mailers, and so on is considered an advertised purchase. Most retailers today have strict policies to ensure that advertised product is available at the time of the advertisement. For this reason, having the product in stock is essential to the integrity of the business.

REORDERS

Reorder allocations are necessary to sell more of a product that is already selling. When something is hot and selling well, if possible—and if it makes good business sense—buyers need to buy more. Keeping a small amount of money available to reorder best sellers will result in extra sales dollars for the bottom line.

NEW RECEIPTS

The term **new receipts** refers to any new product not previously seen in inventory. Maintaining a fresh new product flow is essential to any business. The actual type of new inventory depends on the business; new receipts could range from purchasing all new styles to merely offering a different color. New receipts can also include products from new vendor sources, or they can be new products or collections from existing vendors. It is important to keep new receipts coming into the store. Customers are always eager to see what is new. This is what gives them a reason to keep coming in and a reason to buy.

TEST INVENTORY

Test inventory may be the most overlooked and under-planned category of purchase receipts. The potential for discovering a new trend, a new product, or a new customer need exists within test inventory. Early-adopter consumers are always looking for the newest products. Without test product, product assortments can become outdated and result in sales declines. Although early adopters tend to frequent forward-thinking retailers, every store and every geographical market includes some form of early adopter. For example, a new trend at Neiman Marcus in February might become a new trend at Macy's in August.

By planning small amounts of test inventory, buyers always have fresher assortments that translate into frequent and interested customers. When buyers travel to market, it is important for them to have money to spend on something new and exciting. Buyers who have no money for test inventory have to pass up such opportunities and could lose important profit opportunities.

Test inventory can be a small dollar amount or percentage that is used only in specific test markets. For example, a large department store with hundreds or thousands of units might place test inventory into only 20 units in strategic geographic regions. On the other hand, a single-unit boutique owner might plan test inventory for a specific month—such as when their early adopters tend to shop. No matter what the product category, buyers always have opportunities to test new products and must plan accordingly.

OFF-PRICE SPECIALS

Off-price specials are slightly different from promotional purchases. Although they may be offered to the customer at a special discount or sale price, off-price specials are typically initiated by the vendor supplier. These off-price specials are usually overstocks by the vendor, which in turn offers them to its best retail store customers at a percentage off the regular wholesale price. Immediate sale opportunities sometimes arise for the buyer to pass the savings along to the consumer. At other times, vendors offer these special items to the retailer to boost profitability. Chapters 13 and 14 discuss ways of providing these additional profit margins.

RESERVES

Reserve allocations can be the most challenging for the buyer, yet they are essential for good business decision making. Planning for the "what if" scenarios can make or break a season.

Reserves function much like a personal savings account. What if sales decline? The result is that inventory rises, markdowns increase, and profitability decreases. Buyers who hold some money in reserve have not spent all of their purchase money and thus have a small cushion to prevent inventory from rising further.

On the flip side, what if a new test item is hot, and the buyers lack the test money to buy the inventory? Innovative new products or inspiring new designers or vendors may have entered the market after the merchandising plan was created six months or a year earlier. Having money available in reserve gives the buyer additional money to make the purchase and capitalize on the opportunity.

Reserve inventory for a small retail store is absolutely necessary. Small retailers lack abundant cash flows to camouflage inventory problems. Holding money for the "what-if" scenarios can sometimes determine whether a retailer stays in business or must close. Large retailers have significantly more flexibility. One buyer or division may have extra money available while another may not; but in total, everything remains balanced. As with markdowns, some large stores hold reserves at the divisional merchandise manager (DMM) or general merchandise manager (GMM) level. This practice allows greater flexibility within a division and shifts the decision making to the higher level for the good of the team and the overall store. Because most large retailers measure performance through team results, contributing inventory dollars or markdowns to the team reserve funds can benefit everyone.

The amount of reserve allocation varies but should not be less than 10 percent of the monthly purchase receipt plan. For example, if the purchase plan for the month of May is $362.0, then the reserve allocation should be no less than $36.2. To maintain gross margin profitability and inventory turnover, the response to slow sales is to decrease inventory levels. This can be difficult, if not impossible, when the money has already been spent in the market. Therefore, holding a percentage of inventories in reserve is the prudent and responsible way of managing a retail business.

Remember that the purchase receipt plan is a guide, and it can be manipulated. This process must be carried out with thoughtful analysis and planning. Buyers are often faced with manipulating dollars between months to avoid the possibility of a negative impact on profit. At the same time, blatant overspending with little or no regard for the purchase plan is irresponsible and could have serious consequences, such as job loss or store closure. By carefully managing purchase receipts, buyers can ensure proper inventory balance. If the inventory is too low, customer's needs are not met and sales will decline. If the inventory is too high, customers are overwhelmed, sales floors are cluttered, and customers move to more comfortable shopping environments. Following a thoughtful plan that includes calculating the total purchase receipt plan and allocating purchase categories readies the buyer to attend market and purchase the necessary inventory to deliver profitable results.

Practice Problems

1. Suppose you are the DMM of footwear for a large department store. The DMM direct reports encompass four buyerships that include Comfort, Athletic, Dress, and Special Occasion footwear. Apply percentages to the purchase receipt plan for each buyer.

Buyer Basic	New	Test	Reorder	Special Order	Reserve
Comfort					
Athletic					
Dress					
Special Occasion					

Explain why you planned each category in this way.

2. You are a small-business owner and buyer with four retail stores. Your stores specialize in gift items and are located in tourist resort towns. Considering the six categories of purchase receipts, how might you plan purchase receipts? Explain your decision-making process.

3. You are the holiday trim buyer for a discount store. It is eight weeks before Thanksgiving. Your plan is as follows:

Holiday Trim					
Basic	New	Test	Reorder	Special Order	Reserve
30%	39%	15%	5%	1%	10%

a. How would you apportion the following categories?
   Ornaments
   Lights
   Indoor Décor
   Outdoor Décor
   Cards and Wrap

b. If lights are selling at a 50 percent greater pace than planned, how might you adjust orders?

c. If a high percentage of your inventory is imported and has a 12-week lead time, what precautions might you take to ensure maximum sales?

PRICING STRATEGIES

Determining retail prices is the critical factor in achieving profitability. Planning markup strategies vary by business but are usually generally accepted percentages within a business category. Markup strategies for private-label fashion products can be as high as 80 to 90 percent. Yet the markup for designer fashions could be 50 percent, and it is even less for small appliances. Overall pricing is determined by initial markup (IMU) and cumulative markup (CMU).

INITIAL MARKUP

IMU is the **initial markup** placed on the product when it arrives in the store. This is usually the full price that the customer pays at the point of sale. (There are some circumstances where markup cancellations are involved, but for a basic understanding we will use the definition above.) IMU can be calculated as a percentage. For example, if the cost of a T-shirt is $5.10 and the department has an IMU plan of 68 percent, the retail price would be $15.94.

Cost ÷ Cost Complement = IMU

$5.10 ÷ (100 − 68% = 32%)

$5.10 ÷ 32% = $15.94

The price of $15.94 is rounded to an even $16.00. Rounding initiates an IMU of 68.1%.

Check: Retail − Cost ÷ Retail = IMU

IMU can also be calculated using a keystone process.

Keystone consists of simply doubling the cost price. Using the earlier example for a T-shirt priced at $5.10, the keystone retail price is $10.20. Other keystone methods are known as keystone plus. The **keystone plus** method doubles the price and then adds a specific dollar amount or percentage, usually between $1 and $10. Using the same T-shirt and a keystone + $5 would result in pricing the T-shirt at $15.20. As in the percentage example, the T-shirt price usually is rounded to $15.00 or $16.00 (rounding up or down depends on the business or on the item itself).

IMU Practice Problems

1. What is retail if cost is $538.00 and markup is 52 percent?

2. What is retail if cost is $62.50 and markup is keystone? Keystone + $5? Keystone + 10 percent?

3. What is cost if retail is $158.00 and markup is 58.3 percent?

4. What is cost if retail is $62.00 and markup is keystone + $2?

5. What is markup if cost is $4.75 and retail is $11.50?

6. What is markup if cost is $238.00 and retail is $578.00?

CUMULATIVE MARKUP

CMU is the **cumulative markup** of the life of the product or of the entire inventory. Cumulative markup calculates the overall markup from the IMU through all phases of markdowns. For instance, consider the example in Table 10.1.

While this T-shirt carries a high markup of 68.1 percent at the start of the life cycle, as markdowns are initiated the markup percentage deteriorates and results in an overall markup of only 59.4 percent. Calculating overall profit at the IMU would yield $3815 (350 T-shirts at a cost of $5.10 and retail of $16.00); yet after markdowns, the profit result is $2615.00 ($4400.00 − $1785), which is $1200.00 less than if the product had been sold 100 percent at full retail.

TABLE 10.1. SALES OF 350 T-SHIRTS			
350 T-shirts at a cost of $5.10 with a retail price of $16.00, with IMU = 68.1%			
188	T-Shirts at full price:	188 × $5.10 = $958.80 cost	188 × $16.00 = $3008 Retail
53	T-Shirts at 25% off:	53 × $5.10 = $270.30 cost	53 × $12.00 = $636 Retail ($16.00 − 25% = $12.00)
80	T-Shirts at 50% off:	80 × $5.10 = $408.00 cost	80 × $8.00 = $640 Retail ($16.00 − 50% = $8.00 Retail)
29	T-Shirts at 75% off:	29 × $5.10 = $147.90 cost	29 × $4.00 = $116.00 Retail ($16.00 − 75% = $4.00 Retail)
TOTAL SHIRTS SOLD = 350 at $1785.00 cost			$4400.00 Retail
TOTAL Retail Sales − TOTAL Cost Sales ÷ TOTAL Retail Sales = CMU (Cumulative markup) ($4400.00 − $1785.00) ÷ $4400.00 = 59.4%			

CMU Practice Problems

1. Calculate CMU based on the following denim business.

   Five-pocket jean: cost $18.50, retail $55.00, 1,200 total quantity purchased. Forty percent of the inventory is sold at regular price. The buyer decides to take a reduction of 40 percent on the remaining inventory. After 30 days, only 25 percent of the reduced inventory has sold. Subsequently the buyer takes firm action and reduces the remaining inventory to 75 percent off until there is nothing left. Calculate the CMU.

2. Add to the above five-pocket jean the following additional style.

   Boot-cut jean: cost $21.00, IMU 62 percent, 2500 total quantity purchased. Fifty percent of the inventory is sold at regular price. The buyer decides to take a reduction on 1250 pairs at a 25 percent discount for two weeks and sells 500 pairs; the remaining inventory returns to regular price. At the end of the season, 50 pairs are left, and they are reduced to clear out at 60 percent off until nothing is left.
   Calculate the overall CMU for these two styles of jeans.

TERMINOLOGY

basic replenishment: A form of reorder; dependable products with a predictable sales pattern, profit margin, and turnover.

cumulative markup (CMU): Markup of the product throughout its life span. Calculates the overall markup from the IMU through all phases of markdowns.

initial markup (IMU): Markup placed on the product when it arrives in the store.

keystone: The process of doubling the cost price.

keystone plus: Pricing strategy of doubling the cost price plus an additional percentage or dollar amount, usually between $1 and $10.

new receipts: New product that previously has not been seen in inventory.

off-price specials: Usually overstocks by the vendor, who in turn offers them to its best customers at a percentage off the regular wholesale price. Immediate sale opportunities may arise for the buyer to pass the savings along to the customer.

promotional and/or advertised: Any product that will be used for a sale or point-of-purchase event.

reorders: Money available to reorder best sellers.

reserve: Purchase money not spent; it acts as a small cushion to prevent inventory from rising further or for use in capitalizing on new product entries.

special orders: Orders placed particularly for the customer, usually with written consent to order the items and agreement to pay fully upon arrival.

test inventory: Small amounts of inventory that are new and unknown. This inventory is typically noticed by early adopters and often translates into reorders.

FORMULAS

$$\text{IMU} = \text{Cost} \div \text{Cost Complement}$$

$$\text{e.g., } 32\% = \$45.00 \div (100 - 68\%)$$

$$\$140.63 \text{ or } \$141.00 = \$45.00 \div 32\%$$

$$\text{CMU} = \text{Total Cost Sales} - \text{Total Retail Sales} \div \text{Total Retail Sales}$$

$$\text{e.g., } 48.1\% = \$1432.6 - \$2761.2 \div \$2761.2$$

11

CLASSIFICATION IDENTIFICATION AND PLANNING

With the six-month planning complete, a top-down process allows buyers to plan for smaller classifications of business and gives them greater control over business decisions. Understanding individual classifications of business within the total plan supports improved management of each smaller classification. Before planning such classifications, however, the buyer must identify the product classifications.

MODELS OF CLASSIFICATION PLANNING

Classifications are related groups of products that can be viewed in smaller units within the total business. Classifications can be developed in many ways, depending on the business. Here are some models of classification planning:

• Vendor or Resource

• Silhouette

• Fabrication

• Size

• Color

• Lifestyle

- Price
- Trend

These models for classification planning represent only a few possibilities. Specific businesses may use other criteria to plan classifications.

DETERMINING PRODUCT CLASSIFICATIONS

Internal forces, such as overall company strategy and related business segments within the company, can affect classification planning. Planning decisions can also be influenced by external forces such as competition and resource structure. While each of these forces is important, understanding how to classify products begins with the customer.

Buyers need to focus on questions like these: Why do my customers by this product? What drives their buying decision? What is my store's business strategy? The answers to these questions will guide buyers in identifying classifications as well as in completing the planning process.

Looking at the models listed earlier and understanding which model to use requires some thought about the pros and cons of each (Table 11.1).

Each of the classification models described in Table 11.1 represents the driving force behind customer decisions. If customers shop only by brand recognition, and vendor relationships are essential to business success, then a vendor or resource classification strategy is utilized. Conversely, if vendors are constantly changing and products are quickly in or out of style, a trend strategy is more beneficial in driving decisions and thus increasing sales.

EXERCISE

1. Identify a classification model type for the following businesses. Name possible classifications based on the model chosen. Justify your decisions and consider all alternatives.
   a. Kitchen electrics
   b. Men's ties
   c. Children's footwear
   d. Jeans
   e. Hair products
   f. Women's sweaters
   g. Socks

To further analyze selling and subsequently plan for future stock and sales, many retailers also consider subclassification planning or product trait identification. For example, a business may be classified by vendor or resource and subclassified by silhouette. The general process for multilevel planning is similar to the planning process discussed in this chapter. To better understand classification planning, the next step is to calculate the financial plan from the total six-month plan.

TABLE 11.1. CLASSIFICATION TYPES: PLANNING PROS AND CONS		
Classification	**Pros**	**Cons**
Vendor or Resource	• Isolates vendor profitability. • Streamlines purchase decisions. • Appropriate for brand-conscious businesses. • Improves vendor relations.	• Less viable for small-scale vendors or businesses with large numbers of vendors. • Difficult to manage inconsistency in vendors.
Silhouette	• Highlights strong- and weak-selling silhouettes to make better buying decisions.	• Difficult to manage long term due to changing silhouettes.
Fabrication	• Seasonal and performance fabric trends are easily tracked for upturns and downturns. • Especially good for understanding new entries.	• Less viable for hard lines. • Could be adapted for technological differentiators.
Size	• Size can range from clothing size to tire size where trends in selling are highlighted. • Shifts in buying patterns can be quickly maneuvered. • Ease in identifying manufacturer sizing variances.	• Not appropriate for predetermined case-pack businesses.
Color	• Use in businesses that rely heavily on color trends, such as home furnishings or accessories. Think about the bath towel wall; color is essential. • Basic departments such as T-shirts can also benefit from color classifications. Any retail environment where product is merchandised and sold by color is a possible candidate for this class.	• Related product businesses would not benefit from colorized classifications, because the collection of products is the key selling feature.
Lifestyle	• Use in businesses that cover casual, business, and special occasion; could be lifestyle oriented. Examples: footwear, jewelry, or tabletop. • Small boutique retailers could benefit from this strategy when multiple lifestyles are part of the overall store.	• Not appropriate where the buying department is already a lifestyle. • Less important for basic products or some hard-line businesses.
Price	• Beneficial for price-oriented retailers that merchandise by price point.	• Geared only to low-price or clearance strategies.
Trend	• Beneficial for tracking trend curve customer acceptance and identifying emerging trends.	• Appropriate only to trend-oriented products. • Environments that change too quickly could be missing opportunities. • May not be appropriate for strong branded products where brand is more important than trend.

SEARCH THE NET

➤ The purpose of this activity is to become aware of classifications and how to further break down businesses for better tracking and analysis. While this exercise may not necessarily be the way a retailer actually classifies its business, it can provide some insight and practice to become aware of many classification possibilities. Visit the Internet sites of a variety of retailers. Analyze each website and determine how that retailer might classify merchandise. Identify subclassification or product trait organization. Compare how different types of retailers classify. Contrast how similar retailers take varied approaches: What are the pros and cons as a consumer? How do you shop? Do you find some retailer websites easier to navigate than others? If you have access to a smart phone, visit the sites of other retailers on your phone. How easy is it to navigate? Would you make a purchase

(continued)

APPLICATION

Once the classifications have been established, the buyer's next step is to review historical sales history and project future sales based on market knowledge. This chapter takes a conservative approach to planning that gives a basic understanding of the process. With further knowledge and expertise, buyers could carefully manipulate the classification plan while always keeping the total six-month plan intact.

In this application, you will plan the jewelry department described here.

Department: Jewelry

Classifications: Possible options include vendor or resource, silhouette, or color—or in this case metal type, which could also be fabrication. The sample problem uses the silhouette model with classifications as follows:

Earring
Bracelet
Necklace
Pin
Ring
Other (Always leave room to plan for something unknown. There could be a hot new trend in watches or ankle bracelets. Anything new can be classified as "Other," so that it can be isolated and tracked for future relevance.)

Determine what percentage of the total business each classification represents. Remember that business trends vary; if earrings are hot one season, they may decline the next and necklaces will be the new trend. For this exercise, assign the percentages based on your own knowledge about jewelry in the area where you live.

Use the grid in Table 11.2 to calculate last year's percentages and project how this year will break down.

Notice the two classification increases for bracelet and pin (in bold). Perhaps major stars in a new blockbuster movie are wearing bracelets and pins.

TABLE 11.2. GRID TO CALCULATE LAST YEAR'S PERCENTAGES AND PROJECT THIS YEAR'S PERCENTAGES		
Classification	**Actual % Total Last Year**	**Plan % Total This Year**
Earring	38%	32%
Bracelet	22%	**26%**
Necklace	17%	15%
Pin	9%	**16%**
Ring	11%	9%
Other	3%	2%
TOTAL	100%	100%

Because such events influence how customers buy, buyers need to adjust future purchases in anticipation of new trends. Using the percentages given in the grid, a basic financial plan by classification can be calculated.

Note that this plan is at the total level. A more detailed plan would outline varied percentages by month for a more accurate projection of the plan. The purpose of this plan is for exposure to the process and baseline planning. In addition, notice that markdowns have not been accounted for in this plan. The reason is that some businesses are likely to incur more markdowns, while others may not. For baseline planning purposes, the markdowns have been planned only at the total level and not at the classification level.

CALCULATING THE FINANCIAL PLAN BY CLASSIFICATION

To calculate the classification plan the process begins with the total level 6 month plan and then breaks down the classification plan on a separate spread sheet. Using Excel Spreadsheets 11-A1 and 11-A2 calculate the classification plan. See Appendix B for full-size versions of all Excel Spreadsheets.

1. Using Excel Spreadsheet 11-A1, calculate sales, markdowns, stock using the STS method, and purchases. Complete the plan for last year actual and this year.

2. Using Excel Spreadsheet 11-A2, apply the percentages for this year's plan as follows:

    Earring: 32%

(continued)

from your phone? How a retailer classifies product may hold the key to whether you make a purchase or leave the site. What correlations or inconsistencies do you see in a retailer's Internet presence versus their brick-and-mortar presence?

	A	B	C	D	E	F	G	H	I
1	Actual - Last Year								
2	Plan	Aug	Sept	Oct	Nov	Dec	Jan	Total	Actual Markdown
3	Beg.Month Stock	301.8	367.4	347.1	420.0	906.9	254.4	2597.6	$255.0 / 15.1%
4	Sales	195.2	238.6	225.4	272.7	588.9	165.2	1686.0	Sales Change +6.2%
5	Markdowns	36.4	22.1	18.7	22.9	122.1	32.8	255	Average Stock
6	Purchases	297.2	240.4	317	782.5	58.5	256.5	1952.1	PLN 432.3 ACT 415.7
7	End Month Stock	367.4	347.1	420.0	906.9	254.4	312.5	2608.3	Turnover
8									PLN 3.90 ACT 4.06
9	Future Sales	Feb	Mar	Apr					WOS/STS
10		202.9	151.3	142.7					PLN 1.54 ACT 1.48
11									Average Sales
12									$ 281.0
13									
14	Plan - This Year								
15	Plan							Total	Actual Markdown
16	Beg.Month Stock								/ 15.8%
17	Sales								Sales Change +18.2%
18	Markdowns								Average Stock
19	Purchases								PLN ACT
20	End Month Stock								Turnover
21	Future Sales	Feb	Mar	Apr					PLN 3.93 ACT
22									WOS/STS
23									
24									Mark-Up

EXCEL SPREADSHEET 11-A1.

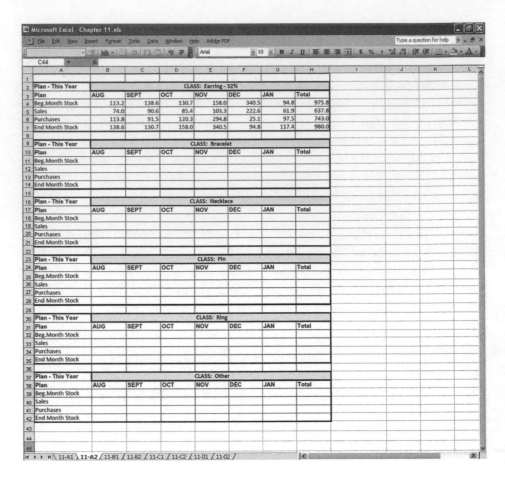

EXCEL SPREADSHEET **11-A2**.

3. Calculate 32% of each variable by month from the six-month plan.

Beg. Month Stock Aug.: $353.6 × 32\% = \$113.2$
Beg. Month Stock Sept.: $433.0 × 32\% = \$138.6$
Beg. Month Stock Oct.: $408.5 × 32\% = \$130.7$
Beg. Month Stock Nov.: $493.9 × 32\% = \$158.0$
Beg. Month Stock Dec.: $1064.1 × 32\% = \$340.5$
Beg. Month Stock Jan.: $296.1 × 32\% = \$94.8$
End Month Stock Jan.: $366.9 × 32\% = \$117.4$

4. Fill in each month's end-of-month (EOM) stock.

Aug.: $138.6   Sept.: $130.7   Oct.: $158.0   Nov.: $340.5   Dec.: $94.8

5. Sales Aug.: $231.1 × 32\% = \$74.0$
Sales Sept.: $283.0 × 32\% = \$90.6$
Sales Oct.: $267.0 × 32\% = \$85.4$
Sales Nov.: $322.8 × 32\% = \$103.3$
Sales Dec.: $695.5 × 32\% = \$222.6$
Sales Jan.: $193.5 × 32\% = \$61.9$

6. Purchases Aug.: $355.5 × 32% = $113.8
Purchases Sept.: $285.9 × 32% = $91.5
Purchases Oct.: $375.4 × 32% = $120.3
Purchases Nov.: $921.3 × 32% = $294.8
Purchases Dec.: $78.3 × 32% = $25.1
Purchases Jan.: $304.7 × 32% = $97.5

7. Continue calculating each classification based on the planned percentage:

Bracelet: 26%

Necklace: 15%

Pin: 16%

Ring: 9%

Other: 2%

Once the classification plans are complete, the buyer has a clear understanding of how to maximize purchase decisions while in market. Specific product sales results are also crucial to the decision-making process and will be discussed further in Chapter 12. The classification plan, however, provides the road map to success by breaking down the total plan and highlighting specific opportunities and downturns in the business. The classification plan described in this chapter only outlines the basic process. A skilled buyer or planner would use this plan as a baseline starting point and make adjustments as necessary for the business. What is important in this chapter is to gain an understanding of identifying and beginning to outline the planning process at the classification level.

Your Turn

Using your own knowledge and business research, use these spreadsheets to gain a further understanding of identifying classifications and more practice planning baseline classification financial components. Make decisions and complete the classification plans for these businesses:

1. Excel Spreadsheet 11-B1 is a men's dress shirt business. Identify possible classifications for planning; estimate last year actual percentages, and predict this year planned percentages. Apply the percentages from the total plan into the classification plan in Excel Spreadsheet 11-B2.

2. Excel Spreadsheet 11-C1 is a women's evening wear business. Identify possible classifications for planning; estimate last year actual percentages, and predict this year planned percentages. Apply the percentages from the total plan into the classification plan in Excel Spreadsheet 11-C2.

3. Excel Spreadsheet 11-D1 is a designer accessory business. Identify possible classifications for planning; estimate last year actual percentages, and predict this year planned percentages. Apply the percentages from the total plan into the classification plan in Excel Spreadsheet 11-D2.

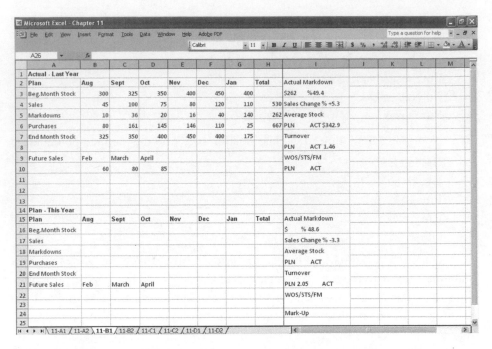

Excel Spreadsheet 11-B1.

Excel Spreadsheet 11-B2.

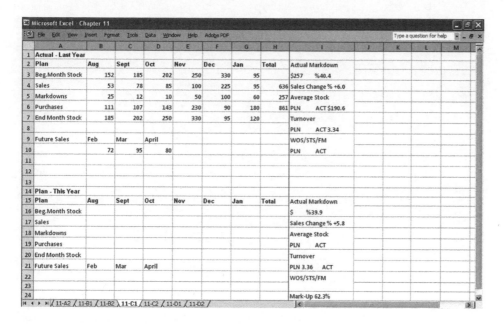

EXCEL SPREADSHEET 11-C1.

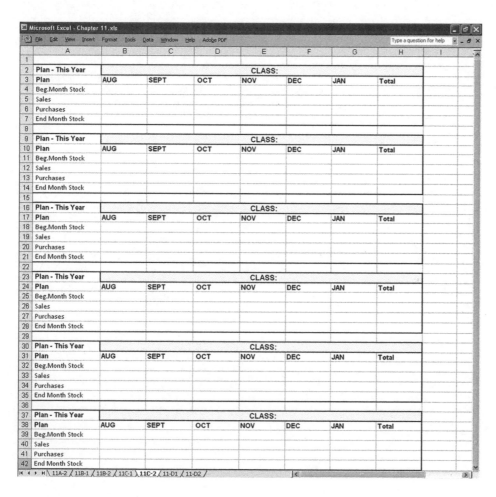

EXCEL SPREADSHEET 11-C2.

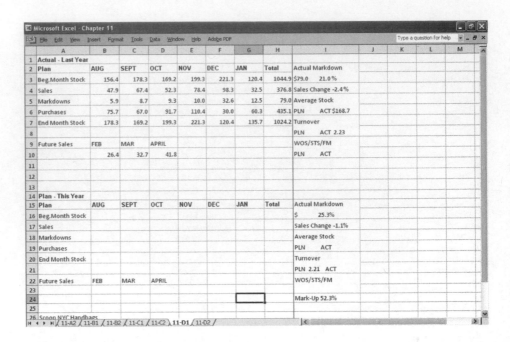

EXCEL SPREADSHEET 11-D1.

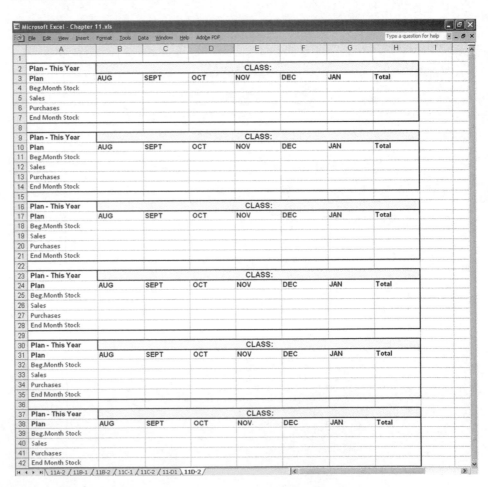

EXCEL SPREADSHEET 11-D2.

CREATE IT IN EXCEL!

Begin with the completed STS plan (7J) for the jewelry department (see Figure 11.1).

Using the Excel worksheet for class planning (Figure 11.2), calculate this year's plan for each class (Table 11.3).

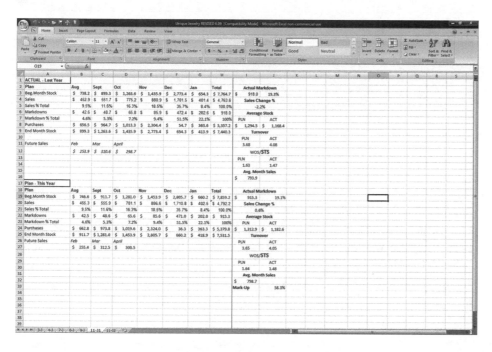

FIGURE 11.1 Completed STS Plan (7-J) for the Jewelry Department.

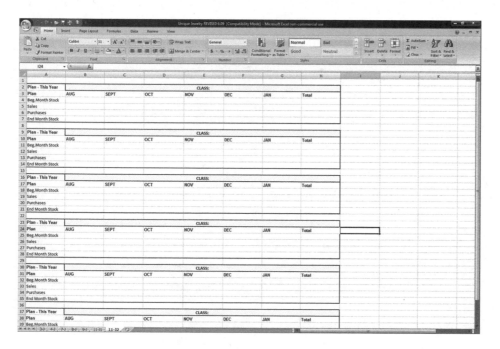

FIGURE 11.2 Jewelry Department Class Plan.

TABLE 11.3. CALCULATE THIS YEAR'S PLAN

Classification	Plan % Total This Year
Earring	38%
Bracelet	18%
Necklace	21%
Pin	12%
Ring	8%
Other	3%
TOTAL	100%

Spreadsheets can be linked together by using functions in Excel. In the example below (Figure 11.3), select the *fx* tool and enter the value argument.

Enter the data by selecting the Month BOM and multiplying it by the percentage for the month. The formula can then be copied across the columns (see Figures 11.4 and 11.5).

Continue using the *fx* function key to enter the value, and multiply by the assigned percentage for each classification (see Figure 11.6).

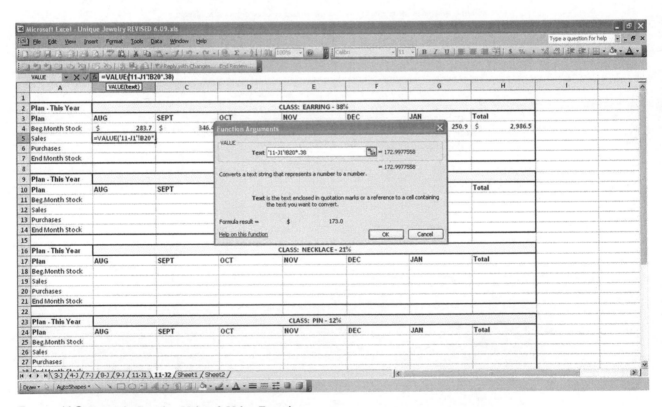

FIGURE 11.3 Formula Creation Using *fx* Value Function.

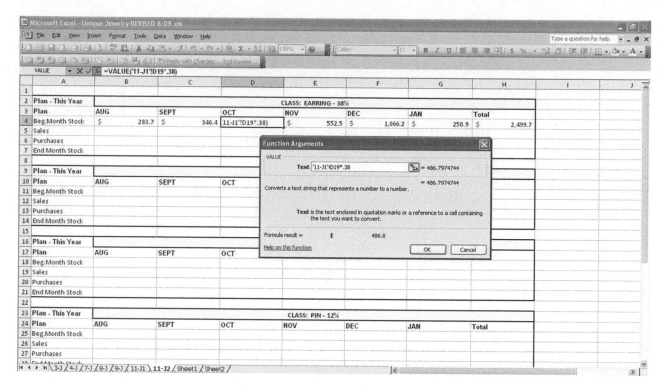

FIGURE 11.4 Value Function Data.

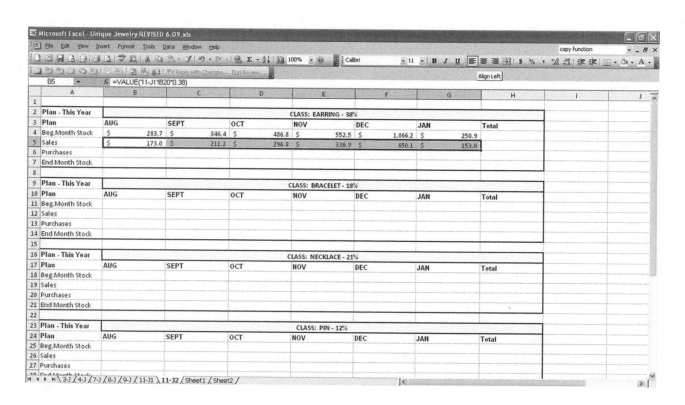

FIGURE 11.5 Copy Value Function.

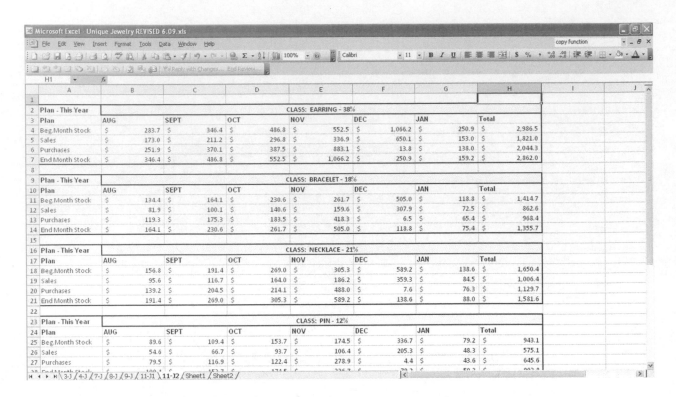

FIGURE 11.6 Class Plan Complete Using Value Function.

TERMINOLOGY

classifications: Related groups of products that can be viewed in smaller units within a total business.

12

ASSORTMENT PLANNING AND HOW MUCH TO BUY

Each step of the buying process introduces another level of planning and decision making. The plan began with a total season plan and was then broken down into a classification plan. The classification plan works in conjunction with further analysis of assortments to determine exactly what to buy. The process of assortment planning is the next step, which the buyer can accomplish in several ways.

ASSORTMENT PLANNING

Assortment planning is a process that helps a buyer bridge the gap between the financial classification plan and how the retail store will visually appeal to customers in a way that ultimately encourages them to buy. The three most common methods of assortment planning are style-out, sell-through or selling reports, and trend analysis, including testing new products. Testing is really a subcategory of trend analysis. Although each method serves a specific purpose, buyers often use multiple methods during the planning season.

STYLE-OUT

The **style-out** method is often the most productive, but it is also costly. Style-out requires significant effort and time by the buyer, and the costs of shipping vendors' products to the retailer can be high. Though significant,

these costs can easily pay for themselves when a thoughtful style-out is implemented.

A style-out begins in the market, where the buyers visit many showrooms during the week. By the time market ends, buyers may forget some details about products they saw at the beginning of the week. Photographs, notes, and line sheets are always helpful, but nothing compares to physically comparing products side by side. Style-out analysis is usually conducted seasonally or quarterly. Costs, quality, features, benefits, styling traits, and other attributes are all critical decision factors for the customer and should also be critical to the buyer.

Conducting a style-out can be as simple as reviewing one major brand in one department, or it can involve several brands, departments, and buyers. The process typically begins in market, where the buyer requests the vendor to ship sample product to his or her office. As samples arrive, they are checked in and logged for accurate record keeping and potential expenses. Shipping boxes are generally saved for efficiently returning the product to the vendor. (Samples not shipped back to the vendor create excessive inventory or sample costs; they are usually charged to the buyer and often cannot be resold to the customer.)

Samples are assembled and staged according to business need. Buyers then review each sample and make decisions based on multiple criteria relating to actual sales history. The style-out method also offers the buyer a visual image of how the products will look in the store as well as what the monthly flow of product will reveal. Is the assortment too basic? Does the assortment need another price level? Are the brands well represented? Does the assortment need color to add visual interest? These are just examples of some of the pertinent questions that the buyer must address during the style-out process.

Sell-Through

Sell-through (or selling reports), another method of assortment planning, is often used as a basis for the style-out process. Analysis of historical selling is usually (but not always) an indicator of future sales performance. For large corporate stores, sell-through reports are usually at a high level, such as product classification or subclassification. Stores that use Universal Product Code (UPC) scanners can review further detailed selling by style, color, or size. Small boutique stores that rely on in-store knowledge can take physical inventory counts. Another quick method is to look at the sale or clearance racks to see what sizes or colors remain.

Sell-through reports are easy to review but without sophisticated software can be time-consuming to prepare. The actual analysis can also be time-consuming for stores with an extensive breadth of inventory. Single-unit retail stores with UPC capability and report generation can easily recoup their technology expenses by reinvesting in best-selling inventory that improves profitability. The ideal software programs allow the buyer to input what data they are seeking and then generate the appropriate report. Without this type of software, an assistant buyer or planner will prepare Excel spreadsheets to aid in making an informed decision. A typical sell-through report identifies a product or product category as shown in Table 12.1.

In this example, the sell-through (actual units sold) is the same for both styles listed. The difference is the number of days the product has been available. For the first style, a 37 percent sell-through in 14 days is very good and could indicate a need for reorder. For the second style, that same sell-through in 48 days is considered slow selling and in need of attention. Sell-through reports are very useful, and buyers should always analyze them with an eye for opportunities and challenges.

TABLE 12.1. TYPICAL SELL-THROUGH REPORT

Style #	Beg. Units on Hand	End Units on Hand	Units Sold	% Sold	Time
56321	154	97	57	37%	14 days
56681	154	97	57	37%	48 days

TREND ANALYSIS

Trend analysis, another assortment planning method, is especially important in fashion product businesses. A thorough analysis consisting of plotting trends into a trend curve is essential to understanding where a business has been and where it is going. Most businesses require carefully planned amounts of basic inventory, fashion or trend inventory, and test inventory. Reviewing sales information and placing it on the trend curve will tell a buyer whether to accelerate buying basic, fashion, or test inventory or get out of slow-moving inventory. Trend analysis need not be cumbersome; the data can be reviewed monthly or quarterly—unlike sell-through data, which are generally reviewed weekly.

Analyzing trend curves between departments can also be beneficial. Consider these relationships:

Dresses : Jewelry

Men's Suits : Men's Ties

Coat Silhouettes : Robe Silhouettes

High-Pattern Clothing : Footwear

Three-Quarter Sleeve : Bracelets

Slow-Selling Suits : Increase in Ties

Neck and Sleeve Details : Newness for Robes

Large, Busy Patterns : Simple Footwear

Think of other relationships that could provide future selling clues through trend curve analysis and plot them on the following trend curve.

Attribute	Testing	Incoming	Pre-Peak	Peak	Post-Peak	Decline	Outgoing
AVAILABILITY							
COMPETITION							
PRICE							
MARKET WATCH							
KEY QUESTION							
ACT!							

TESTING

Testing is a critical part of any business. Buyers are remiss if they do not always designate a small amount of money for testing something new. Planning for test product gives buyers a competitive edge in the marketplace, where competitors may not be aware of or ready to buy the new product. Buyers purchase testing products in small amounts and usually for only a few locations. The results of the test will determine if the product has greater viability or needs to be eliminated from inventory.

Incoming product has passed the testing phase, is reordered for test stores, and likely is ordered for another layer of stores. Incoming product could also refer to an expansion of product from multiple vendors.

As discussed in Chapter 6, the product life cycle begins with the testing phase and moves through each cycle before finally exiting the business through markdowns. Each phase of the process can last for weeks, months, or even years. Careful analysis of the cycle will keep assortments fresh and new, which will keep customers buying.

HOW MUCH TO BUY

The next level of planning for buyers involves understanding how much to buy. Using average units and average dollars, a buyer can quickly calculate how much inventory to buy or not to buy. Consider the following scenario using averages as logic instead of taking the time to actually write an order.

The buyer has about $5000 available to spend (this is also called the "open to buy" and will be discussed in greater detail in Chapter 13).

A four-way apparel fixture can accommodate one small collection of related separates. The buyer can compare the capacity of the fixture with the projection of buying the collection.

On one four-way apparel rack, two straight-arm sides can accommodate about 30 units of inventory each; two waterfall-arm sides can accommodate about 14 units of inventory each. The total capacity of the fixture is 88 units. Keep in mind that the fixture's capacity varies with product width and hanger style.

Review of a new collection at market reveals that the ideal assortment includes two pant styles, one skirt, one blazer, one knit top, and one woven top with the following retail prices.

New Collection–Quick Calculation

Pant 1, $62.00: Sizes 4–16 = 7-unit size run + 4 units for key sizes

Pant 2, $68.00: Sizes 4–16 = 7-unit size run + 2 units for key sizes

Skirt, $50.00: Sizes 4–16 = 7-unit size run + 4 units for key sizes

Blazer, $98.00: Sizes 4–16 = 7-unit size run + 2 units for key sizes

Knit Top in three colors, $32.00:

Sizes S–XL = 4-unit size run × 3 colors = 12 units × 2 for key item

Woven Top in two colors, $42.00:

Sizes 4–16 = 7-unit size run = 14 units

Total = 54 units + 4 for key sizes

Total = 82 units

Calculate the average retail at $58:

82 units × $58 = $4756

The buyer can make a quick decision to purchase the collection. While this exercise may have taken several minutes to calculate, buyers become skilled at making this type of quick average calculation to assist with buying decisions. If the quick calculation looks like the buyer can make the buy, he or she will continue with a more in-depth order-writing process that will involve an analysis of sales history, size needs, silhouette needs, fabric needs, etc.

Another use of averages involves looking at total months purchase plans and calculating averages. If a total purchase plan for a month is $527.0, the task of buying the product can be daunting. Breaking down the total into units helps to make the task clearer. At an average retail price of $78.00, the buyer can quickly surmise that 6756 units are to be purchased. As discussed earlier in the chapter and in classification planning (Chapter 11), the 6756 units are further broken down into small categories to make the purchase decision easier to manage and less intimidating.

APPLICATION

Using the classification plan established in Chapter 11 and Excel Spreadsheet 11A-2, complete the unit plan as shown in Table 12.2. Assume the average retail price by classifications shown here.

TABLE 12.2. AVERAGE RETAIL		
Classification	**Plan % Total TY** [As completed in Excel Spreadsheet 11-A2]	**Average Retail**
Earring	32%	$78.00
Bracelet	26%	$175.00
Necklace	15%	$215.00
Pin	16%	$91.00
Ring	9%	$63.00
Other	2%	$54.00
TOTAL	100%	$124.00

1. Using Excel Spreadsheet 11-A2, apply the average retail prices from Table 12.2 and calculate the UNITS TO BUY for each classification and enter them in Spreadsheet 12A.

August Purchases	$113.8	÷	$78.00	=	1459 units
September	$91.5	÷	$78.00	=	1173 units
October	$120.3	÷	$78.00	=	1542 units

November	$294.8	÷	$78.00	=	3779 units
December	$25.1	÷	$78.00	=	322 units
January	$97.5	÷	$78.00	=	1250 units

Continue this process through all classifications. Understanding how many units to buy per months provides the buyer with a realistic unit expectation to maximize sales through managed purchasing.

CREATE IT IN EXCEL!

Begin with the completed classification plan from Chapter 11 using Figure 11.6. Table 12-3 provides the average retail to calculate UNITS TO BUY for each classification. Enter them in Excel Spreadsheet 12-J.

TABLE 12.3. AVERAGE RETAIL		
Classification	**Plan % Total LY** [As completed in Figure 11.6]	**Average Retail**
Earring	38%	$83.00
Bracelet	18%	$190.00
Necklace	21%	$225.00
Pin	12%	$86.00
Ring	8%	$68.00
Other	3%	$61.00
TOTAL	100%	$131.00

1. Using Figure 11.6, apply the average retail prices from Table 12.3 and calculate the UNITS TO BUY for each classification and enter them in Excel Spreadsheet 12-J.

August Purchases	$251.9	÷	$83.00	=	3035 units
September	$370.1	÷	$83.00	=	4459 units
October	$387.5	÷	$83.00	=	4668 units
November	$883.1	÷	$83.00	=	10,640 units
December	$13.8	÷	$83.00	=	166 units
January	$138.0	÷	$83.00	=	1662 units

In Cell B7 enter: = B6/E2   result 3034 units
In Cell C7 enter: = C6/E2   result 4459 units
In Cell C8 enter: = D6/E2   result 4668 units

Be sure to format cells in the unit row to number with three decimal places. Continue this process through all classifications. Understanding how many units to buy per months provides the buyer with a realistic unit expectation to maximize sales through managed purchasing.

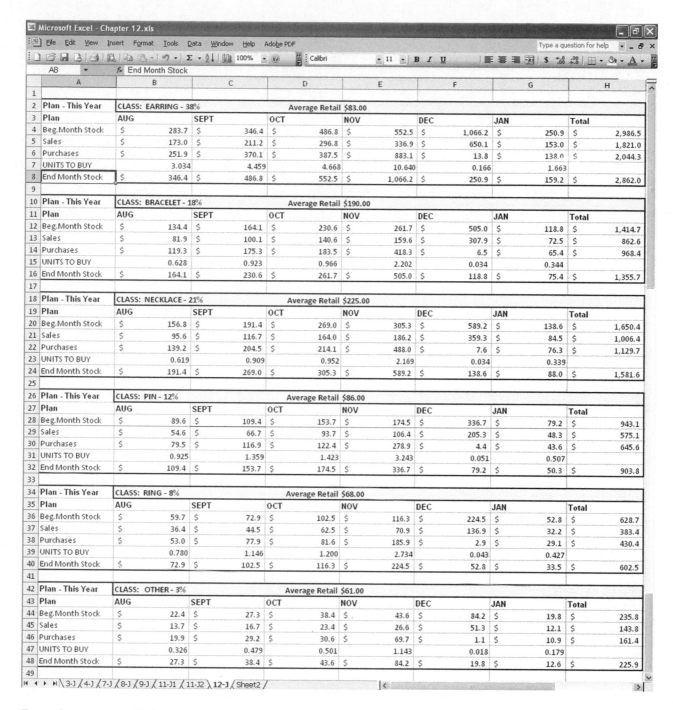

	Microsoft Excel - Chapter 12.xls							
	A	B	C	D	E	F	G	H
1								
2	**Plan - This Year**	CLASS: EARRING - 38%			Average Retail $83.00			
3	Plan	AUG	SEPT	OCT	NOV	DEC	JAN	Total
4	Beg.Month Stock	$ 283.7	$ 346.4	$ 486.8	$ 552.5	$ 1,066.2	$ 250.9	$ 2,986.5
5	Sales	$ 173.0	$ 211.2	$ 296.8	$ 336.9	$ 650.1	$ 153.0	$ 1,821.0
6	Purchases	$ 251.9	$ 370.1	$ 387.5	$ 883.1	$ 13.8	$ 138.0	$ 2,044.3
7	UNITS TO BUY	3.034	4.459	4.668	10.640	0.166	1.663	
8	End Month Stock	$ 346.4	$ 486.8	$ 552.5	$ 1,066.2	$ 250.9	$ 159.2	$ 2,862.0
9								
10	**Plan - This Year**	CLASS: BRACELET - 18%			Average Retail $190.00			
11	Plan	AUG	SEPT	OCT	NOV	DEC	JAN	Total
12	Beg.Month Stock	$ 134.4	$ 164.1	$ 230.6	$ 261.7	$ 505.0	$ 118.8	$ 1,414.7
13	Sales	$ 81.9	$ 100.1	$ 140.6	$ 159.6	$ 307.9	$ 72.5	$ 862.6
14	Purchases	$ 119.3	$ 175.3	$ 183.5	$ 418.3	$ 6.5	$ 65.4	$ 968.4
15	UNITS TO BUY	0.628	0.923	0.966	2.202	0.034	0.344	
16	End Month Stock	$ 164.1	$ 230.6	$ 261.7	$ 505.0	$ 118.8	$ 75.4	$ 1,355.7
17								
18	**Plan - This Year**	CLASS: NECKLACE - 21%			Average Retail $225.00			
19	Plan	AUG	SEPT	OCT	NOV	DEC	JAN	Total
20	Beg.Month Stock	$ 156.8	$ 191.4	$ 269.0	$ 305.3	$ 589.2	$ 138.6	$ 1,650.4
21	Sales	$ 95.6	$ 116.7	$ 164.0	$ 186.2	$ 359.3	$ 84.5	$ 1,006.4
22	Purchases	$ 139.2	$ 204.5	$ 214.1	$ 488.0	$ 7.6	$ 76.3	$ 1,129.7
23	UNITS TO BUY	0.619	0.909	0.952	2.169	0.034	0.339	
24	End Month Stock	$ 191.4	$ 269.0	$ 305.3	$ 589.2	$ 138.6	$ 88.0	$ 1,581.6
25								
26	**Plan - This Year**	CLASS: PIN - 12%			Average Retail $86.00			
27	Plan	AUG	SEPT	OCT	NOV	DEC	JAN	Total
28	Beg.Month Stock	$ 89.6	$ 109.4	$ 153.7	$ 174.5	$ 336.7	$ 79.2	943.1
29	Sales	$ 54.6	$ 66.7	$ 93.7	$ 106.4	$ 205.3	$ 48.3	575.1
30	Purchases	$ 79.5	$ 116.9	$ 122.4	$ 278.9	$ 4.4	$ 43.6	645.6
31	UNITS TO BUY	0.925	1.359	1.423	3.243	0.051	0.507	
32	End Month Stock	$ 109.4	$ 153.7	$ 174.5	$ 336.7	$ 79.2	$ 50.3	$ 903.8
33								
34	**Plan - This Year**	CLASS: RING - 8%			Average Retail $68.00			
35	Plan	AUG	SEPT	OCT	NOV	DEC	JAN	Total
36	Beg.Month Stock	$ 59.7	$ 72.9	$ 102.5	$ 116.3	$ 224.5	$ 52.8	628.7
37	Sales	$ 36.4	$ 44.5	$ 62.5	$ 70.9	$ 136.9	$ 32.2	383.4
38	Purchases	$ 53.0	$ 77.9	$ 81.6	$ 185.9	$ 2.9	$ 29.1	$ 430.4
39	UNITS TO BUY	0.780	1.146	1.200	2.734	0.043	0.427	
40	End Month Stock	$ 72.9	$ 102.5	$ 116.3	$ 224.5	$ 52.8	$ 33.5	$ 602.5
41								
42	**Plan - This Year**	CLASS: OTHER - 3%			Average Retail $61.00			
43	Plan	AUG	SEPT	OCT	NOV	DEC	JAN	Total
44	Beg.Month Stock	$ 22.4	$ 27.3	$ 38.4	$. 43.6	$ 84.2	$ 19.8	235.8
45	Sales	$ 13.7	$ 16.7	$ 23.4	$ 26.6	$ 51.3	$ 12.1	143.8
46	Purchases	$ 19.9	$ 29.2	$ 30.6	$ 69.7	$ 1.1	$ 10.9	161.4
47	UNITS TO BUY	0.326	0.479	0.501	1.143	0.018	0.179	
48	End Month Stock	$ 27.3	$ 38.4	$ 43.6	$ 84.2	$ 19.8	$ 12.6	225.9
49								

EXCEL SPREADSHEET 12-J.

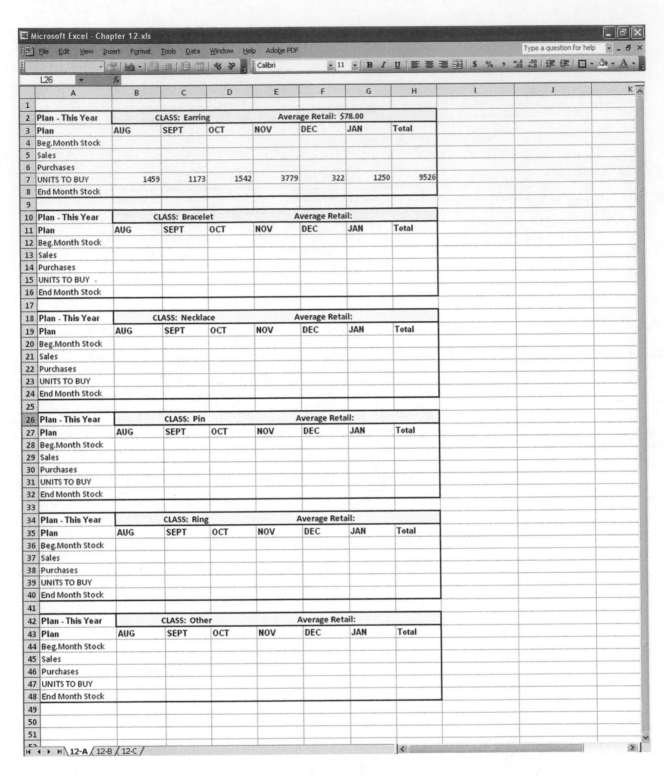

	A	B	C	D	E	F	G	H	I	J	K
1											
2	Plan - This Year		CLASS: Earring			Average Retail: $78.00					
3	Plan	AUG	SEPT	OCT	NOV	DEC	JAN	Total			
4	Beg.Month Stock										
5	Sales										
6	Purchases										
7	UNITS TO BUY	1459	1173	1542	3779	322	1250	9526			
8	End Month Stock										
9											
10	Plan - This Year		CLASS: Bracelet			Average Retail:					
11	Plan	AUG	SEPT	OCT	NOV	DEC	JAN	Total			
12	Beg.Month Stock										
13	Sales										
14	Purchases										
15	UNITS TO BUY .										
16	End Month Stock										
17											
18	Plan - This Year		CLASS: Necklace			Average Retail:					
19	Plan	AUG	SEPT	OCT	NOV	DEC	JAN	Total			
20	Beg.Month Stock										
21	Sales										
22	Purchases										
23	UNITS TO BUY										
24	End Month Stock										
25											
26	Plan - This Year		CLASS: Pin			Average Retail:					
27	Plan	AUG	SEPT	OCT	NOV	DEC	JAN	Total			
28	Beg.Month Stock										
29	Sales										
30	Purchases										
31	UNITS TO BUY										
32	End Month Stock										
33											
34	Plan - This Year		CLASS: Ring			Average Retail:					
35	Plan	AUG	SEPT	OCT	NOV	DEC	JAN	Total			
36	Beg.Month Stock										
37	Sales										
38	Purchases										
39	UNITS TO BUY										
40	End Month Stock										
41											
42	Plan - This Year		CLASS: Other			Average Retail:					
43	Plan	AUG	SEPT	OCT	NOV	DEC	JAN	Total			
44	Beg.Month Stock										
45	Sales										
46	Purchases										
47	UNITS TO BUY										
48	End Month Stock										
49											
50											
51											

12-A / 12-B / 12-C /

EXCEL SPREADSHEET 12-A.

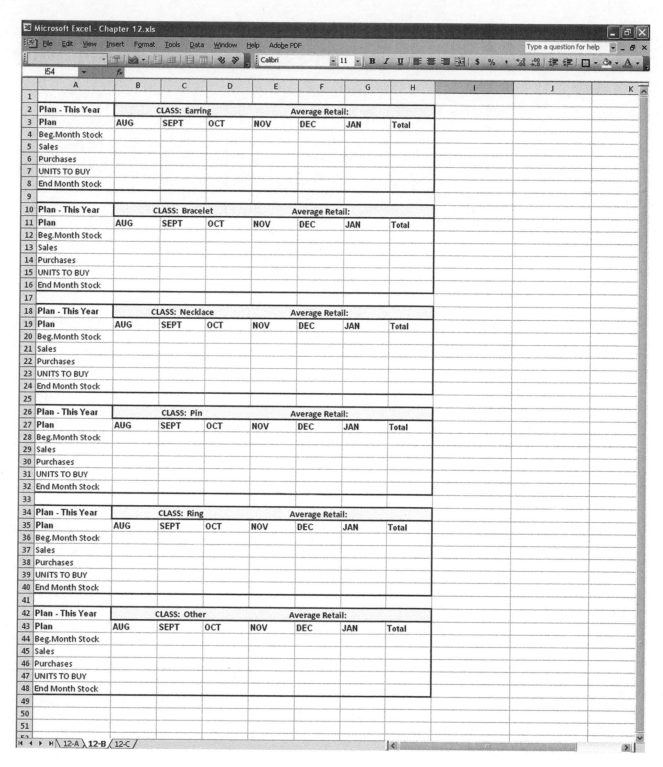

EXCEL SPREADSHEET 12-B.

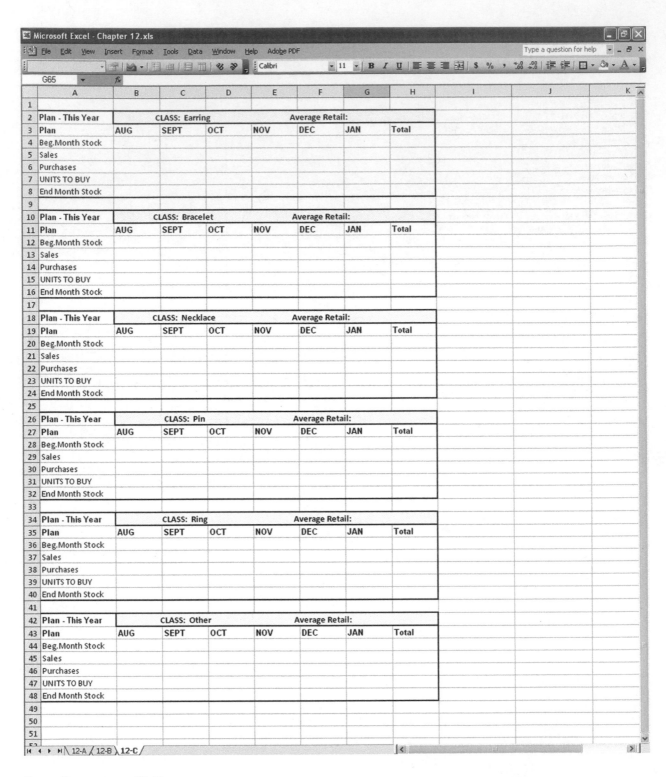

EXCEL SPREADSHEET 12-C.

YOUR TURN

Select two completed classification plans from Chapter 11.

- 11B Men's Dress Shirts
- 11C Women's Eveningwear
- 11D Designer Accessories

After researching an appropriate retailer for the product category, determine a pricing structure by classification. Using Excel Spreadsheets 12-B and 12-C, calculate UNITS TO BUY.

After completing Excel Spreadsheets 12-B and 12-C, select one classification for further assortment analysis. Using online sources, actual store visits, industry publications, or other sources, plot product from one classification—e.g., patterned dress shirts—onto a trend curve analysis. Complete the following exercises:

1. Describe how the analysis was conducted.

2. Review UNITS TO BUY for one month, and make a projection for purchases in testing, incoming, pre-peak, and peak purchases. Use a trend curve plot or Excel spreadsheet.

   a. Are the unit projections reasonable or are adjustments necessary?

3. While hindsight is always 20/20, using a variety of planning tools will yield more careful assessment of each stage of the trend curve. Calculate the percentage of each inventory phase for the month.

TERMINOLOGY

assortment planning: Is a process that helps a buyer bridge the gap between the financial classification plan and how the retail store will visually appeal to customers in a way that will ultimately encourage them to buy.

style out: An assortment planning method in which buyers review product samples and decide which ones to purchase.

sell-through: An assortment planning method in which buyers review selling reports—units of product sold, and how quickly—in deciding which ones to purchase.

trend analysis: An assortment planning method in which buyers analyze trend curves in determining which products to purchase.

13

FORECASTING AND VENDOR RELATIONSHIPS

After weeks and sometimes months of careful planning, all plans eventually become forecasts. Forecasting in-season results, managing the open-to-buy process, and maintaining vendor relationships are all essential buyer functions.

FORECASTING

Forecasting moves the planning process into real-time, actual results, and projected forecasts of future performance. Because the plan itself was completed at a moment in time, it does not include external threats and challenges or new business opportunities that became known six months later. While the forecasting process is intended to manage business decisions using current data and to re-project future results, it is also intended to aid buyers in maximizing new opportunities, correcting course on poor performance, and partnering with vendors every step of the way. Forecasting can be completed using new and ongoing business knowledge, or it can be completed on a strictly statistical basis. Financial analysts within the planning group might review forecasts based only on numerical trends. Conversely, the buyer has greater insight and business knowledge that could impact how the business is forecast into the future. What is important is to strike a balance between analytical

analysis (quantitative) and knowledge-based analysis (qualitative) in order to maximize profit and sales results.

VENDOR RELATIONSHIPS

Vendor relationships are one of the most complex aspects of the buyer's job. Thus far, a buyer's life has involved countless hours spent calculating all of the variables that affect profitability. With concrete, black-and-white results, buyers are armed to build, end, or maintain relationships with vendors. Managing these personal relationships can be challenging—and sometimes quite rewarding. Finding the balance between interpersonal skills and financial performance involves varied approaches at different times. Whatever the circumstances, buyers need to remember that although they have the power to buy or not to buy product, success is built on mutually beneficial relationships.

Buyers and vendors both want the same thing: profitable sales. However, maintaining customers' trust falls largely into the buyer's hands. Thus, buyers must always act in the best interest of the customer while protecting overall profitability. When buyers become too difficult to work with or overly demanding, they literally have the power to put a small vendor out of business. Managing the relationship to ensure that each party has ownership and interest in the profitability will result in building a long-term, collaborative business.

Buyers and vendors have several levers to consider in establishing profit margins. Buyers typically are committed to an overall six-month plan, but for each vendor, multiple strategies can be applied to result in the overall desired performance outcome. Some of these strategies are as follows:

- *Markdowns.* Slow-selling product is not going to improve with age. It needs to be addressed as soon as possible so that it can be zeroed out and new desirable inventory can be purchased. The cost of markdowns can be shared or in some cases completely absorbed by the vendor.

- *Return to vendor.* If product is not selling well in one region or store but selling well in another, there may be an opportunity to return the product to the vendor, who in turn sends it to a retailer who is successfully selling the product.

- *Additional dating.* Allowing extra time to pay for product can be beneficial in improving cash flows. This strategy is often used for new store openings, when the product needs to arrive far earlier than the store opening.

- *Discount terms.* Discount terms are also favorable to profitability and are usually extended to stores with significant orders or stores that can pay more rapidly. Discount terms are negotiated at the point of order. Some examples would include a 2 percent discount if paid within 10 days, known as 2/10 net 30; or if paid within 10 days, the retailer is entitled to a 2 percent discount or no discount if paid in 30 days. Another form of discount might include purchase of 100 or more units of a specific item and receiving a 10 percent discount on that item. Although these discounts may seem small, when multiplied over several vendors or several months, they can add tens of thousands of profit dollars to the bottom line.

- *Off-price buys.* Vendors sometimes need to clear out excess inventory, and they are willing to do so at a discount. Buyers can take advantage of these savings and run short-term promotions to drive sales.

- *First or exclusive products.* Buyers who negotiate for early deliveries or exclusive products have the first-mover advantage. Often this situation makes customers feel an urgency to buy because the product has limited availability. To add profit through increased markup, these products can sometimes be priced slightly higher.

- *Cooperative advertising.* Advertising costs can range from inexpensive Internet coverage to store catalog to full-page color advertising in the latest magazine or spotlights in a weekly promotional circular. But with each initiative comes a cost, and sharing that cost between retailer and vendor can be profitable for both parties. Vendors can expect larger sales orders for advertised product, and both parties count on increased traffic and sales from any advertising. Cost sharing between vendor and retailer encourages partnership in decision making.

- *Order cancellation.* Buyers never want to find themselves in the position of needing to cancel orders. However, this is one strategy buyers can use to improve results, and it becomes especially useful when orders are shipped late. Orders shipped after the cancellation date are no longer legally binding and may be subject to cancellation by the buyer.

- *Partial order cancellation.* Making a partial cancellation is another possible tactic. By canceling a percentage of the order, or the order for a particularly overstocked store location, buyers can accomplish their goals without severely damaging the vendor's bottom line. Implementing this strategy can be done across many vendors thereby not significantly affecting any one vendor but rather spreading the cancellation across many to improve results and maintain relationships.

- *Auto replenishment and build orders.* Outlining a plan for automatic replenishment is a proactive measure for both parties. Establishing automatic replenishment enables the computer system to analyze the business, and it prevents basic inventory from running out. Keeping basics on hand at all times has significant positive effects for both retailer and vendor. A similar strategy is using what are known as build orders, which typically involve holding trend merchandise for a busy season. This can be particularly effective prior to a holiday season or other business-related peak selling season. Buyers select specific trend merchandise that is projected for future shipments. Orders are placed and released as needed and as negotiated with the vendor. These orders might have a small discount or other favorable profit terms.

- *Backup order placement.* Retail buying can often feel like gazing into a crystal ball. Knowing what to reorder and when can be tricky. Planning for backup orders ahead of time enables buyers to maximize sales and allows vendors to plan ahead.

APPLICATION

Based on the information contained in the following spreadsheets, complete the forecast. Completion of the forecast will require revised calculations of each plan variable (sales, markdowns, purchases, stock levels). Enter each variable change as described in the problem and recalculate each month and compare to plan. Once the forecast is complete, identify decisions to be made that will result in financial improvement. What strategies can be negotiated or implemented?

Using Excel Spreadsheet 13-A, actual results having been recorded through October beginning of month, complete the forecast based on the following information:

Sales

Sales in September were ahead of plan, and you expect the rest of the season to be equally strong. You anticipate that October will yield a 15 percent gain over plan.

The construction plan for renovating one of your best stores was moved from March of next year and will now begin in January; sales will drop by 10 percent.

Purchases

You have just been told that your November shipment from a major supplier has been canceled due to a fire at the warehouse; the order was valued at $115.2. Prepare the forecast, and recalculate average stock, inventory turnover, markdowns, and stock-to-sales (STS) ratio. What adjustments are necessary to remain profitable? How will you accomplish these adjustments, and in what time frame?

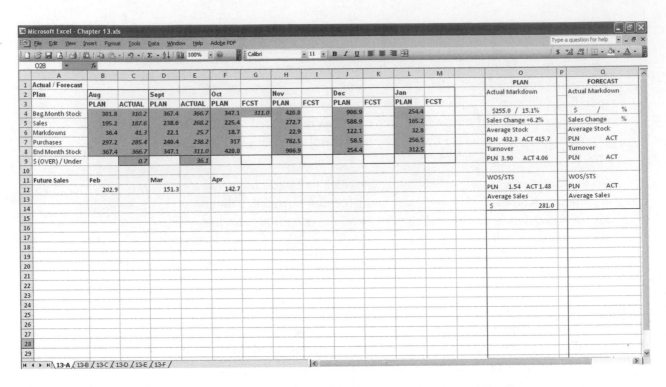

EXCEL SPREADSHEET 13-A.

Using Excel Spreadsheet 13-B, complete the forecast based on the following:

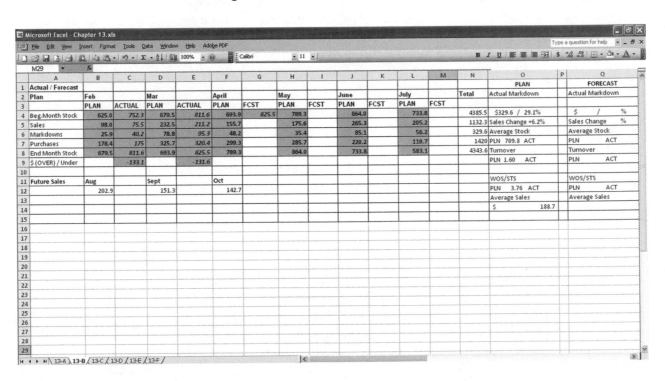

EXCEL SPREADSHEET 13-B.

Using a purely analytical approach, forecast the rest of the season. Prepare the forecast, and recalculate average stock, inventory turnover, markdowns, and STS ratio. What adjustments are necessary to remain profitable? How will you accomplish these adjustments, and in what time frame?

YOUR TURN

EXCEL SPREADSHEET 13-C

It's December, and a major snowstorm is predicted just two weeks before Christmas. Prepare the forecast, and recalculate average stock, inventory turnover, markdowns, and STS ratio. What adjustments are necessary to remain profitable? How will you accomplish these adjustments, and in what time frame?

EXCEL SPREADSHEET 13-D

Your area's favorite baseball team just made it to the World Series! Baseball mania has hit your top five stores, which represent 70 percent of your volume. Everyone is watching baseball instead of shopping. What is your revised forecast up until the games begin in mid-October and beyond? Can you recoup lost sales? If so, how will you do it?

EXCEL SPREADSHEET 13-E

You have just returned from market and found a hot new item. You want to be first in your market to have it in stock, but you are currently overbought. What do you do? The new spring catalog arrived in homes in mid-February. The featured items from your department were not prominently displayed, and your sales are dropping every day. How do you improve sales and reduce inventory?

EXCEL SPREADSHEET 13-F

A company's divisional merchandise manager (DMM) has called a meeting of the seven-member buying team. One buyer in the division has returned from market and sees a million-dollar opportunity to get exclusivity for a new product launch. The opportunity represents potential for significant sales volume that could benefit the whole team. Each buyer is asked to cut his or her own plans by a minimum of 10 percent to support their team members. Beginning with sales, forecast the 10 percent reduction for the season. Complete the forecast by calculating all other variables. The buyer who has spotted this opportunity has a history of being enthusiastic about new product but not always delivering the results. How do you respond? What contingency plans would you put into place just in case the million-dollar opportunity fades?

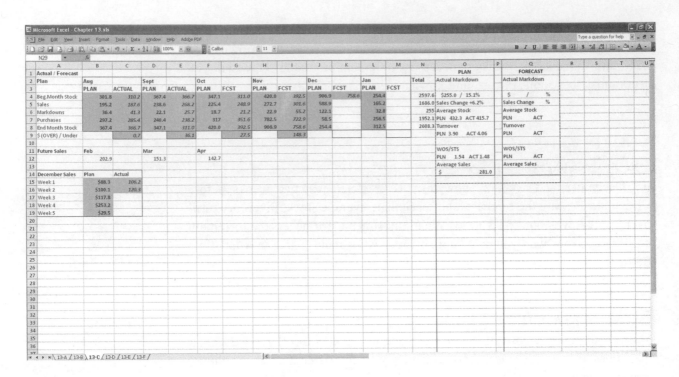

Excel Spreadsheet 13-C.

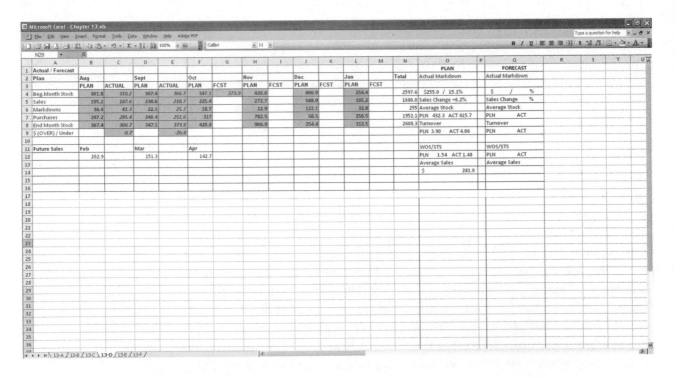

Excel Spreadsheet 13-D.

A BUYER'S LIFE

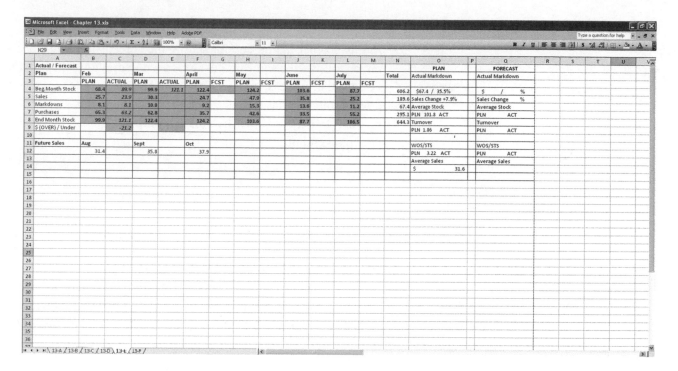

	Feb		Mar		April		May		June		July		Total	PLAN Actual Markdown		FORECAST Actual Markdown
Plan	PLAN	ACTUAL	PLAN	ACTUAL	PLAN	FCST	PLAN	FCST	PLAN	FCST	PLAN	FCST				
Beg.Month Stock	68.4	89.9	99.9	121.1	122.4		124.2		103.6		87.7		606.2	$67.4 / 35.5%		$ / %
Sales	25.7	23.9	30.3		24.7		47.9		35.8		25.2		189.6	Sales Change +7.9%		Sales Change %
Markdowns	8.1	8.1	10.0		9.2		15.3		13.6		11.2		67.4	Average Stock		Average Stock
Purchases	65.3	63.2	62.8		35.7		42.6		33.5		55.2		295.1	PLN 101.8 ACT		PLN ACT
End Month Stock	99.9	121.1	122.4		124.2		103.6		87.7		106.5		644.3	Turnover		Turnover
$ (OVER) / Under		-21.2												PLN 1.86 ACT		PLN ACT
Future Sales	Aug		Sept		Oct									WOS/STS		WOS/STS
	31.4		35.8		37.9									PLN 3.22 ACT		PLN ACT
														Average Sales		Average Sales
														$ 31.6		

Row label: Actual / Forecast

EXCEL SPREADSHEET 13-E.

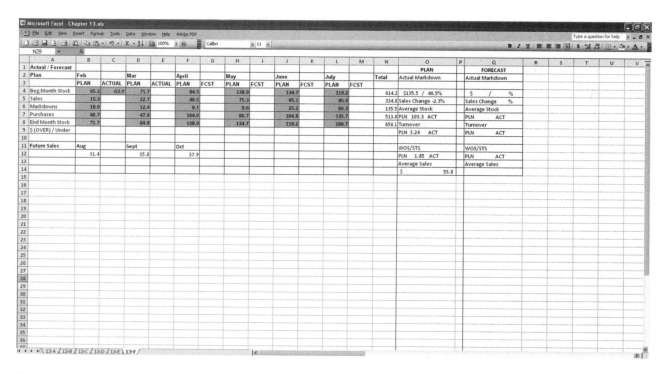

	Feb		Mar		April		May		June		July		Total	PLAN Actual Markdown		FORECAST Actual Markdown
Plan	PLAN	ACTUAL	PLAN	ACTUAL	PLAN	FCST	PLAN	FCST	PLAN	FCST	PLAN	FCST				
Beg.Month Stock	65.2	63.9	71.7		84.5		138.9		134.7		119.2		614.2	$135.5 / 40.5%		$ / %
Sales	15.3		22.7		40.5		75.3		95.1		85.9		334.8	Sales Change -2.3%		Sales Change %
Markdowns	18.9		12.4		9.1		9.6		25.2		60.3		135.5	Average Stock		Average Stock
Purchases	40.7		47.9		104.0		80.7		104.8		135.7		513.8	PLN 103.3 ACT		PLN ACT
End Month Stock	71.7		84.9		138.9		134.7		119.2		108.7		658.1	Turnover		Turnover
$ (OVER) / Under														PLN 3.24 ACT		PLN ACT
Future Sales	Aug		Sept		Oct									WOS/STS		WOS/STS
	31.4		35.8		37.9									PLN 1.85 ACT		PLN ACT
														Average Sales		Average Sales
														$ 55.8		

Row label: Actual / Forecast

EXCEL SPREADSHEET 13-F.

CREATE IT IN EXCEL!

X In this chapter the process of setting the spreadsheet with formulas follows the same process as is seen in previous chapters. Follow the process to enter formulas for stock, sales, markdowns, and purchases. Once complete, calculate the $ amount that is (OVER) or Under by simply comparing the actual end of month stock to the plan end of month stock.

FORMULA

Σ Actual End of Month Stock $/Plan End of Month Stock $

The formula will calculate a positive or negative number. A positive result states that there is additional money available for purchases. A negative result states an overbought situation that will require attention. This number is typically represented in brackets ($0.00).

14

A REPORT CARD: GROSS MARGIN AND CONTRIBUTION

Planning for and executing profitability projections are the final phases of determining business success. Two distinct calculations are made to determine profitability. The first and most common is gross margin. In simple terms, **gross margin** is the profit remaining after costs of goods sold are subtracted from sales. **Contribution** profitability takes gross margin one step further by applying expense charges to the business, thus determining a more accurate profit level. Retailers have differing views on profitability. Although they widely accept gross margin, not all retailers identify expenses and contribution levels as a matter of profit measurement at the buyer level.

CALCULATING GROSS MARGIN

Nearly all retailers measure gross margin as the major indicator of their company's health. Gross margin calculations account for all factors leading to the sale of merchandise in the store. A gross margin calculation includes these factors:

- *Beginning of period (BOP).* Beginning-of-period inventory at cost and retail. BOP may refer to beginning of year, season, quarter, or month.

- *Markup.* The dollar or percentage difference between the price paid for the merchandise and the current retail selling price.

- *Beginning markup (BMU).* Beginning markup of the entire inventory at the beginning of the period being calculated. BMU includes all inventory at all price points. Older inventory that has been marked down has a much lower markup than inventory newly received at full retail price and markup.

- *Receipts.* All merchandise received into the store at cost and retail during the period for which gross margin is calculated.

- *Initial markup (IMU).* Markup for the receipts received into the store upon their arrival.

- *Freight.* Retailers must pay the freight charges of shipping the inventory from the vendor to the store or distribution center, so freight is accounted for at cost only. It is important to note that the buyer and vendor can negotiate freight charges; however, general practice is that freight is paid by the retailer.

- *Stock available.* Cost and retail totals of the inventory of the specified time

- *Sales.* Net retail sales for the specified period of the gross margin calculation. Keep in mind that net sales are what the customer actually paid for the merchandise.

- *Markdowns.* Net retail markdowns for the specified period of the gross margin calculation. If a vendor helps pay for markdowns, this number will be reduced by whatever amount the vendor contributes. For example, if gross markdowns are $10.0, and the vendor pays for half, then the net markdown for the buyer is $5.0.

- *Shortage.* Inventory shortage is generally planned as an allocation based on percentage of sales and calculated as a dollar amount. Once the physical inventory is completed, the shortage allocation is adjusted to reflect actual retail dollar results.

- *Employee discount.* As with shortage, the employee discount is planned as an allocation based on percentage of sales and calculated as a dollar amount.

- *End-of-period (EOP) inventory.* Inventory held at the end of the period at cost and retail.

- *Cost of goods sold (COGS).* The difference between what was sold at retail and specific costs associated with preparing the merchandise to sell.

- *Cumulative markup (CMU).* The markup for the entire inventory available during the specified period. CMU combines the BOP inventory and subsequent markup with all new receipts and subsequent markup to identify the markup for all inventories during the specified period.

- *Workroom expenses.* Expenses associated with selling merchandise that are incurred by the selling department (e.g., alterations).

- *Cash discount (CD).* Any discounts negotiated between the buyer and the vendor, such as a discount for paying invoices within ten days or discounts associated with late shipments.
- *Gross margin $.* The actual dollar profit of the business.
- *Gross margin %.* The percentage of profit as a percent of sales.

Gross margin planning is completed at the start of each season and is constantly measured and forecasted throughout the season. Showing seasonal and yearly improvement to gross margin is a critical success factor for every buyer. Measuring gross margin profitability can be viewed against last year numbers or as a top-down planning function for the total company. While gross margin is an essential measurement for large-store buyers, specialty store or boutique buyers may be more concerned about contribution percentage, because it incorporates some operational expenses.

CONTRIBUTION PLANNING

Contribution planning accounts for expenses in the business that more clearly reflect its health. This planning includes advertising, payroll, supply chain, selling and store processing, inventory storage, headquarters, and interest on inventory. Although a small-boutique owner may not incur all of these expenses, they remain critical in determining profitability. For example, if a buyer reports gross margin profits of $50.0 but incurs advertising expenses of $45.0, the profit is eroded to only $5.0. Planning for expenses and subsequent contribution levels forces the buyer to monitor all expenses associated with selling the product. Additionally for the boutique owner, all expenses are accounted for and factored into overall profitability of the business through P&L statements.

After completing the season gross margin and contribution plan, the buyer monitors progress toward achieving the plan each month. As seen in Chapter 13, to achieve the plan, a buyer forecasts progress in future months and makes changes to affect those months and remain profitable. Buyers can use several adjustments, or levers, to affect financial profit projections. To maximize profits, buyers decide how to improve business and who to partner with in the process. Other decisions include reducing future order liability, partnering with vendors for markdown money or shared advertising expenses, returning slow-selling inventory to vendors, or seeking higher levels of pre-ticketing and UPC usage. Each of these actions can contribute to the overall health of the business and can be focused on specific vendors. Strategizing both short- and long-term plans with vendors can improve results over time and make seasonal negotiations more productive.

Besides overseeing the total planning process, the buyer may also plan and forecast gross margin and contribution for individual vendors. This allows the buyer to isolate over-performing vendors from underperforming vendors and negotiate accordingly. This process also reinforces vendor relations and encourages vendors to take an active role in achieving profitability, which in turn allows their product to remain in the store assortment.

APPLICATION
CALCULATE THE GROSS MARGIN PLAN BASED ON A FULL SEASON

Using Excel Spreadsheet 14-A, calculate gross margin. See Appendix B for full-size versions of all Excel Spreadsheets.

Line 1

Enter the beginning of period (BOP) stock level at retail, using the beginning markup (BMU) percentage; calculate the BOP at cost.

BOP = $670.0 retail

BMU = 58.3%

100% − 58.3% = 41.7%

$670.0 × 41.7% = $279.4 BOP at cost

Line 2

Enter the purchase receipts for the full season at retail, using the initial markup (IMU) percentage; calculate the purchase receipts at cost.

Purchase receipts = $885.0 retail

IMU = 60.0%

100% − 60.0% = 40.0%

$885.0 × 40.0% = $354.0 purchase receipts at cost

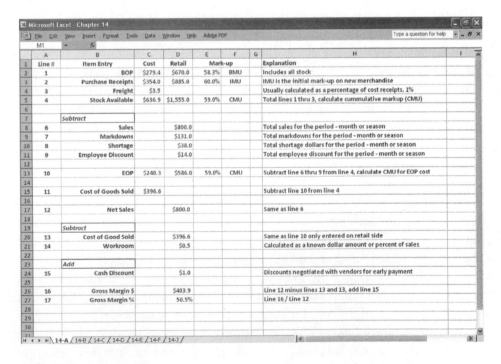

Line #	Item Entry	Cost	Retail	Mark-up		Explanation
1	BOP	$279.4	$670.0	58.3%	BMU	Includes all stock
2	Purchase Receipts	$354.0	$885.0	60.0%	IMU	IMU is the initial mark-up on new merchandise
3	Freight	$3.5				Usually calculated as a percentage of cost receipts, 1%
4	Stock Available	$636.9	$1,555.0	59.0%	CMU	Total lines 1 thru 3, calculate cummulative markup (CMU)
Subtract						
6	Sales		$800.0			Total sales for the period - month or season
7	Markdowns		$131.0			Total markdowns for the period - month or season
8	Shortage		$38.0			Total shortage dollars for the period - month or season
9	Employee Discount		$14.0			Total employee discount for the period - month or season
10	EOP	$240.3	$586.0	59.0%	CMU	Subtract line 6 thru 9 from line 4, calculate CMU for EOP cost
11	Cost of Goods Sold	$396.6				Subtract line 10 from line 4
12	Net Sales		$800.0			Same as line 6
Subtract						
13	Cost of Good Sold		$396.6			Same as line 10 only entered on retail side
14	Workroom		$0.5			Calculated as a known dollar amount or percent of sales
Add						
15	Cash Discount		$1.0			Discounts negotiated with vendors for early payment
16	Gross Margin $		$403.9			Line 12 minus lines 13 and 13, add line 15
17	Gross Margin %		50.5%			Line 16 / Line 12

EXCEL SPREADSHEET 14-A.

Line 3

Calculate freight charges by applying a percentage of 1 percent to cost receipts.

$354.0 \times 1\% = \$3.5$ freight entered as cost

Line 4

1. Calculate stock available by adding the Cost column of BOP, purchase receipts, and freight.

2. Calculate stock available by adding the Retail column of BOP, purchase receipts, and freight.

3. Calculate cumulative markup (CMU).

$(\$1555.0 - \$636.9) \div \$1555.0 = 59.0\%$

Lines 6 through 9

At retail only, enter total season.

Sales: $800.0

Markdowns: $131.0

Shortage: $38.0

Employee Discount: $14.0

Line 10

1. Determine end of period (EOP), beginning with retail stock available ($1555.0). Subtract sales, markdowns, shortage, and employee discount.

$\$1555.0 - \$800.0 - \$131.0 - \$38.0 - \$14.0 = \$586.0$

2. Calculate EOP at cost by applying 59.0% CMU to $586.0.

EOP = $586.0 retail
CMU = 59.0%
$100\% - 59.0\% = 41.0\%$
$\$586.0 \times 41.0\% = \$240.3$ EOP at cost

Line 11

Determine cost of goods sold by subtracting EOP at cost from stock available at cost.

$\$636.9 - \$240.3 = \$396.6$ cost of goods sold

Line 12

Enter net sales from total sales: $800.0

Line 13

In the Retail column, enter cost of goods sold: $396.6

Line 14

In the Retail column, enter workroom expenses: $0.5

Line 15

In the Retail column, enter cash discount: $1.0

Line 16

Determine gross margin $ (GM$), beginning with sales and subtracting cost of goods sold and workroom and then adding cash discount.

$800.0 − $396.6 − $.5 + $1.0 = $403.9 gross margin $

Line 17

Calculate gross margin % by dividing GM$ into sales

$403.9 ÷ $800.0 = 50.5% gross margin %

CONTRIBUTION PROFITABILITY

Determining contribution as profitability refers to a more realistic level of profit measurement. Contribution profitability is a key factor for single-store boutique owners because it further subtracts expense items that contribute to selling merchandise in the store. Although contribution provides a more realistic view of profit, it does not account for operational expenses such as rent, electricity, telephone, and so on that are seen on an organization's profit and loss statements. Expense items calculated for contribution profitability are as follows.

NET ADVERTISING

All advertising costs money. From a paper flyer handed out in the mall to an advertisement in *Vogue*, expenses need to be controlled and reconciled. In some cases vendors are willing to share in these costs and contribute cooperative advertising. The amount reflected in net advertising is after such cooperative agreements. For example, if an advertisement costs $20.0 and is negotiated as a 50–50 split between the retailer and the vendor, the net expense to the retailer would be $10.0.

SUPPLY CHAIN

The buyer usually calculates expenses associated with the supply chain as a percentage of purchase receipts and then applies them as a dollar amount to the contribution plan. Supply chain items include the expenses associated with warehouse functions such as trucking, warehouse costs, merchandise ticketing, and so forth. Supply chain expenses are typical of large retailers with centralized distribution centers. Retailers who use EDI and UPC strategies have lower supply chain costs because the cost of ticketing the merchandise is absorbed into merchandise processing with the vendor.

SELLING/STORE PROCESSING

Selling and store processing costs are associated with in-store processing such as ticketing, inventory intake processes, steaming of goods, and any other function that requires human effort to prepare merchandise to be sold.

Storage

Most businesses do not incur storage costs, but businesses that carry over inventory from season to season may be accountable for storing the excess inventory. An example of carryover inventory is Christmas lights, which do not change from year to year. Additionally, storage costs are calculated for businesses that use warehouse facilities and ship direct to customers from the warehouse. This expense arises for many tabletop businesses, such as fine china.

Interest on Inventory

By maintaining optimal levels of inventory, buyers can ensure efficient use of the organization's cash. When retailers use credit lines to buy inventory, they accrue interest on the debt that needs to be accounted for as an expense.

Headquarters

Going on a buying trip, visiting stores, and managing a staff all have associated costs. Headquarters expenses account for these costs and deduct them from gross margin. If a buyer wants to improve profitability he or she might consider one less night in New York or consolidate store visits. Being aware of such expenses by making buyers accountable improves the overall health of the business and eliminates frivolous spending.

As noted earlier in the chapter, each of the preceding expenses can also be accounted for through profit and loss statements, but applying them to individual buyer profitability or vendor profitability begins to more closely reflect true profit margins.

In most organizations, profitability accounts for as much as 75 percent or more of a buyer's performance review. Thus, achieving key profit variables of sales, inventory turnover, gross margin, and contribution are the critical success factors of the position. Not only are these success factors essential measurements for a buyer's success, but these results are measured for the organization's general merchandise manager (GMM) and divisional merchandise manager (DMM). Making all levels of the buying function accountable for key profit levels ensures teamwork and business ownership. For boutique owners, accounting profit and loss statements are true indicators of actual profitability. Whether you are a corporate retail buyer or a small-business owner, operating a business at a profit is expected at all levels.

Calculate the Contribution Plan Based on a Full Season

Using Excel Spreadsheet 14-B, calculate contribution.

Continuing from Excel Spreadsheet 14-A, subtract expenses from gross margin and calculate contribution.

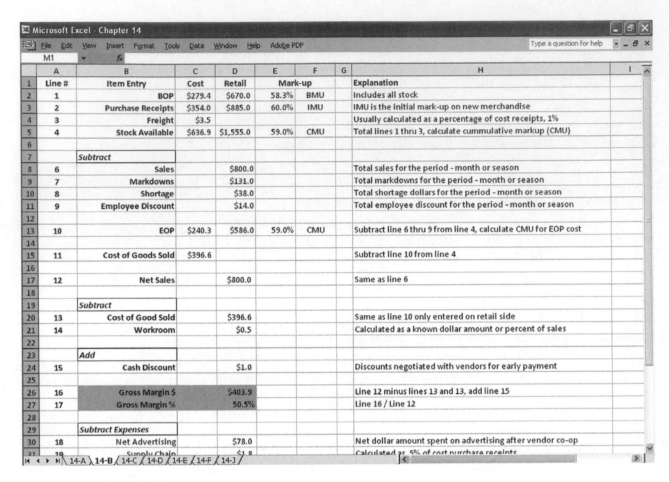

	A	B	C	D	E	F	G	H	I
1	Line #	Item Entry	Cost	Retail	Mark-up			Explanation	
2	1	BOP	$279.4	$670.0	58.3%	BMU		Includes all stock	
3	2	Purchase Receipts	$354.0	$885.0	60.0%	IMU		IMU is the initial mark-up on new merchandise	
4	3	Freight	$3.5					Usually calculated as a percentage of cost receipts, 1%	
5	4	Stock Available	$636.9	$1,555.0	59.0%	CMU		Total lines 1 thru 3, calculate cummulative markup (CMU)	
6									
7		Subtract							
8	6	Sales		$800.0				Total sales for the period - month or season	
9	7	Markdowns		$131.0				Total markdowns for the period - month or season	
10	8	Shortage		$38.0				Total shortage dollars for the period - month or season	
11	9	Employee Discount		$14.0				Total employee discount for the period - month or season	
12									
13	10	EOP	$240.3	$586.0	59.0%	CMU		Subtract line 6 thru 9 from line 4, calculate CMU for EOP cost	
14									
15	11	Cost of Goods Sold	$396.6					Subtract line 10 from line 4	
16									
17	12	Net Sales		$800.0				Same as line 6	
18									
19		Subtract							
20	13	Cost of Good Sold		$396.6				Same as line 10 only entered on retail side	
21	14	Workroom		$0.5				Calculated as a known dollar amount or percent of sales	
22									
23		Add							
24	15	Cash Discount		$1.0				Discounts negotiated with vendors for early payment	
25									
26	16	Gross Margin $		$403.9				Line 12 minus lines 13 and 13, add line 15	
27	17	Gross Margin %		50.5%				Line 16 / Line 12	
28									
29		Subtract Expenses							
30	18	Net Advertising		$78.0				Net dollar amount spent on advertising after vendor co-op	
31	19	Supply Chain		$1.8				Calculated as 5% of cost purchase receipts	

Sheet tabs: 14-A, **14-B**, 14-C, 14-D, 14-E, 14-F, 14-J

EXCEL SPREADSHEET 14-B.

Line 18

In the Retail column, enter net advertising expenses: $78.0.

Line 19

In the Retail column, enter supply chain as 0.5% of purchase receipts: $1.8.

Line 20

In the Retail column, enter selling/store processing as 0.3% of purchase receipts: $1.1.

Line 21

In the Retail column, enter storage as a flat dollar amount: $0.2.

Line 22

In the Retail column, enter interest on inventory as 3% of cost purchase receipts: $10.6.

Line 23

In the Retail column, enter headquarters as 1% of retail sales: $8.0.

Line 24

Determine contribution $ beginning with gross margin $ and subtracting net advertising, supply chain, selling/store processing, storage, interest on inventory, and headquarters.

$403.9 − $78.0 − $1.8 − $1.1 − $.2 − $10.6 − $8.0 = $304.2 contribution $

Line 25

Calculate contribution % by dividing contribution $ by sales.

$304.2 ÷ $800.0 = 38.0% contribution %

YOUR TURN

Complete Excel Spreadsheets 14-C through 14-F, and calculate gross margin and contribution as indicated.

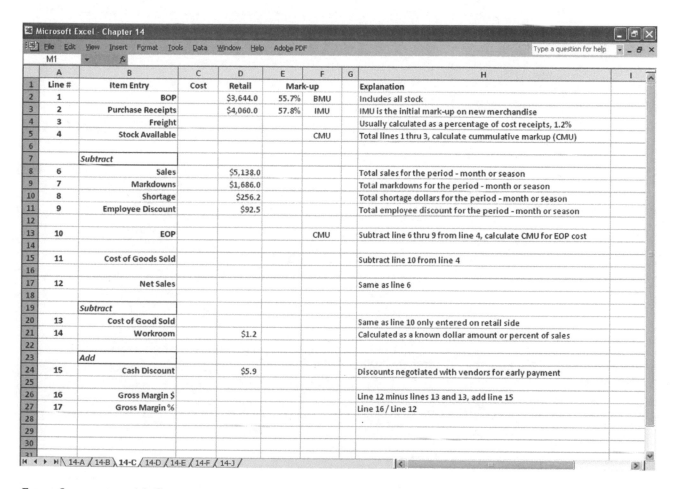

EXCEL SPREADSHEET 14-C.

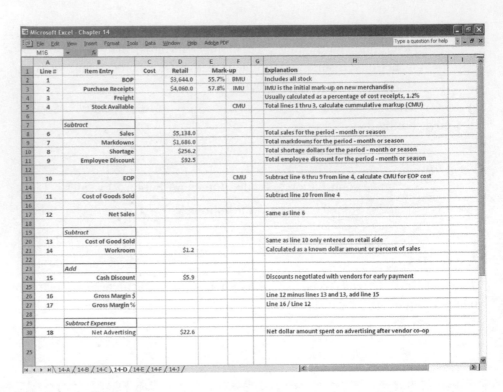

EXCEL SPREADSHEET 14-D.

Line #	Item Entry	Cost	Retail	Mark-up		Explanation
1	BOP		$3,644.0	55.7%	BMU	Includes all stock
2	Purchase Receipts		$4,060.0	57.8%	IMU	IMU is the initial mark-up on new merchandise
3	Freight					Usually calculated as a percentage of cost receipts, 1.2%
4	Stock Available				CMU	Total lines 1 thru 3, calculate cummulative markup (CMU)
	Subtract					
6	Sales		$5,138.0			Total sales for the period - month or season
7	Markdowns		$1,686.0			Total markdowns for the period - month or season
8	Shortage		$256.2			Total shortage dollars for the period - month or season
9	Employee Discount		$92.5			Total employee discount for the period - month or season
10	EOP				CMU	Subtract line 6 thru 9 from line 4, calculate CMU for EOP cost
11	Cost of Goods Sold					Subtract line 10 from line 4
12	Net Sales					Same as line 6
	Subtract					
13	Cost of Good Sold					Same as line 10 only entered on retail side
14	Workroom		$1.2			Calculated as a known dollar amount or percent of sales
	Add					
15	Cash Discount		$5.9			Discounts negotiated with vendors for early payment
16	Gross Margin $					Line 12 minus lines 13 and 13, add line 15
17	Gross Margin %					Line 16 / Line 12
	Subtract Expenses					
18	Net Advertising		$22.6			Net dollar amount spent on advertising after vendor co-op

EXCEL SPREADSHEET 14-D.

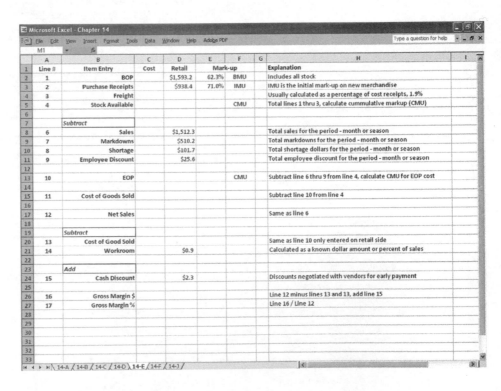

Line #	Item Entry	Cost	Retail	Mark-up		Explanation
1	BOP		$1,593.2	62.3%	BMU	Includes all stock
2	Purchase Receipts		$938.4	71.0%	IMU	IMU is the initial mark-up on new merchandise
3	Freight					Usually calculated as a percentage of cost receipts, 1.9%
4	Stock Available				CMU	Total lines 1 thru 3, calculate cummulative markup (CMU)
	Subtract					
6	Sales		$1,512.3			Total sales for the period - month or season
7	Markdowns		$510.2			Total markdowns for the period - month or season
8	Shortage		$101.7			Total shortage dollars for the period - month or season
9	Employee Discount		$25.6			Total employee discount for the period - month or season
10	EOP				CMU	Subtract line 6 thru 9 from line 4, calculate CMU for EOP cost
11	Cost of Goods Sold					Subtract line 10 from line 4
12	Net Sales					Same as line 6
	Subtract					
13	Cost of Good Sold					Same as line 10 only entered on retail side
14	Workroom		$0.9			Calculated as a known dollar amount or percent of sales
	Add					
15	Cash Discount		$2.3			Discounts negotiated with vendors for early payment
16	Gross Margin $					Line 12 minus lines 13 and 13, add line 15
17	Gross Margin %					Line 16 / Line 12

EXCEL SPREADSHEET 14-E.

A BUYER'S LIFE

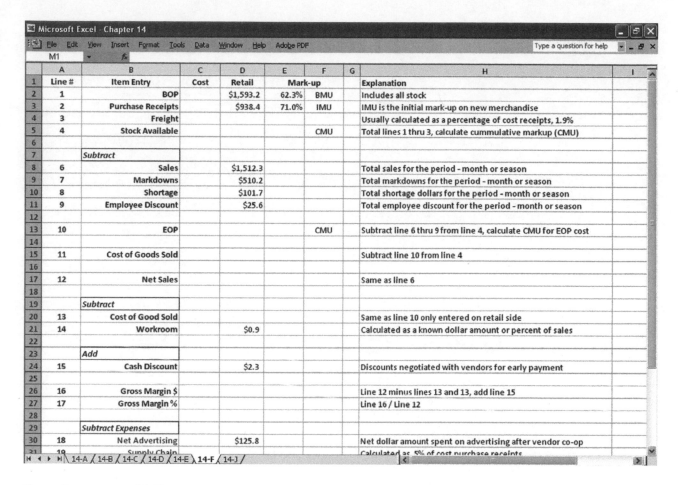

Line #	Item Entry	Cost	Retail	Mark-up		Explanation
1	BOP		$1,593.2	62.3%	BMU	Includes all stock
2	Purchase Receipts		$938.4	71.0%	IMU	IMU is the initial mark-up on new merchandise
3	Freight					Usually calculated as a percentage of cost receipts, 1.9%
4	Stock Available				CMU	Total lines 1 thru 3, calculate cummulative markup (CMU)
	Subtract					
6	Sales		$1,512.3			Total sales for the period - month or season
7	Markdowns		$510.2			Total markdowns for the period - month or season
8	Shortage		$101.7			Total shortage dollars for the period - month or season
9	Employee Discount		$25.6			Total employee discount for the period - month or season
10	EOP				CMU	Subtract line 6 thru 9 from line 4, calculate CMU for EOP cost
11	Cost of Goods Sold					Subtract line 10 from line 4
12	Net Sales					Same as line 6
	Subtract					
13	Cost of Good Sold					Same as line 10 only entered on retail side
14	Workroom		$0.9			Calculated as a known dollar amount or percent of sales
	Add					
15	Cash Discount		$2.3			Discounts negotiated with vendors for early payment
16	Gross Margin $					Line 12 minus lines 13 and 13, add line 15
17	Gross Margin %					Line 16 / Line 12
	Subtract Expenses					
18	Net Advertising		$125.8			Net dollar amount spent on advertising after vendor co-op
19	Supply Chain					Calculated as 5% of cost purchase receipts

EXCEL SPREADSHEET 14-F.

CREATE IT IN EXCEL!

CALCULATE THE GROSS MARGIN PLAN FOR THE JEWELRY DEPARTMENT BASED ON THE FULL SEASON FOR PLAN THIS YEAR

Gather data from Excel Spreadsheet 11-J. Using Excel Spreadsheet 14-J, calculate gross margin.

Line 1

Enter the beginning of period (BOP) stock level at retail, using the beginning markup (BMU) percentage, then calculate the BOP at cost (see Figure 14.1).

BOP = $746.6 Retail
BMU = 58.3%
100% − 58.3% = 41.7%
$746.6 × 41.7% = $311.3 BOP at cost

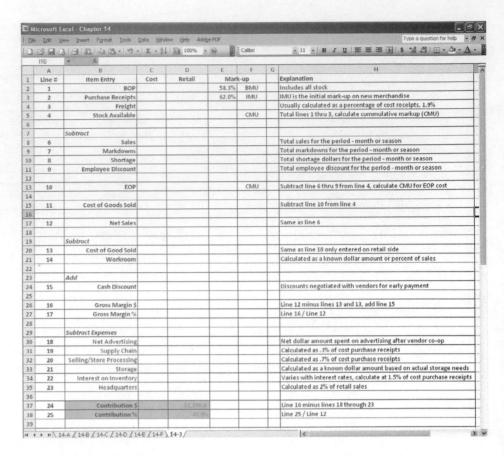

Excel Spreadsheet 14-J.

Line 2

Enter the purchase receipts for the full season at retail, using the initial markup (IMU) percentage, then calculate the purchase receipts at cost (see Figure 14.2).

Purchase receipts = $4792.2 retail
IMU = 62.0%
100% − 62.0% = 38.0%
$4792.2 × 38.0% = $2044.3 purchase receipts at cost

Line 3

Calculate freight charges by applying a percentage of 1% to cost receipts (see Figure 14.3).

$2044.3 × 1% = $20.4 freight entered as cost

Line 4

1. Calculate stock available by adding the Cost column of BOP, purchase receipts, and freight.

2. Calculate stock available by adding the Retail column of BOP, purchase receipts, and freight.

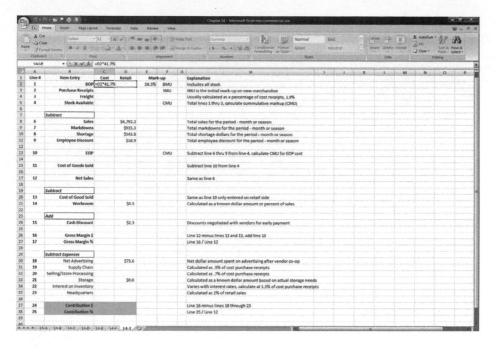

FIGURE 14.1 Calculating BOP.

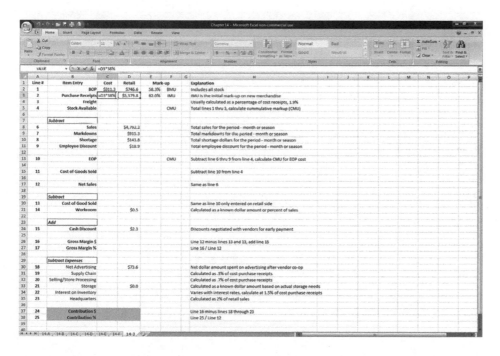

FIGURE 14.2 Calculate Receipts.

3.   Calculate cumulative markup (CMU).

$6126.4 – $2376.1 ÷ 6126.4 = 61.2% (see Figure 14.4).

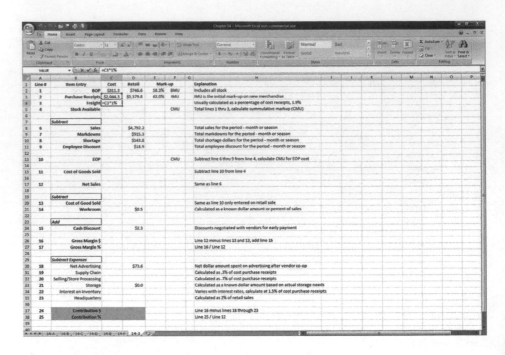

FIGURE 14.3 Calculate Freight Based on Percentage of Receipts.

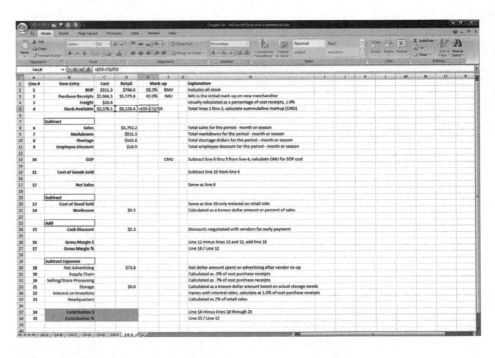

FIGURE 14.4 Calculate Stock Available.

Lines 6 through 9

At retail only, enter total season.

Sales: $4792.2

A BUYER'S LIFE

Markdowns: $915.3

Shortage: $143.8

Employee discount: $18.9

Line 10

1. Determine end of period (EOP), beginning with retail stock available ($6126.4). Subtract sales, markdowns, shortage, and employee discount.

   $6126.4 – $4792.2 – $915.3 – $143.8 – $18.9 = $256.2

2. Calculate EOP at cost by applying 61.2% CMU to $256.2.

   EOP = $256.2 retail

   CMU = 61.2%

   100% – 61.2% = 38.8%

   $256.2 × 38.8% = $99.4 EOP at cost (See Figure 14.5.)

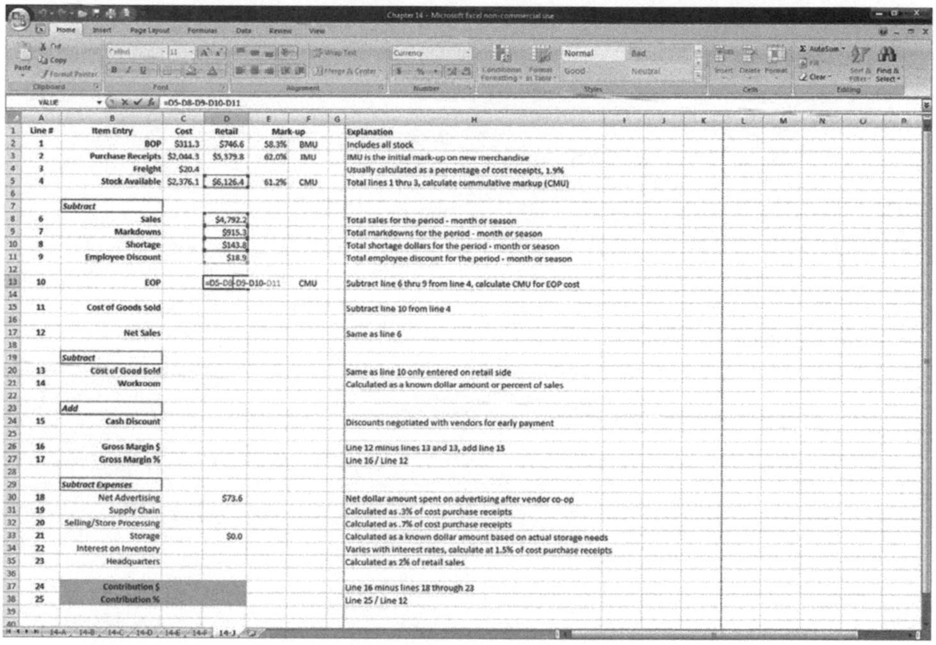

Line #	Item Entry	Cost	Retail	Mark-up		Explanation
1	BOP	$311.3	$746.6	58.3%	BMU	Includes all stock
2	Purchase Receipts	$2,044.3	$5,379.8	62.0%	IMU	IMU is the initial mark-up on new merchandise
3	Freight	$20.4				Usually calculated as a percentage of cost receipts, 1.9%
4	Stock Available	$2,376.1	$6,126.4	61.2%	CMU	Total lines 1 thru 3, calculate cummulative markup (CMU)
	Subtract					
6	Sales		$4,792.2			Total sales for the period - month or season
7	Markdowns		$915.3			Total markdowns for the period - month or season
8	Shortage		$143.8			Total shortage dollars for the period - month or season
9	Employee Discount		$18.9			Total employee discount for the period - month or season
10	EOP		=D5-D8-D9-D10-D11		CMU	Subtract line 6 thru 9 from line 4, calculate CMU for EOP cost
11	Cost of Goods Sold					Subtract line 10 from line 4
12	Net Sales					Same as line 6
	Subtract					
13	Cost of Good Sold					Same as line 10 only entered on retail side
14	Workroom					Calculated as a known dollar amount or percent of sales
	Add					
15	Cash Discount					Discounts negotiated with vendors for early payment
16	Gross Margin $					Line 12 minus lines 13 and 13, add line 15
17	Gross Margin %					Line 16 / Line 12
	Subtract Expenses					
18	Net Advertising		$73.6			Net dollar amount spent on advertising after vendor co-op
19	Supply Chain					Calculated as .3% of cost purchase receipts
20	Selling/Store Processing					Calculated as .7% of cost purchase receipts
21	Storage		$0.0			Calculated as a known dollar amount based on actual storage needs
22	Interest on Inventory					Varies with interest rates, calculate at 1.5% of cost purchase receipts
23	Headquarters					Calculated as 2% of retail sales
24	Contribution $					Line 16 minus lines 18 through 23
25	Contribution %					Line 25 / Line 12

FIGURE 14.5 Calculate EOP.

Line 11

Determine cost of goods sold by subtracting EOP at cost from stock available at cost (see Figure 14.6).

$2376.1 – $99.4 = $2276.7 cost of goods sold

Line 12

Enter net sales from total sales: $4792.2

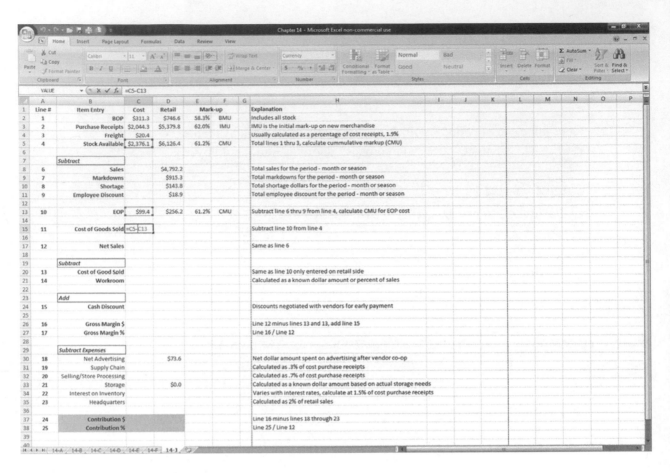

FIGURE 14.6 Calculate Cost of Goods Sold (COGS).

Line 13

In the Retail column, enter cost of goods sold: $2,276.7

Line 14

In the Retail column, enter workroom expenses: $0.5

Line 15

In the Retail column, enter cash discount: $2.3

Line 16

Determine gross margin $ (GM$), beginning with sales and subtracting cost of goods sold and workroom and then adding cash discount (see Figure 14.7).

$4792.2 – $2276.7 – $.5 + $2.3 = $2517.3 gross margin $

Line 17

Calculate gross margin % by dividing GM$ into sales (see Figure 14.8).

$2517.3 ÷ $4792.2 = 52.5% gross margin %

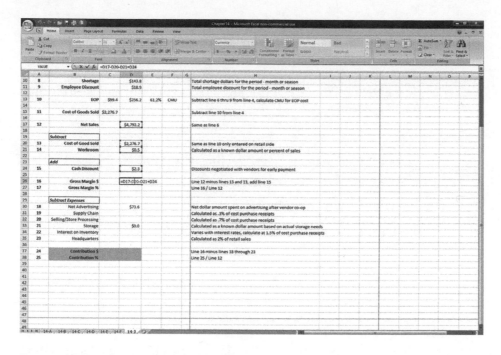

FIGURE 14.7 Calculate Gross Margin Dollars.

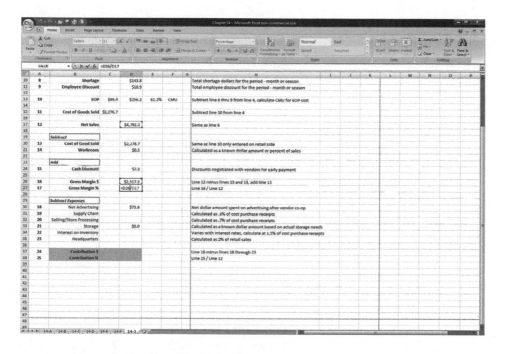

FIGURE 14.8 Calculate Gross Margin Percentage.

CALCULATE THE CONTRIBUTION PLAN FOR JEWELRY DEPARTMENT

Continuing from Excel Spreadsheet 14-J, subtract expenses from gross margin and calculate contribution.

Line 18

In the Retail column, enter net advertising expenses: $73.6.

Line 19

In the Retail column, enter supply chain as 0.3% of purchase receipts: $6.1 (see Figure 14.9).

Line 20

In the Retail column, enter selling/store processing as 0.7% of purchase receipts: $14.3 (see Figure 14.10).

Line 21

In the Retail column, enter storage as a flat dollar amount of zero.

Line 22

In the Retail column, enter interest on inventory as 1.5% of cost purchase receipts: $30.7 (see Figure 14.11).

Line 23

In the Retail column, enter headquarters as 2% of retail sales: $95.8 (see Figure 14.12).

Line 24

Determine contribution $, beginning with gross margin $ and subtracting net advertising, supply chain, selling/store processing, storage, interest on inventory, and headquarters (see Figure 14.13).

$2517.3 – $73.6 – $6.1 – $14.3 – $30.7– $95.8 = $2296.8 contribution $

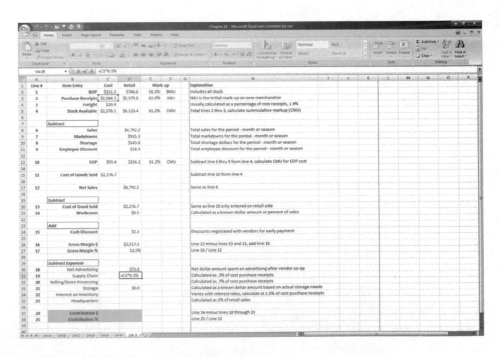

FIGURE 14.9 Calculate Contribution Expenses.

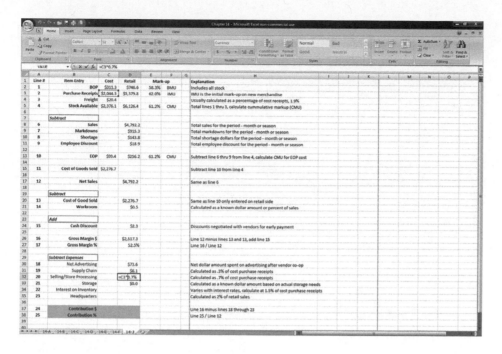

FIGURE 14.10 Contribution Expenses continued.

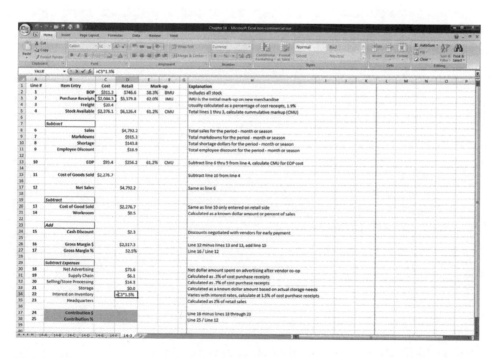

FIGURE 14.11 Contribution Expenses continued.

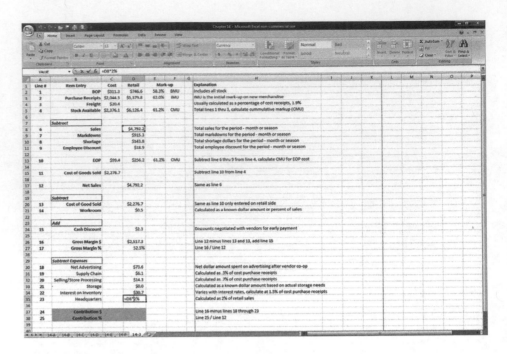

FIGURE 14.12 Contribution Expenses continued.

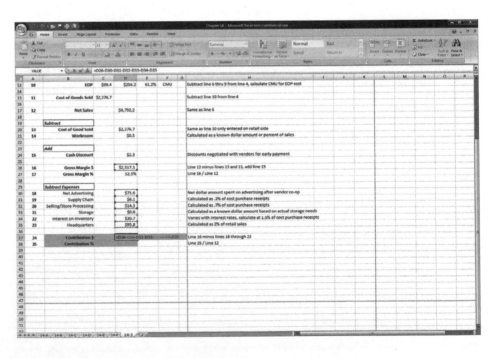

FIGURE 14.13 Calculate Contribution Dollars.

A BUYER'S LIFE

Line 25

Calculate contribution % by dividing contribution $ into sales (see Figure 14.14).

$2296.8 ÷ $4792.2 = 47.9% contribution %

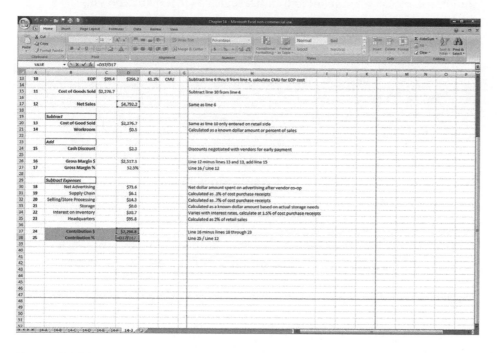

FIGURE **14.14** Calculate Contribution Percentage.

TERMINOLOGY

contribution: A calculation that takes *gross margin* one step further by applying expense charges to the business and thus determining a more accurate profit level.

contribution $: The actual dollar profit of the business *after* subtracting expenses.

contribution %: The actual percentage of profit of the business as a percent of sales *after* subtracting expenses.

gross margin: The profit remaining after costs of goods sold are subtracted from sales.

gross margin $: The actual dollar profit of the business before expenses.

gross margin %: The percentage of profit as a percent of sales before expenses.

FORMULAS

Beginning-of-period (BOP) inventory at cost when retail and beginning stock markup (BMU) are known:

Retail BOP $ × (100% – BMU%)

Example:

$$\$946.6 \times (100\% - 57.2\%)$$
$$\$946.6 \times 42.8\% = \$405.1$$

Purchases at cost when retail and initial markup (IMU) are known:

Retail Purchases $ × (100% – IMU%)

Example:

$$\$5479.8 \times (100\% - 61\%)$$
$$\$5479.8 \times 39\% = \$2137.1$$

Cumulative stock markup (CMU) %

CMU = (Stock Available at Retail − Stock Available at Cost) ÷ Stock Available at Retail

Example:

$$(\$6426.4 - \$2572.6) \div \$6426.4 = 60\%$$

$ stock available at cost

Cost BOP$ + Cost Purchase Receipt $ + Freight = Cost Stock Available $

e.g., $405.1 + $2137.1 + $30.4 = $2572.6

$ stock available at retail

Retail BOP$ + Retail Purchase Receipt $ = Retail Stock Available $

Example:

$946.6 + $5479.8 = $6426.4 Cost of goods sold

Cost of Goods Sold = Stock Available Cost $ – End-of-Period (EOP) Cost $

e.g., $2572.6 – $205.7 = $2366.9

End of period $ at cost

EOP Cost $ = Retail Stock Available $ – Sales $ – Markdown $ – Shortage $ – Employee Discount $ × (100% – CMU%)

Example:

$$(\$6426.4 - \$4994.2 - \$715.3 - \$173.8 - \$28.9) \times (100 - 40.0\%)$$
$$= \$205.7$$

End of period $ at retail

> Retail Stock Available – Sales – Markdowns – Shortage – Employee Discount = EOP Retail Stock Available

> *Example:*

> $6426.4 – $4994.2 – $715.3 – $173.8 – $28.9 = $514.2

Gross margin $

> Gross Margin $ = Net Sales $ – Cost of Goods Sold $ – Workroom $ + Cash Discount $

> *Example:*

> $4994.2 – $2366.9 – $5.0 + $4.2 = $2626.5

Gross margin %

> Gross Margin % = Gross Margin $ ÷ Net Sales $

> *Example:*

> $2626.5 ÷ $4994.2 = 52.6%

Contribution $

> Contribution $ = Gross Margin $ – Net Advertising $ – Supply Chain $ – Selling/Store Processing $ – Storage $ – Interest on Inventory $ – Headquarters Expense $

> *Example:*

> $2626.5 – $152.0 – $5.3 – $12.2 – $36.9 – $109.0 = $2311.1

Contribution %

> Contribution % = Contribution $ ÷ Net Sales $

> *Example:*

> $2311.1 ÷ $4994.2 = 46.3%

GLOSSARY

Aging inventory: A product that is usually three months or older and is no longer viable.

Allocator: This entry-level planning position is also referred to as an analyst. Allocators or analysts are responsible for allocating orders to stores.

Assistant buyer or clerical: This entry-level merchandising position reports to the buyer and functions as support. This position often entails task-oriented duties of order distribution, order tracking, and vendor follow-up. There is limited decision making in this position.

Associate buyer: The associate buyer reports to the buyer, often has a limited buying responsibility, and is involved in most decision making and negotiations.

Associate planner: The associate planner reports to the planner or DPM within the planning organization. This position provides analysis and forecasting to the planner and buyer.

Assortment planning: A process that helps a buyer bridge the gap between the financial classification plan and how the retail store will visually appeal to customers in a way that will ultimately encourage them to buy.

Average inventory and/or **average stock:** The average amount of inventory dollars or units spread over a specified period of time (usually six months).

Back-stock inventory: Any product that is physically in the store yet located in a stockroom or other area that is not accessible to the customer.

Basic replenishment: A form of reorder; dependable products with a predictable sales pattern, profit margin, and turnover.

Booked: The result of an accounting process that charges any dollar amount to the financial budget. *Booked* could refer to sales, inventory, markdowns, or any other business phase that affects the financial budget.

Bottom up: A planning process that operates in the opposite direction of the top-down approach whereby the plan begins with the buyer and works up to the CEO.

Buyer: The buyer reports to the DMM and has responsibility for a specific area within the DMM area. One buyer may be responsible for special-occasion dresses, while another is responsible for career dresses. The buyer has specific bottom-line financial responsibility to the organization, which can account for as much as 80 percent of his or her annual review.

Classifications: Related groups of products that can be viewed in smaller units within a total business.

Competitive price matching: The reduction of price, usually through a point-of-sale markdown, to meet a competitor price.

Contribution: A calculation that takes *gross margin* one step further by applying specific expense charges to the business and thus determining a more accurate profit level.

Contribution $: The actual dollar profit of the business *after* subtracting specific expenses.

Contribution %: The actual percentage of profit of the business as a percent of sales *after* subtracting specific expenses.

Crossover career: A corporate career path in which individuals move horizontally within an organization, attaining a mix of skills along the way. Crossover career paths cross an individual between stores, merchandising, and/or planning.

Cumulative markup (CMU): Markup of the product throughout its life span. Calculates the overall markup from the IMU through all phases of markdowns.

Customer preference: What customers want, when they want it, and at what price they want it.

Damaged and defective: The reduction of inventory dollars based on product that can no longer be sold and is either physically given away to charity or destroyed.

Damaged and defective inventory: Product that is physically and financially owned by the retailer but is unsalable.

Decline phase: The phase during which products may still be widely available, but inventory is no longer being replenished and products are consistently on sale.

Demographic: Statistical information about the customer. Demographic information is often obtained through government census or market survey.

Divisional merchandise manager (DMM): Reporting to the GMM and having responsibility for a range of products within a broad area. For example, a DMM in women's might have responsibility for dresses. The DMM has significant financial responsibility.

Divisional planning manager (DPM): Reporting to the GPM and having planning responsibility for a range of product. The DPM is typically aligned with one or more **DMMs**. The DPM has significant financial responsibility.

Economic factors: Issues of the overall economy such as unemployment and inflation that affect a consumer's confidence related to purchases they make.

Electronic data interchange (EDI): A virtual, paperless exchange of information between vendor and retailer.

Electronic inventory: Inventory that has left the vendor but is still in transit to the retail store. This inventory may be with the freight carrier, in a distribution center, or simply on a truck waiting to be unloaded at the store.

Employee discount: A reduction in price taken for employee purchases.

Floor inventory: Any product physically on the selling floor and accessible to customers.

4-5-4 or 4-4-5: Refers to the fiscal calendar. The year is broken down into complete weeks, Sunday through Saturday. The numbers refer to the number of weeks in the given month. (See the fiscal calendar in Appendix XX.)

Front loading: Delivering most of the inventory at the start of a season or month.

General merchandise manager (GMM): Oversees a broad-range merchandise category, such as men's, women's, or home. The GMM is typically a vice president, reports to the president or CEO, and has a high level of financial responsibility.

General planning manager (GPM): A planning director who oversees the planning for broad-range merchandise categories. The GPM is typically a vice president, reports to the president or CEO, and has a high level of financial responsibility.

Gross margin: The profit remaining after costs of goods sold are subtracted from sales.

Gross margin $: The actual dollar profit of the business before expenses.

Gross margin %: The percentage of profit as a percent of sales before expenses.

High inventory turnover: Inventory that moves in and out of inventory quickly. This category typically includes high-fashion or highly perishable products with a limited shelf life.

Historical sales: Analysis of past sales results, which may include specified time periods, past product performance, or past vendor performance. It could also include current sales trends as they relate to historical sales performance.

Holiday/event shift: The shift in business when a holiday or major storewide event moves from one fiscal month into another.

Incoming phase: The phase during which products are still relatively new but gaining popularity. Such products are sold at full retail price.

Initial markup (IMU): Markup placed on the product when it arrives in the store.

Inventory: Any physical product or invisible product expressed as a dollar amount and booked into the financial budget.

Inventory on hold: Items that are on hold for customers but have not yet been paid for by the customer.

Inventory turnover: The number of times, within a specified period (usually a six-month season) per season, that inventory is bought, sold, and replaced.

Invisible inventory: Inventory that is not physically present or visible but has been booked into the budget. Examples include electronic inventory, shortage inventory, repair inventory, and transfer inventory.

Keystone: The process of doubling the cost price.

Keystone plus: Pricing strategy of doubling the cost price plus an additional percentage or dollar amount, usually between $1 and $10. This accounts for variability in new inventory and sales fluctuation.

Life stage: Considers factors related to family size and life cycle. Life stage can vary by geographic region and has a significant impact on disposable income.

Low inventory turnover: Inventory that has an unlimited or long shelf life. These products do not change rapidly, and their price remains constant.

Markdown: Any reduction of the original retail price.

Markdown cadence: The rate at which markdowns are implemented and the relationship to sell-through.

Markdown liabilities: The total of inventory categories not meeting sales expectations; in the broadest terms, all inventory is a liability.

Maximum capacity: The maximum amount of inventory units that can be housed within a fixture and within a physical floor space allocation without obstructing traffic patterns or overflowing product fixture limitations.

Medium inventory turnover: Inventory that has a limited shelf life, usually seasonal. These products do not change frequently and may be sold at full retail price for most of a season.

Merchandising organization: Refers to all levels of product decision making and vendor negotiation. Members of the merchandising organization have a significant financial obligation to earn profit for the company.

Minimum capacity: The minimum amount of inventory units that can be housed within a fixture and within a physical floor space allocation. Minimum capacity is the smallest amount of inventory possible without deterring sales.

New receipts: New product that previously has not been seen in inventory.

Off-price specials: Usually overstocks by the vendor, who in turn offers them to its best customers at a percentage off the regular wholesale price. Immediate sale opportunities may arise for the buyer to pass the savings along to the customer.

Outgoing phase: The final phase of the product life cycle, characterized by permanent markdowns at all levels with a goal to liquidate the inventory to zero.

Peak phase: The phase during which products are widely distributed and at many price points.

Percentage change (% change): Denotes the percentage change from one season (spring to spring) or month (May to May) to the next.

Percentage total (% total): The percentage total that one month represents to the total season.

Permanent markdown: Markdowns that are permanently reduced and will incur further reductions until the product is gone.

PEST analysis: Identification of external environmental factors including political, environmental, social, and technological influences.

Planner: The planner reports to the DPM and has a close working relationship with the buyer. With the buyer, the planner forecasts and plans the business on an ongoing basis.

Planning organization: Refers to the financial planning that affects the merchandising organization.

Point-of-sale markdown (POS markdown): Temporary reductions in price, taken at the cash register during checkout, that will return to regular full price after a specified number of days.

Poor planning/timing: May be related to delayed shipment, goods being ordered too late, or goods being ordered too early; one cause of markdowns.

Post-peak phase: The phase during which products have higher volume and wide distribution but are often seen on sale.

Pre-peak phase: The phase during which product is carried in all locations, and may also be seen from a variety of manufacturers or price points, but is generally still sold at full retail price.

Product decision making: All-encompassing decision making to buy or not buy product(s) based on overall analysis of demographics, psychographics, life stage, and historical sales.

Product life cycle analysis: The process of mapping products or categories into the life-cycle spectrum. The analysis includes testing, incoming, pre-peak, peak, post-peak, decline, and outgoing phases. Also known as *trend curve analysis*.

Product market analysis: A process used to pinpoint specific issues within the product category.

Promotional and/or advertised: Any product that will be used for a sale or point-of-purchase event.

Promotional markdown: A price reduction processed as a POS markdown but categorized as a consistent markdown by year, month, or season.

Psychographic: Involves the assumptions about a customer based on demographic information. Assumptions about a customer's personality, social class, and lifestyle are examples of psychographic assumptions.

Purchase receipts: The amount of inventory needed each month in order to maintain BOM stock levels.

Reorders: Money available to reorder best sellers.

Regional trends or events: Specific events such as weather, or the politics within a city or region, that affect product and price.

Repair inventory: Inventory that is booked and owned but may be out of the store for repair.

Reserve: Purchase money not spent; it acts as a small cushion to prevent inventory from rising further or for use in capitalizing on new product entries.

Sales: An amount reflecting the retail price that consumers pay for the merchandise they receive.

Sales total: The total sales for a period of time. For the purposes of this text it is usually all six months of a season.

Seasonality: Factor describing the trend that some products that have a limited season for selling, particularly products intended for use in cold or hot weather.

Sell-through: Amount of product or inventory sold, expressed as a percentage sold through from the original amount received.

Shelf life: The amount of time a product can remain in inventory or on the shelf until it can no longer be sold at full value.

Shortage: The manually calculated reduction of inventory dollars based on anticipated theft or paperwork errors. Upon completion of a physical inventory, usually once per year, shortage dollars are permanently removed from stock dollars.

Shortage inventory: A shortage that is determined from theft or paperwork error but remains booked to inventory even if the inventory does not exist. Shortage inventory is projected on a regular basis and is updated for accuracy following a physical inventory count.

Silo career: A corporate career path that places individuals in one specific silo or area of expertise. Individuals move vertically through careers in one specified area of merchandising, planning, or stores.

Six-month plan: Refers to the process and variables of business planning for a period of time, usually January through June or July through December.

Slow seller: A product that is not meeting sell-through expectations. This product is typically in the inventory for up to 3 months without significant sell-through.

Special orders: Orders placed particularly for the customer, usually with written consent to order the items and agreement to pay fully upon arrival.

Stock-outs: Inventory that sells too quickly and is unavailable.

Stock-to-sales (STS) method of inventory: The calculation of inventory levels planned as a ratio to planned sales.

Stores organization: Refers to the physical store where merchandise is sold to the customer.

Style out: An assortment planning method in which buyers review product samples and decide which ones to purchase.

SWOT analysis: Identification of the business's internal strengths and weaknesses as well as the external opportunities and threats.

Test inventory: Small amounts of inventory that are new and unknown. This inventory is typically noticed by early adopters and often translates into reorders.

Testing phase: The phase during which a generally small amount of inventory is strategically placed in test locations and sold at full retail price.

Top down: A planning process that begins with the chief executive officer (CEO) or board of directors.

Transfer inventory: Inventory that is transferred between store locations. The sending store is booked for the inventory until it is fully received by the receiving store. Transfer of dollar ownership in the accounting process occurs either at the sender or receiver but may be physically invisible while in transit. Store policy varies as to when the dollar transfer of ownership occurs yet the overall retail store owns the inventory.

Trend: A tendency displayed in the areas of fashion, lifestyle, or statistics.

Trend analysis: An assortment planning method in which buyers analyze trend curves in determining which products to purchase.

Trend curve or product life-cycle analysis: The process of mapping products or categories into the life-cycle spectrum. The analysis includes testing, incoming, pre-peak, peak, post-peak, decline, and outgoing stages.

Trend cycles: The product life-cycle stage based on customer preferences.

Universal Product Code (UPC): Bar code identification system that allows product data to be scanned rather than entered manually.

Vendor negotiation: Working with vendors and suppliers either preseason, midseason, or postseason to strategize financial partnerships that may include assisting with the costs of marking down inventory.

Visible inventory: Any inventory that can be seen or touched within the retail store.

Warehouse inventory: Typically, household or hard-line products that are stored at a secondary location but are readily available to ship direct to customers.

Weeks-of-supply (WOS) method of inventory: The calculation of monthly inventory needs based on planned sales for a specified number of weeks. This method more accurately accounts for variability in new inventory and sales fluctuations.

APPENDIX A

FORMULAS

Formula Component	Numerical Sample
Total Sales $ =	
Sales Change % =	
This Year $ Sales Plan =	
Month Sales % Total =	
Month $ Sales =	
Total Markdown $ =	
Monthly Markdown % Total =	
Season Markdown % Total =	
Average Stock = (when BOM's are not known)	
Average Stock = (when BOM's are known)	
Turnover =	
Average Monthly Sales =	

(Formula Components continued on following page)

Formula Component	Numerical Sample
STS Ratio =	
Average Monthly Sales =	
Average Stock =	
Monthly Average Sales =	
Weeks of Supply =	
Purchases =	
IMU =	
CMU =	
BMU =	
BOP $ at Cost =	
Cost $ =	
$ Stock Available at Cost =	
$ Stock Available at Retail =	
Cost of Goods Sold =	
End of Period $ at Cost =	
End of Period $ at Retail =	
Gross Margin $ =	
Gross Margin % =	
Contribution $ =	
Contribution % =	

APPENDIX B

EXCEL SPREADSHEETS

	A	B	C	D	E	F	G	H	I
1	**Actual - Last Year**								
2	**Plan**	**Feb**	**Mar**	**April**	**May**	**June**	**July**	**Total**	Actual Markdown
3	Beg.Month Stock								
4	Sales	$15.0	$22.0	$40.0	$75.0	$95.0	$85.0	$332.0	Sales Change % +3.3%
5	Sales % Total								
6	Markdowns								Average Stock
7	Markdown % Total								
8	Purchases								PLN ACT
9	End Month Stock								Turnover
10									PLN ACT
11	Future Sales	Aug	Sept	Oct					WOS/STS/FM
12									PLN ACT
13									
14									
15									
16	**Plan - This Year**								
17	**Plan**	**Feb**	**Mar**	**April**	**May**	**June**	**July**	**Total**	Actual Markdown
18	Beg.Month Stock								$
19	Sales								Sales Change % +12.3
20	Sales % Total								
21	Markdowns								Average Stock
22	Markdown % Total								
23	Purchases								PLN ACT
24	End Month Stock								Turnover
25	Future Sales	Aug	Sept	Oct					PLN ACT
26									WOS/STS/FM
27									Mark-Up
28									
29									
30									

Sheet tabs: 3-A / 3-B / 3-C / 3-D / 3-E / 3-F / 3-G / 3-J

EXCEL SPREADSHEET 3-A.

Actual – Last Year

Plan	Feb	Mar	April	May	June	July	Total	Actual Markdown
Beg.Month Stock								
Sales							$969.5	Sales Change % +3.3%
Sales % Total	18.4%	18.9%	18.7%	21.2%	12.5%	10.3%		
Markdowns								Average Stock
Markdown % Total								
Purchases								PLN ACT
End Month Stock								Turnover
								PLN ACT
Future Sales	Aug	Sept	Oct					WOS/STS/FM
								PLN ACT

Plan – This Year

Plan	Feb	Mar	April	May	June	July	Total	Actual Markdown
Beg.Month Stock								$
Sales								Sales Change % +5.7%
Sales % Total								
Markdowns								Average Stock
Markdown % Total								
Purchases								PLN ACT
End Month Stock								Turnover
Future Sales	Aug	Sept	Oct					PLN ACT
								WOS/STS/FM
								Mark-Up

Excel Spreadsheet 3-B.

	A	B	C	D	E	F	G	H	I
1	**Actual - Last Year**								
2	**Plan**	**Aug**	**Sept**	**Oct**	**Nov**	**Dec**	**Jan**	**Total**	Actual Markdown
3	Beg.Month Stock								
4	Sales	$19.2	$10.3	$15.8	$55.6	$121.2	$99.9		Sales Change % -8.9%
5	Sales % Total								
6	Markdowns								Average Stock
7	Markdown % Total								
8	Purchases								PLN ACT
9	End Month Stock								Turnover
10									PLN ACT
11	Future Sales	Feb	Mar	Apr					WOS/STS/FM
12									PLN ACT
13									
14									
15									
16	**Plan - This Year**								
17	**Plan**	**Aug**	**Sept**	**Oct**	**Nov**	**Dec**	**Jan**	**Total**	Actual Markdown
18	Beg.Month Stock								$
19	Sales								Sales Change % -7.2%
20	Sales % Total								
21	Markdowns								Average Stock
22	Markdown % Total								
23	Purchases								PLN ACT
24	End Month Stock								Turnover
25	Future Sales	Feb	Mar	Apr					PLN ACT
26									WOS/STS/FM
27									
28									Mark-Up
29									
30									

EXCEL SPREADSHEET 3-C.

Home | Insert | Page Layout | Formulas | Data | Review | View | Add-Ins

M32

	A	B	C	D	E	F	G	H	I
1	Actual - Last Year								
2	Plan	Aug	Sept	Oct	Nov	Dec	Jan	Total	Actual Markdown
3	Beg.Month Stock								
4	Sales	$27.5	$38.2	$41.1	$73.6	$255.5	$20.9		Sales Change % +8.8%
5	Sales % Total								
6	Markdowns								Average Stock
7	Markdown % Total								
8	Purchases								PLN ACT
9	End Month Stock								Turnover
10									PLN ACT
11	Future Sales	Feb	Mar	Apr					WOS/STS/FM
12									PLN ACT
13									
14									
15									
16	Plan - This Year								
17	Plan	Aug	Sept	Oct	Nov	Dec	Jan	Total	Actual Markdown
18	Beg.Month Stock								$
19	Sales								Sales Change % +4.2%
20	Sales % Total								
21	Markdowns								Average Stock
22	Markdown % Total								
23	Purchases								PLN ACT
24	End Month Stock								Turnover
25	Future Sales	Feb	Mar	Apr					PLN ACT
26									WOS/STS/FM
27									
28									Mark-Up
29									
30									

3-A / 3-B / 3-C / 3-D / 3-E / 3-F / 3-G / 3-I

EXCEL SPREADSHEET 3-D.

N39

	A	B	C	D	E	F	G	H	I
1	**Actual - Last Year**								
2	**Plan**	**Feb**	**Mar**	**April**	**May**	**June**	**July**	**Total**	Actual Markdown
3	Beg.Month Stock								
4	Sales	$110.9	$178.3	$150.9	$161.2	$95.3	$88.7		Sales Change % +18.3%
5	Sales % Total								
6	Markdowns								Average Stock
7	Markdown % Total								
8	Purchases								PLN ACT
9	End Month Stock								Turnover
10									PLN ACT
11	Future Sales	Aug	Sept	Oct					WOS/STS/FM
12									PLN ACT
13									
14									
15									
16	**Plan - This Year**								
17	**Plan**	**Feb**	**Mar**	**April**	**May**	**June**	**July**	**Total**	Actual Markdown
18	Beg.Month Stock								$
19	Sales								Sales Change % +14.9%
20	Sales % Total								
21	Markdowns								Average Stock
22	Markdown % Total								
23	Purchases								PLN ACT
24	End Month Stock								Turnover
25	Future Sales	Aug	Sept	Oct					PLN ACT
26									WOS/STS/FM
27									Mark-Up
28									
29									
30									

3-A / 3-B / 3-C / 3-D / 3-E / 3-F / 3-G / 3-J

EXCEL SPREADSHEET 3-E.

	A	B	C	D	E	F	G	H	I
1	**Actual - Last Year**								
2	**Plan**	**Feb**	**Mar**	**April**	**May**	**June**	**July**	**Total**	Actual Markdown
3	Beg.Month Stock								
4	Sales	$10.3	$11.7	$11.2	$15.9	$30.6	$18.2	$97.9	Sales Change % -15.4%
5	Sales % Total								
6	Markdowns								Average Stock
7	Markdown % Total								
8	Purchases								PLN ACT
9	End Month Stock								Turnover
10									PLN ACT WOS/STS/FM
11	Future Sales	Aug	Sept	Oct					PLN ACT
12									
13									
14									
15									
16	**Plan - This Year**								
17	**Plan**	**Feb**	**Mar**	**April**	**May**	**June**	**July**	**Total**	Actual Markdown
18	Beg.Month Stock								$
19	Sales								Sales Change % -12.9%
20	Sales % Total								
21	Markdowns								Average Stock
22	Markdown % Total								
23	Purchases								PLN ACT
24	End Month Stock								Turnover
25	Future Sales	Aug	Sept	Oct					PLN ACT
26									WOS/STS/FM
27									
28									Mark-Up
29									
30									

EXCEL SPREADSHEET 3-F.

	A	B	C	D	E	F	G	H	I
1	**Actual - Last Year**								
2	**Plan**	**Aug**	**Sept**	**Oct**	**Nov**	**Dec**	**Jan**	**Total**	Actual Markdown
3	Beg.Month Stock								
4								$2,490.4	Sales Change % -2.2%
5	Sales % Total	10.2%	12.3%	15.6%	17.1%	40.8%	4.0%		
6	Markdowns								Average Stock
7	Markdown % Total								
8	Purchases								PLN ACT
9	End Month Stock								Turnover
10									PLN ACT
11	Future Sales	Feb	Mar	April					WOS/STS/FM
12									PLN ACT
13									
14									
15									
16	**Plan - This Year**								
17	**Plan**	**Aug**	**Sept**	**Oct**	**Nov**	**Dec**	**Jan**	**Total**	Actual Markdown
18	Beg.Month Stock								$
19	Sales								Sales Change % -8.3%
20	Sales % Total								
21	Markdowns								Average Stock
22	Markdown % Total								
23	Purchases								PLN ACT
24	End Month Stock								Turnover
25	Future Sales	Feb	Mar	April					PLN ACT
26									WOS/STS/FM
27									PLN ACT
28									Mark-Up
29									
30									

EXCEL SPREADSHEET 3-G.

ACTUAL - Last Year

Plan	Aug	Sept	Oct	Nov	Dec	Jan	Total		
Beg.Month Stock								**Actual Markdown**	
Sales	$ 452.9	$ 551.7	$ 775.2	$ 880.9	$ 1,701.5	$ 401.4		$ 918.0	19.3%
Sales % Total								**Sales Change %**	
Markdowns									−2.2%
Markdown % Total								**Average Stock**	
Purchases								PLN	ACT
End Month Stock								**Turnover**	
								PLN	ACT
Future Sales	Feb	Mar	April					**WOS/STS**	
	$ 253.9	$ 310.6	$ 298.7					PLN	ACT
								Avg. Month Sales	

Plan - This Year

Plan	Aug	Sept	Oct	Nov	Dec	Jan	Total		
Beg.Month Stock								**Actual Markdown**	
Sales									19.1%
Sales % Total								**Sales Change %**	
Markdowns									0.6%
Markdown % Total								**Average Stock**	
Purchases								PLN	ACT
End Month Stock								**Turnover**	
Future Sales	Feb	Mar	April					PLN	ACT
								WOS/STS	
								PLN	ACT
								Avg. Month Sales	
								Mark-Up	58.3%

EXCEL SPREADSHEET 3-J.

	A	B	C	D	E	F	G	H	I	J	K
1	Actual - Last Year										
2	Plan	Feb	Mar	April	May	June	July	Total	Actual Markdown		
3	Beg.Month Stock								$92.2		
4	Sales	$85.9	$96.2	$89.3	$110.4	$78.9	$72.1		Sales Change % +6.7%		
5	Sales % Total										
6	Markdowns	$8.3	$15.2	$9.6	$28.3	$18.4	$12.5		Average Stock		
7	Markdown % Total										
8	Purchases								PLN ACT		
9	End Month Stock								Turnover		
10									PLN ACT		
11	Future Sales	Aug	Sept	Oct					WOS/STS/FM		
12									PLN ACT		
13											
14											
15											
16	Plan - This Year										
17	Plan	Feb	Mar	April	May	June	July	Total	Actual Markdown		
18	Beg.Month Stock								$86.6		
19	Sales								Sales Change % +8.2		
20	Sales % Total										
21	Markdowns								Average Stock		
22	Markdown % Total										
23	Purchases								PLN ACT		
24	End Month Stock								Turnover		
25	Future Sales	Aug	Sept	Oct					PLN ACT		
26									WOS/STS/FM		
27											
28									Mark-Up		
29											
30											

EXCEL SPREADSHEET 4-A.

	A	B	C	D	E	F	G	H	I
1	**Actual - Last Year**								
2	**Plan**	**Feb**	**Mar**	**April**	**May**	**June**	**July**	**Total**	Actual Markdown
3	Beg.Month Stock								15.7%
4	Sales							$1,131.5	Sales Change % +3.3%
5	Sales % Total	16.4%	17.3%	16.7%	20.8%	15.5%	13.3%		
6	Markdowns								Average Stock
7	Markdown % Total	23.2%	20.5%	13.0%	21.1%	13.4%	8.8%		
8	Purchases								PLN ACT
9	End Month Stock								Turnover
10									PLN ACT
11	Future Sales	Aug	Sept	Oct					WOS/STS/FM
12									PLN ACT
13									
14									
15									
16	**Plan - This Year**								
17	**Plan**	**Feb**	**Mar**	**April**	**May**	**June**	**July**	**Total**	Actual Markdown
18	Beg.Month Stock								$160.0
19	Sales								Sales Change % -5.7%
20	Sales % Total								
21	Markdowns								Average Stock
22	Markdown % Total								
23	Purchases								PLN ACT
24	End Month Stock								Turnover
25	Future Sales	Aug	Sept	Oct					PLN ACT
26									WOS/STS/FM
27									PLN ACT
28									Mark-Up
29									
30									

EXCEL SPREADSHEET 4-B.

Actual - Last Year

Plan	Aug	Sept	Oct	Nov	Dec	Jan	Total	
Beg.Month Stock								Actual Markdown
								26.4%
Sales	$58.9	$75.7	$72.6	$105.4	$275.6	$60.9	$649.1	Sales Change % -8.9%
Sales % Total								
Markdowns	$18.8	$15.6	$12.6	$15.3	$78.6	$30.2		Average Stock
Markdown % Total								
Purchases								PLN ACT
End Month Stock								Turnover
								PLN ACT
Future Sales	Feb	Mar	Apr					WOS/STS/FM
								PLN ACT

Plan - This Year

Plan	Aug	Sept	Oct	Nov	Dec	Jan	Total	
Beg.Month Stock								Actual Markdown
								$201.6
Sales								Sales Change % +17.2%
Sales % Total								
Markdowns								Average Stock
Markdown % Total								
Purchases								PLN ACT
End Month Stock								Turnover
Future Sales	Feb	Mar	Apr					PLN ACT
								WOS/STS/FM
								Mark-Up

EXCEL SPREADSHEET 4-C.

	A	B	C	D	E	F	G	H	I	J	K
1	**Actual - Last Year**										
2	**Plan**	**Aug**	**Sept**	**Oct**	**Nov**	**Dec**	**Jan**	**Total**	Actual Markdown		
3	Beg.Month Stock								$164.5		
4	Sales	$27.5	$38.2	$41.1	$73.6	$255.5	$20.9	$456.8	Sales Change % +8.8%		
5	Sales % Total										
6	Markdowns								Average Stock		
7	Markdown % Total	10%	16%	13%	9%	35%	17%				
8	Purchases								PLN ACT		
9	End Month Stock								Turnover		
10									PLN ACT		
11	Future Sales	Feb	Mar	Apr					WOS/STS/FM		
12									PLN ACT		
13											
14											
15											
16	**Plan - This Year**										
17	**Plan**	**Aug**	**Sept**	**Oct**	**Nov**	**Dec**	**Jan**	**Total**	Actual Markdown		
18	Beg.Month Stock								$161.8		
19	Sales								Sales Change % +4.2%		
20	Sales % Total										
21	Markdowns								Average Stock		
22	Markdown % Total										
23	Purchases								PLN ACT		
24	End Month Stock								Turnover		
25	Future Sales	Feb	Mar	Apr					PLN ACT		
26									WOS/STS/FM		
27									Mark-Up		
28											
29											
30											

EXCEL SPREADSHEET 4-D.

	Aug	Sept	Oct	Nov	Dec	Jan	Total		
ACTUAL - Last Year									
Plan	**Aug**	**Sept**	**Oct**	**Nov**	**Dec**	**Jan**	**Total**	**Actual Markdown**	
Beg.Month Stock								$ 918.0	19.3%
Sales	$ 452.9	$ 551.7	$ 775.2	$ 880.9	$1,701.5	$ 401.4	$4,763.6	**Sales Change %**	
Sales % Total	9.5%	11.6%	16.3%	18.5%	35.7%	8.4%	100.0%	-2.2%	
Markdowns	$ 42.6	$ 48.7	$ 65.8	$ 85.9	$ 472.4	$ 202.6	$ 918.0	**Average Stock**	
Markdown % Total								PLN	ACT
Purchases									
End Month Stock								**Turnover**	
								PLN	ACT
Future Sales	*Feb*	*Mar*	*April*					**WOS/STS**	
	$ 253.9	$ 310.6	$ 298.7					PLN	ACT
								Avg. Month Sales	
Plan - This Year									
Plan	**Aug**	**Sept**	**Oct**	**Nov**	**Dec**	**Jan**	**Total**	**Actual Markdown**	
Beg.Month Stock									19.1%
Sales	$ 455.3	$ 555.9	$ 781.1	$ 886.6	$1,710.8	$ 402.5	$4,792.2	**Sales Change %**	
Sales % Total	9.5%	11.6%	16.3%	18.5%	35.7%	8.4%	100.0%	0.6%	
Markdowns								**Average Stock**	
Markdown % Total								PLN	ACT
Purchases									
End Month Stock								**Turnover**	
Future Sales	*Feb*	*Mar*	*April*					PLN	ACT
								WOS/STS	
								PLN	ACT
								Avg. Month Sales	
								Mark-Up	58.3%

EXCEL SPREADSHEET 4-J.

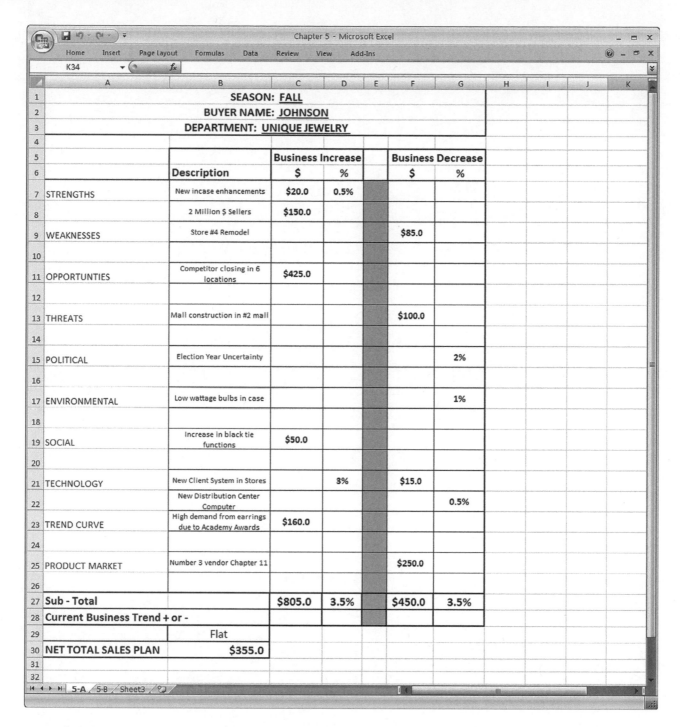

EXCEL SPREADSHEET 5-A.

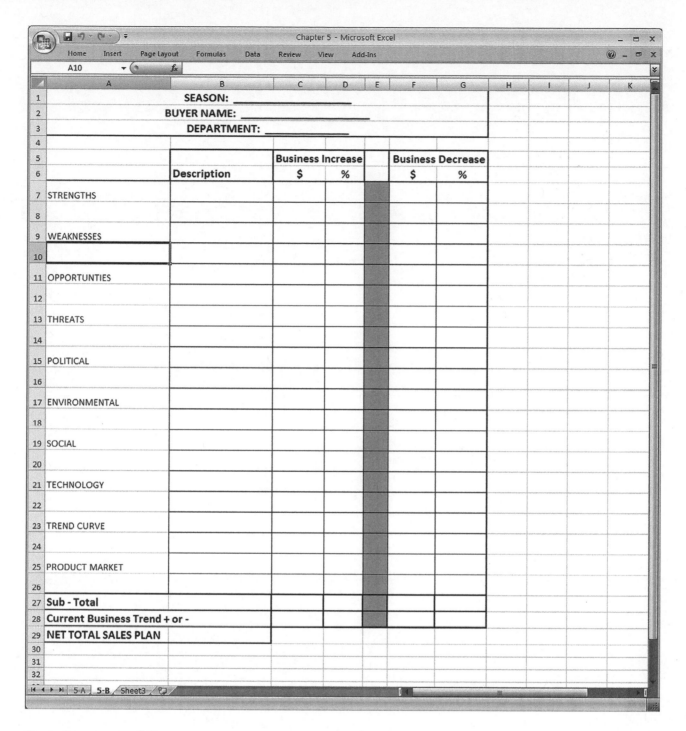

EXCEL SPREADSHEET 5-B.

Actual - Last Year

Plan	Feb	Mar	April	May	June	July	Total	Actual Markdown
Beg.Month Stock	325.4	330.9	335.7	398.6	297.4	278.3		
Sales	178.6	185.2	187.1	211.4	165.3	155.2		Sales Change % +5.3
Markdowns	18.2	25.6	22.1	72.3	40.1	15.7		Average Stock
Purchases								PLN ACT
End Month Stock						272.4		Turnover
								PLN ACT
Future Sales	Aug	Sept	Oct					WOS/STS/FM
								PLN ACT

Plan - This Year

Plan	Feb	Mar	April	May	June	July	Total	Actual Markdown
Beg.Month Stock							17.7%	$
Sales								Sales Change % (5.3)
Markdowns								Average Stock
Purchases								PLN ACT
End Month Stock								Turnover
Future Sales	Aug	Sept	Oct					PLN 3.25 ACT
								WOS/STS
								Mark-Up

EXCEL SPREADSHEET 6-A.

Actual - Last Year

Plan	Aug	Sept	Oct	Nov	Dec	Jan	Total	
Beg.Month Stock	28.7	41.3	48.6	95.4	275.2	88.6		Actual Markdown
Sales	12.6	22.4	25.7	40.9	165.6	25.3		Sales Change % +5.3
Markdowns	3.2	4.1	4.5	6.8	12.5	5.2		Average Stock
Purchases								PLN ACT
End Month Stock						52.1		Turnover
								PLN ACT
Future Sales	Aug	Sept	Oct					WOS/STS/FM
								PLN ACT

Plan - This Year

Plan	Aug	Sept	Oct	Nov	Dec	Jan	Total	
Beg.Month Stock								Actual Markdown
Sales								$ 17.7%
Markdowns								Sales Change % (5.3)
Purchases								Average Stock
End Month Stock								PLN $85.6 ACT
Future Sales	Aug	Sept	Oct					Turnover
								PLN 3.25 ACT
								WOS/STS
								Mark-Up

EXCEL SPREADSHEET 6-B.

	A	B	C	D	E	F	G	H	I
1	**Actual - Last Year**								
2	**Plan**	**Aug**	**Sept**	**Oct**	**Nov**	**Dec**	**Jan**	**Total**	Actual Markdown
3	Beg.Month Stock	110.7	110.1	106.6	115.2	139.4	122.5		
4	Sales	19.1	20.2	15.6	19.7	38.5	19.6		Sales Change % +3.5
5	Markdowns	5.6	4.1	4.4	2.8	8.6	6.3		Average Stock
6	Purchases								PLN ACT
7	End Month Stock						110.8		Turnover
8									PLN ACT
9	Future Sales	Aug	Sept	Oct					WOS/STS/FM
10									PLN ACT
11									
12									
13									
14	**Plan - This Year**								
15	**Plan**	**Aug**	**Sept**	**Oct**	**Nov**	**Dec**	**Jan**	**Total**	Actual Markdown
16	Beg.Month Stock								$ 17.7%
17	Sales								Sales Change % +5.5
18	Markdowns								Average Stock
19	Purchases								PLN ACT
20	End Month Stock								Turnover
21	Future Sales	Aug	Sept	Oct					PLN 1.2 ACT
22									WOS/STS
23									
24									Mark-Up
25									
26									
27									

6-A / 6-B / 6-C

Excel Spreadsheet 6-C.

Actual - Last Year

Plan	Aug	Sept	Oct	Nov	Dec	Jan	Total	Actual Markdown
Beg.Month Stock								
Sales	87.0	124.9	110.3	88.6	105.3	48.3	564.4	Sales Change %
Markdowns	10.2	15.3	12.9	11.5	31.8	17.2	98.9	Average Stock
Purchases								PLN ACT
End Month Stock								Turnover
								PLN 4.12 ACT
Future Sales	Feb	Mar	Apr					WOS/STS
	52.1	68.9	72.3					PLN ACT
								Avg. Monthly Sales

Plan - This Year

Plan							Total	Actual Markdown
Beg.Month Stock								$130.1
Sales								Sales Change +18.2%
Markdowns								Average Stock
Purchases								PLN ACT
End Month Stock								Turnover
Future Sales	Feb	Mar	Apr					PLN 3.98 ACT
								WOS/STS
								PLN ACT
								Avg. Monthly Sales
								Mark-Up

EXCEL SPREADSHEET 7-A.

Home · Insert · Page Layout · Formulas · Data · Review · View · Add-ins

L33

Actual - Last Year

Plan	Aug	Sept	Oct	Nov	Dec	Jan	Total	
Beg.Month Stock								Actual Markdown
Sales	12.6	22.4	25.7	40.9	125.6	25.3		Sales Change % +5.3
Markdowns	3.2	4.1	4.5	6.8	12.5	5.2		Average Stock
Purchases								PLN ACT
End Month Stock								Turnover
								PLN ACT
Future Sales	Feb	Mar	Apr					WOS/STS
	30.1	55.2	48.6					PLN ACT

Plan - This Year

Plan	Aug	Sept	Oct	Nov	Dec	Jan	Total	
Beg.Month Stock								Actual Markdown
Sales							17.7%	$
Markdowns								Sales Change % (5.3)
Purchases								Average Stock
End Month Stock								PLN $85.6 ACT
Future Sales	Feb	Mar	Apr					Turnover
								PLN 3.25 ACT
								WOS/STS
								Mark-Up

7-A 7-B 7-C 7-D 7-E

EXCEL SPREADSHEET 7-B.

Home | Insert | Page Layout | Formulas | Data | Review | View | Add-Ins

Actual - Last Year

Plan	Feb	Mar	Apr	May	June	July	Total	
Beg.Month Stock								Actual Markdown
Sales								Sales Change % (-2.2)
Markdowns								Average Stock
Purchases								PLN ACT
End Month Stock								Turnover
								PLN 3.44 ACT
Future Sales	Aug	Sept	Oct					WOS/STS/FM
								PLN ACT

Plan - This Year

Plan	Feb	Mar	Apr	May	June	July	Total	
Beg.Month Stock								Actual Markdown %
Sales	18.8	21.9	20.6	29.6	20.8	16.2		Sales Change % +1.3
Markdowns	1	3.2	3.5	8.2	2.2	1.5		Average Stock
Purchases								PLN ACT
End Month Stock								Turnover
Future Sales	Aug	Sept	Oct					PLN 3.56 ACT
	17.5	22.3	21.4					WOS/STS
								Mark-Up

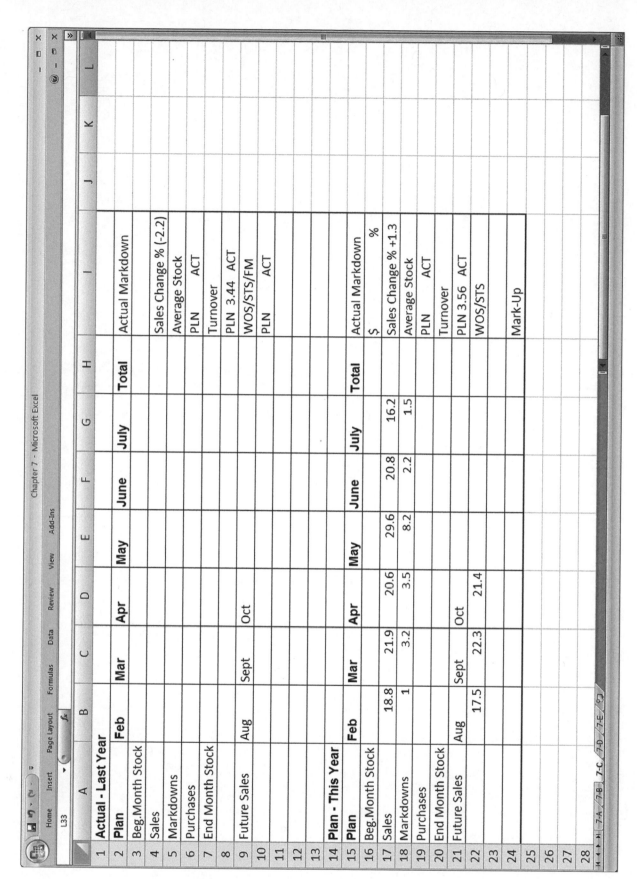

EXCEL SPREADSHEET 7-C.

Actual - Last Year

Plan	Feb	Mar	Apr	May	June	July	Total	
Beg.Month Stock								Actual Markdown
Sales	1100.0	2400.0	2200.0	2000.0	2400.0	1100.0	11200.0	Sales Change % +12.9
Markdowns	140.0	280.0	280.0	630.0	520.0	280.0	2130.0	Average Stock
Purchases								PLN ACT
End Month Stock								Turnover
								PLN 1.88 ACT
Future Sales	Aug	Sept	Oct					WOS/STS
	1050.0	1800.0	1550.0					PLN ACT

Plan - This Year

Plan	Feb	Mar	Apr	May	June	July	Total	
Beg.Month Stock								Actual Markdown
Sales								$
Markdowns								Sales Change % (-7.3)
Purchases								Average Stock
End Month Stock								PLN ACT
Future Sales	Aug	Sept	Oct					Turnover
								PLN 1.95 ACT
								WOS/STS
								Mark-Up

EXCEL SPREADSHEET 7-D.

Actual - Last Year

Plan	Feb	Mar	Apr	May	June	July	Total	Actual Markdown
Beg.Month Stock								
Sales								Sales Change % +.2
Markdowns	7.2	12.9	14.5	62.6	25.2	15.3		Average Stock
Purchases								PLN ACT
End Month Stock								Turnover
Future Sales	Aug	Sept	Oct					PLN 2.02 ACT
								WOS/STS/FM
								PLN ACT

Plan - This Year

Plan	Feb	Mar	Apr	May	June	July	Total	Actual Markdown
Beg.Month Stock								$
Sales	135.9	252.6	295.3	410.2	195.7	88.6		Sales Change % +.5
Markdowns								Average Stock
Purchases								PLN ACT
End Month Stock								Turnover
Future Sales	Aug	Sept	Oct					PLN 2.10 ACT
								WOS/STS
								Mark-Up

EXCEL SPREADSHEET 7-E.

ACTUAL - Last Year

Plan	Aug	Sept	Oct	Nov	Dec	Jan	Total		
Beg. Month Stock								**Actual Markdown**	
Sales	$ 452.9	$ 551.7	$ 775.2	$ 880.9	$ 1,701.5	$ 401.4	$ 4,763.6	$ 918.0	19.3%
Sales % Total	9.5%	11.6%	16.3%	18.5%	35.7%	8.4%	100.0%	**Sales Change %**	-2.2%
Markdowns	$ 42.6	$ 48.7	$ 65.8	$ 85.9	$ 472.4	$ 202.6	$ 918.0	**Average Stock**	
Markdown % Total	4.6%	5.3%	7.2%	9.4%	51.5%	22.1%	100%	PLN	ACT 100%
Purchases									
End Month Stock								**Turnover**	
								PLN	ACT
Future Sales	Feb	Mar	April					3.68	
	$ 253.9	$ 310.6	$ 298.7					**WOS/STS**	
								PLN	ACT
								Avg. Month Sales	

Plan - This Year

Plan	Aug	Sept	Oct	Nov	Dec	Jan	Total		
Beg. Month Stock								**Actual Markdown**	
Sales	$ 455.3	$ 555.9	$ 781.1	$ 886.6	$ 1,710.8	$ 402.5	$ 4,792.2	$ 915.3	19.1%
Sales % Total	9.5%	11.6%	16.3%	18.5%	35.7%	8.4%	100.0%	**Sales Change %**	0.6%
Markdowns	$. 42.5	$ 48.6	$ 65.6	$ 85.6	$ 471.0	$ 202.0	$ 915.3	**Average Stock**	
Markdown % Total	4.6%	5.3%	7.2%	9.4%	51.5%	22.1%	100%	PLN	ACT
Purchases									
End Month Stock								**Turnover**	
Future Sales	Feb	Mar	April					PLN	ACT
								3.65	
								WOS/STS	
								PLN	ACT
								Avg. Month Sales	
								Mark-Up	58.3%

EXCEL SPREADSHEET 7-J.

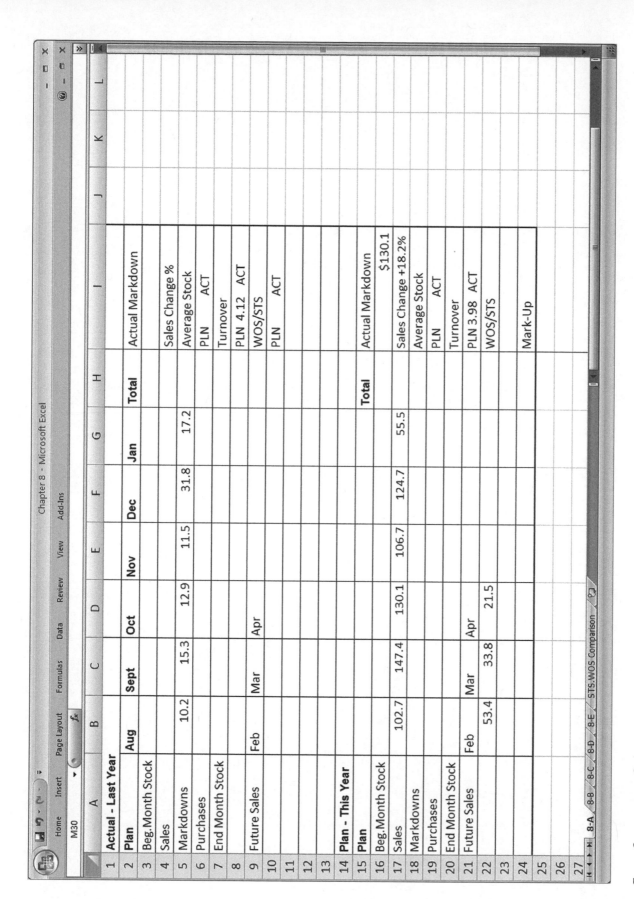

EXCEL SPREADSHEET 8-A.

Home　Insert　Page Layout　Formulas　Data　Review　View　Add-Ins

M30

	A	B	C	D	E	F	G	H	I
1	**Actual - Last Year**								
2	**Plan**	**Aug**	**Sept**	**Oct**	**Nov**	**Dec**	**Jan**	**Total**	Actual Markdown
3	Beg.Month Stock								
4	Sales								Sales Change % +22.3
5	Markdowns		8	10	9	15	12		Average Stock
6							10		PLN　　ACT
7	Purchases								Turnover
8	End Month Stock								PLN　　ACT 1.59
9	Future Sales	Feb	Mar	Apr					WOS/STS
10									PLN　　ACT
11									
12									
13									
14	**Plan - This Year**								
15	**Plan**	**Aug**	**Sept**	**Oct**	**Nov**	**Dec**	**Jan**	**Total**	Actual Markdown
16	Beg.Month Stock						55.3%		$
17	Sales	31.3	35.1	27.5	50.2	37.5	31.4		Sales Change % +25.2
18	Markdowns								Average Stock
19	Purchases								PLN　　ACT
20	End Month Stock								Turnover
21	Future Sales	Feb	Mar	Apr					PLN 2.52 ACT
22		35.1	40.1	43.8					WOS/STS
23									
24									Mark-Up
25									
26									
27									

8-A　**8-B**　8-C　8-D　8-E　STS.WOS Comparison

Excel Spreadsheet 8-B.

M30

Actual - Last Year

	A	B	C	D	E	F	G	H	I
2	Plan	Feb	Mar	Apr	May	June	July	Total	Actual Markdown
3	Beg.Month Stock								
4	Sales		150.6	80.3	120.5	90.4	70.8		Sales Change % +.04
5	Markdowns		10.1	8.2	20.6	9.5	6.8		Average Stock
6	Purchases								PLN ACT
7	End Month Stock								Turnover
8									PLN 3.12 ACT
9	Future Sales	Aug	Sept	Oct					WOS/STS/FM
10		75.9	83.7	81.6					PLN ACT
11									
12									
13									

Plan - This Year

	A	B	C	D	E	F	G	H	I
15	Plan	Feb	Mar	Apr	May	June	July	Total	Actual Markdown
16	Beg.Month Stock								$ 12.6%
17	Sales								Sales Change % +1.8
18	Markdowns								Average Stock
19	Purchases								PLN ACT
20	End Month Stock								Turnover
21	Future Sales	Aug	Sept	Oct					PLN 3.18 ACT
22									WOS/STS
23									
24									Mark-Up
25									
26									
27									

8-A 8-B 8-C 8-D 8-E STS:WOS Comparison

EXCEL SPREADSHEET 8-C.

Actual - Last Year

	Aug	Sept	Oct	Nov	Dec	Jan	Total	
Plan							Total	Actual Markdown
Beg.Month Stock								
Sales	1050.0	1760.0	1550.0	2000.0	1480.0	1220.0		Sales Change % +12.9
Markdowns	62.0	68.0	52.0	175.0	81.0	40.0		Average Stock
Purchases								PLN ACT
End Month Stock								Turnover
								PLN 1.88 ACT
Future Sales	Feb	Mar	Apr					WOS/STS
	1025.0	1430.0	1390.0					PLN ACT

Plan - This Year

	Aug	Sept	Oct	Nov	Dec	Jan	Total	
Plan							Total	Actual Markdown
Beg.Month Stock								$ 4.9%
Sales								Sales Change % (-4.3)
Markdowns								Average Stock
Purchases								PLN ACT
End Month Stock								Turnover
Future Sales	Feb	Mar	Apr					PLN 1.95 ACT
								WOS/STS
								Mark-Up

EXCEL SPREADSHEET 8-D.

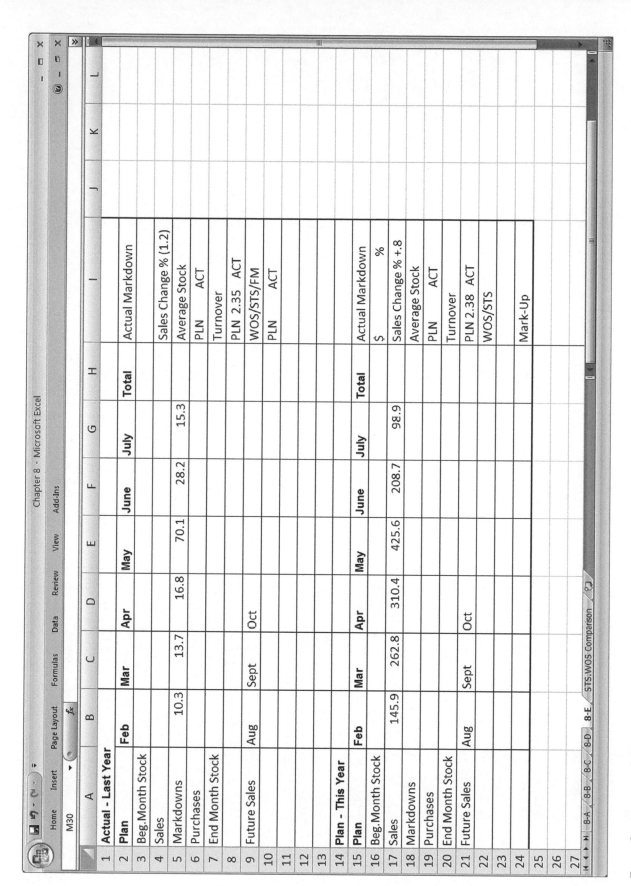

The spreadsheet shows:

M30 | fx

Chapter 8 - Microsoft Excel

Home | Insert | Page Layout | Formulas | Data | Review | View | Add-Ins

	A	B	C	D	E	F	G	H	I
1	**Actual - Last Year**								
2	**Plan**	**Feb**	**Mar**	**Apr**	**May**	**June**	**July**	**Total**	Actual Markdown
3	Beg.Month Stock								
4	Sales								Sales Change % (1.2)
5	Markdowns	10.3	13.7	16.8	70.1	28.2	15.3		Average Stock
6	Purchases								PLN ACT
7	End Month Stock								Turnover
8									PLN 2.35 ACT
9	Future Sales	Aug	Sept	Oct					WOS/STS/FM
10									PLN ACT
11									
12									
13									
14	**Plan - This Year**								
15	**Plan**	**Feb**	**Mar**	**Apr**	**May**	**June**	**July**	**Total**	Actual Markdown
16	Beg.Month Stock								$
17	Sales	145.9	262.8	310.4	425.6	208.7	98.9		Sales Change % +.8
18	Markdowns								Average Stock
19	Purchases								PLN ACT
20	End Month Stock								Turnover
21	Future Sales	Aug	Sept	Oct					PLN 2.38 ACT
22									WOS/STS
23									
24									Mark-Up
25									
26									
27									

8-A | 8-B | 8-C | 8-D | 8-E | STS.WOS Comparison

EXCEL SPREADSHEET 8-E.

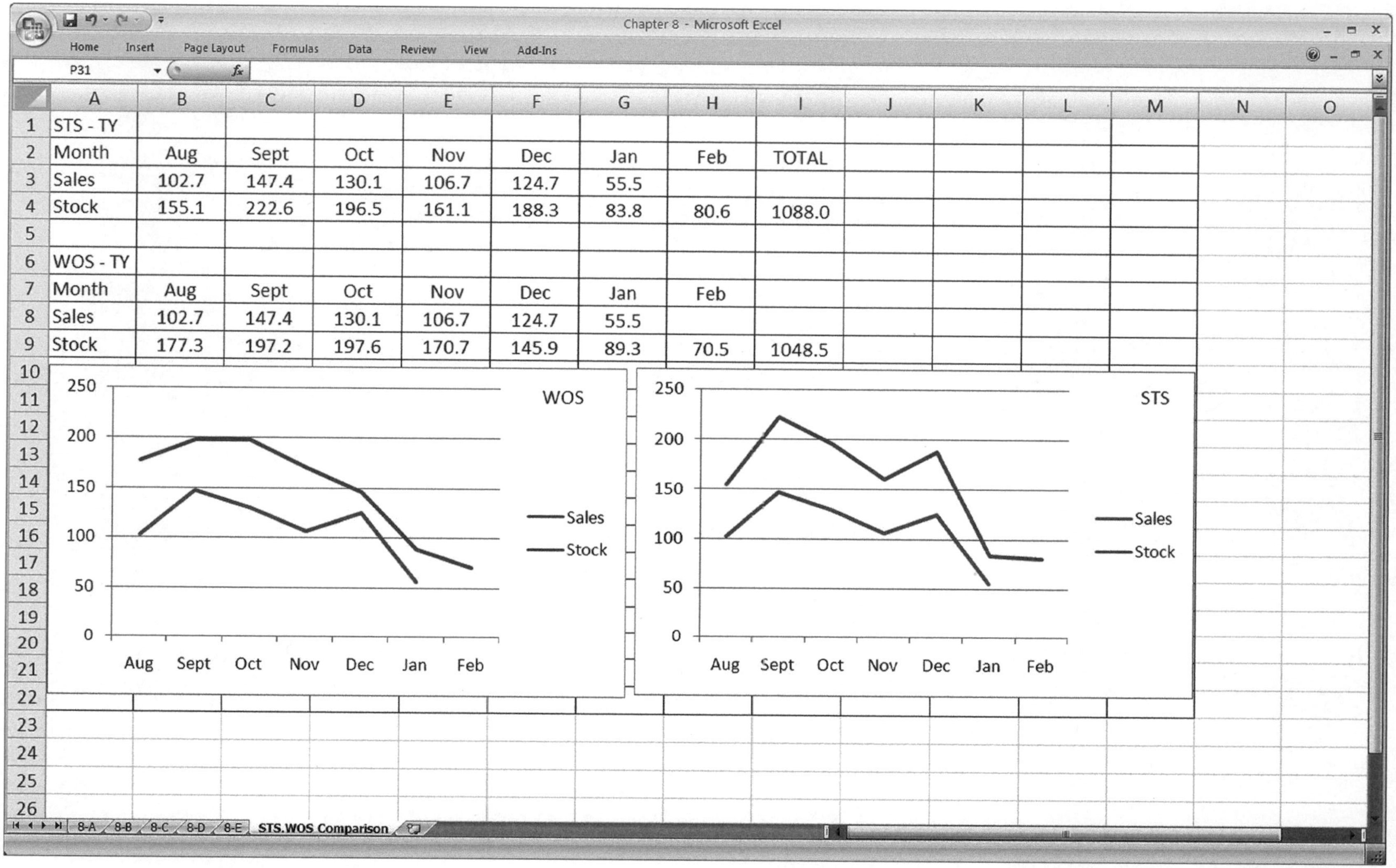

STS - TY								
Month	Aug	Sept	Oct	Nov	Dec	Jan	Feb	TOTAL
Sales	102.7	147.4	130.1	106.7	124.7	55.5		
Stock	155.1	222.6	196.5	161.1	188.3	83.8	80.6	1088.0
WOS - TY								
Month	Aug	Sept	Oct	Nov	Dec	Jan	Feb	
Sales	102.7	147.4	130.1	106.7	124.7	55.5		
Stock	177.3	197.2	197.6	170.7	145.9	89.3	70.5	1048.5

Excel Spreadsheet STS.WOS Comparison.

Unique Jewelry REVISED 6.09 [Compatibility Mode] - Microsoft Excel

ACTUAL - Last Year

Plan	Aug	Sept	Oct	Nov	Dec	Jan	Total	Actual Markdown	
	4	5	4	4	5	4		$ 918.0	19.3%
Beg.Month Stock									
Sales	$ 452.9	$ 551.7	$ 775.2	$ 880.9	$ 1,701.5	$ 401.4	$ 4,763.6	**Sales Change %**	
Sales % Total	9.5%	11.6%	16.3%	18.5%	35.7%	8.4%	100.0%	-2.2%	
Markdowns	$ 42.6	$ 48.7	$ 65.8	$ 85.9	$ 472.4	$ 202.6	$ 918.0	**Average Stock**	
Markdown % Total	4.6%	5.3%	7.2%	9.4%	51.5%	22.1%	100%	PLN	ACT
Purchases									
End Month Stock									100%
								Turnover	
Future Sales	Feb (4)	Mar (5)	April (4)					PLN	ACT
	$ 253.9	$ 310.6	$ 298.7					3.68	
								WOS/STS	
								PLN	ACT
								Avg. Month Sales	

Plan - This Year

Plan	Aug	Sept	Oct	Nov	Dec	Jan	Total	Actual Markdown	
	4	5	4	4	5	4		$ 915.3	19.1%
Beg.Month Stock									
Sales	$ 455.3	$ 555.9	$ 781.1	$ 886.6	$ 1,710.8	$ 402.5	$ 4,792.2	**Sales Change %**	
Sales % Total	9.5%	11.6%	16.3%	18.5%	35.7%	8.4%	100.0%	0.6%	
Markdowns	$ 42.5	$ 48.6	$ 65.6	$ 85.6	$ 471.0	$ 202.0	$ 915.3	**Average Stock**	
Markdown % Total	4.6%	5.3%	7.2%	9.4%	51.5%	22.1%	100%	PLN	ACT
Purchases									
End Month Stock									100%
								Turnover	
Future Sales	Feb (4)	Mar (5)	April (4)					PLN	ACT
								3.65	
								WOS/STS	
								PLN	ACT
								Avg. Month Sales	
								Mark-Up	58.3%

Sheet tabs: 3-J | 4-J | 7-J | 8-J | 9-J | 11-J1 | 11-J2 | 12-J | Sheet2

EXCEL SPREADSHEET 8-J.

Actual - Last Year

Plan	Aug	Sept	Oct	Nov	Dec	Jan	Total	
Beg.Month Stock	$77.5	$135.5	$238.8	$182.0	$520.4	$137.2	$1,291.4	Actual Markdown
Sales	$40.8	$71.3	$125.7	$95.8	$273.9	$72.2	$679.7	$200.9 29.6%
Sales % Total	6.0%	10.5%	18.5%	14.1%	40.3%	10.6%	100.0%	Sales Change N/A
Markdowns	$8.2	$12.3	$18.7	$15.9	$110.7	$35.1	$200.9	PLN $211.1 ACT $195.0 Average Stock
Markdown % Total	4.1%	6.1%	9.3%	7.9%	55.1%	17.5%	100.0%	Turnover
Purchases								PLN 3.22 ACT 3.48
End Month Stock	$135.5	$238.8	$182.0	$520.4	$137.2	$73.3	$1,287.2	WOS/**STS**
								PLN 1.9:1 ACT 1.7:1
Future Sales	Feb	Mar	Apr					Avg. Monthly Sales
	$38.6	$51.7	$58.4					$113.3

Plan - This Year

Plan	Aug	Sept	Oct	Nov	Dec	Jan	Total	
Beg.Month Stock	$75.7	$132.4	$233.3	$177.8	$508.5	$134.0	$1,261.7	Actual Markdown
Sales	$44.6	$77.9	$137.3	$104.6	$299.1	$78.8	$742.3	$179.6 24.2%
Sales % Total	6.0%	10.5%	18.5%	14.1%	40.3%	10.6%	100.0%	Sales Change +9.2%
Markdowns	$7.3	$11.0	$16.7	$14.2	$99.0	$31.4	$179.6	PLN $207.3 ACT $190.4 Average Stock
Markdown % Total	4.1%	6.1%	9.3%	7.9%	55.1%	17.5%	100.0%	Turnover
Purchases								PLN 3.58 ACT 3.90
End Month Stock	$132.4	$233.3	$177.8	$508.5	$134.0	$71.7	$1,257.7	WOS/**STS**
								PLN 1.7:1 ACT 1.5:1
Future Sales	Feb	Mar	Apr					Avg. Monthly Sales
	$42.2	$56.5	$63.7					$123.7
								Mark-Up

Sheet tabs: 9-A STS / 9-B WOS / 9-A and 9-B Comparison / 9-C STS / 9-D WOS / 9-C and 9-D Comparison

EXCEL SPREADSHEET 9-A.

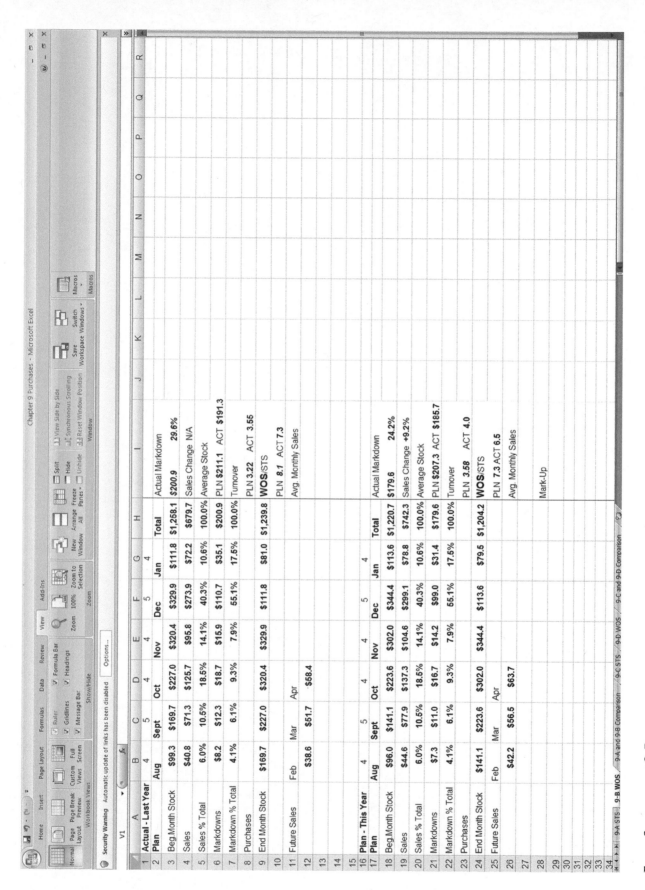

Actual - Last Year

Plan	Aug (4)	Sept (5)	Oct (4)	Nov (4)	Dec (5)	Jan (4)	Total	Actual Markdown
Beg.Month Stock	$99.3	$169.7	$227.0	$320.4	$329.9	$111.8	$1,258.1	$200.9 29.6%
Sales	$40.8	$71.3	$125.7	$95.8	$273.9	$72.2	$679.7	Sales Change N/A
Sales % Total	6.0%	10.5%	18.5%	14.1%	40.3%	10.6%	100.0%	Average Stock
Markdowns	$8.2	$12.3	$18.7	$15.9	$110.7	$35.1	$200.9	PLN $211.1 ACT $191.3
Markdown % Total	4.1%	6.1%	9.3%	7.9%	55.1%	17.5%	100.0%	Turnover
Purchases								
End Month Stock	$169.7	$227.0	$320.4	$329.9	$111.8	$81.0	$1,239.8	PLN 3.22 ACT 3.55
								WOS/STS
Future Sales	Feb	Mar	Apr					PLN 8.1 ACT 7.3
	$38.6	$51.7	$58.4					Avg. Monthly Sales

Plan - This Year

Plan	Aug (4)	Sept (5)	Oct (4)	Nov (4)	Dec (5)	Jan (4)	Total	Actual Markdown
Beg.Month Stock	$96.0	$141.1	$223.6	$302.0	$344.4	$113.6	$1,220.7	$179.6 24.2%
Sales	$44.6	$77.9	$137.3	$104.6	$299.1	$78.8	$742.3	Sales Change +9.2%
Sales % Total	6.0%	10.5%	18.5%	14.1%	40.3%	10.6%	100.0%	Average Stock
Markdowns	$7.3	$11.0	$16.7	$14.2	$99.0	$31.4	$179.6	PLN $207.3 ACT $185.7
Markdown % Total	4.1%	6.1%	9.3%	7.9%	55.1%	17.5%	100.0%	Turnover
Purchases								
End Month Stock	$141.1	$223.6	$302.0	$344.4	$113.6	$79.5	$1,204.2	PLN 3.58 ACT 4.0
Future Sales	Feb	Mar	Apr					WOS/STS
	$42.2	$56.5	$63.7					PLN 7.3 ACT 6.5
								Avg. Monthly Sales
								Mark-Up

Excel Spreadsheet 9-B.

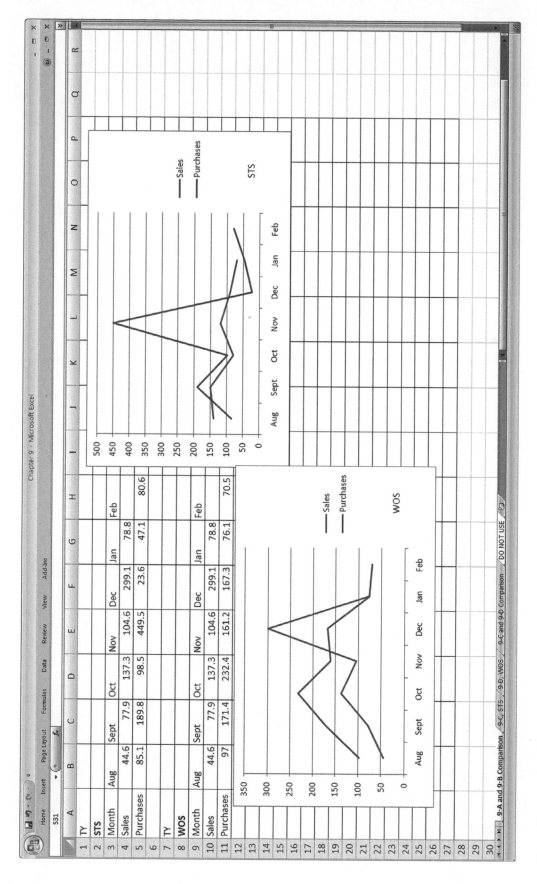

	A	B	C	D	E	F	G	H
1	TY							
2	STS							
3	Month	Aug	Sept	Oct	Nov	Dec	Jan	Feb
4	Sales	44.6	77.9	137.3	104.6	299.1	78.8	
5	Purchases	85.1	189.8	98.5	449.5	23.6	47.1	80.6
6								
7	TY							
8	WOS							
9	Month	Aug	Sept	Oct	Nov	Dec	Jan	Feb
10	Sales	44.6	77.9	137.3	104.6	299.1	78.8	
11	Purchases	97	171.4	232.4	161.2	167.3	76.1	70.5

EXCEL SPREADSHEET 9-A AND 9-B COMPARISON.

Actual - Last Year

	Plan	Aug	Sept	Oct	Nov	Dec	Jan	Total	Actual Markdown
2									Actual Markdown
3	Beg.Month Stock								
4	Sales	1050.0	1760.0	1550.0	2000.0	1480.0	1220.0		Sales Change % +12.9
5	Markdowns	62.0	68.0	52.0	175.0	81.0	40.0		Average Stock
6	Purchases								PLN ACT
7	End Month Stock								Turnover
8									PLN 1.88 ACT
9	Future Sales	Feb	Mar	Apr					WOS/STS
10		1025.0	1430.0	1390.0					PLN ACT
11									
12									
13									

Plan - This Year

	Plan	Aug	Sept	Oct	Nov	Dec	Jan	Total	Actual Markdown
15									Actual Markdown
16	Beg.Month Stock								$ 4.9%
17	Sales								Sales Change % (-4.3)
18	Markdowns								Average Stock
19	Purchases								PLN ACT
20	End Month Stock								Turnover
21	Future Sales	Feb	Mar	Apr					PLN 1.95 ACT
22									WOS/STS
23									
24	REVISE								Mark-Up
25									
26									
27									

9-A and 9-B Comparison | 9-C, STS | 9-D, WOS | 9-C and 9-D Comparison | DO NOT USE

EXCEL SPREADSHEET 9-C, STS.

	A	B	C	D	E	F	G	H	I
1	Actual - Last Year								
2	Plan	Aug	Sept	Oct	Nov	Dec	Jan	Total	Actual Markdown
3	Beg.Month Stock								
4	Sales	1050.0	1760.0	1550.0	2000.0	1480.0	1220.0		Sales Change % +12.9
5	Markdowns	62.0	68.0	52.0	175.0	81.0	40.0		Average Stock
6	Purchases								PLN ACT
7	End Month Stock								Turnover
8		Feb	Mar	Apr					PLN 1.88 ACT
9	Future Sales								WOS/STS
10		1025.0	1430.0	1390.0					PLN ACT
11									
12									
13									
14	Plan - This Year								
15	Plan	Aug	Sept	Oct	Nov	Dec	Jan	Total	Actual Markdown
16	Beg.Month Stock							4.9%	$
17	Sales								Sales Change % (-4.3)
18	Markdowns								Average Stock
19	Purchases								PLN ACT
20	End Month Stock								Turnover
21	Future Sales	Feb	Mar	Apr					PLN 1.95 ACT
22									WOS/STS
23									
24	REVISE								Mark-Up
25									
26									
27									

Excel Spreadsheet 9-D, WOS.

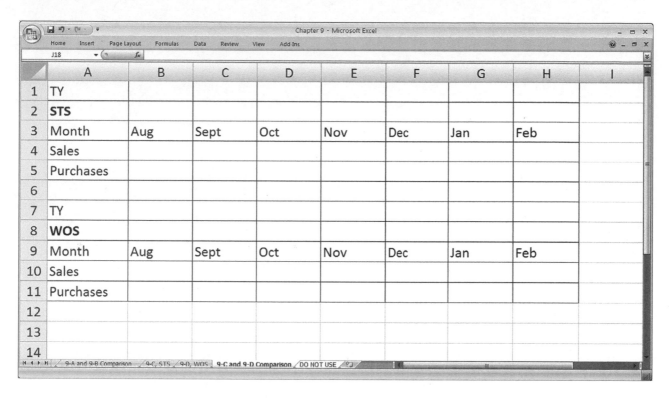

EXCEL SPREADSHEET 9-C AND 9-D COMPARISON.

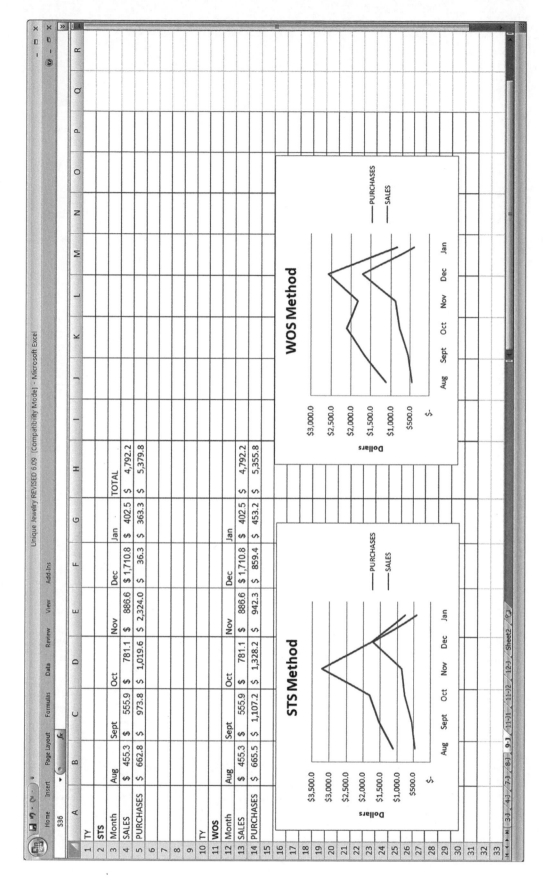

EXCEL SPREADSHEET 9-J.

Actual - Last Year

Plan	Aug	Sept	Oct	Nov	Dec	Jan	Total	Actual Markdown
Beg.Month Stock	301.8	367.4	347.1	420.0	906.9	254.4	2597.6	$255.0 / 15.1%
Sales	195.2	238.6	225.4	272.7	588.9	165.2	1686.0	Sales Change +6.2%
Markdowns	36.4	22.1	18.7	22.9	122.1	32.8	255	Average Stock
Purchases	297.2	240.4	317	782.5	58.5	256.5	1952.1	PLN 432.3 ACT 415.7
End Month Stock	367.4	347.1	420.0	906.9	254.4	312.5	2608.3	Turnover
								PLN 3.90 ACT 4.06
Future Sales	Feb	Mar	Apr					WOS/STS
	202.9	151.3	142.7					PLN 1.54 ACT 1.48
								Average Sales
								$ 281.0

Plan - This Year

Plan							Total	Actual Markdown
Beg.Month Stock								/ 15.8%
Sales								Sales Change +18.2%
Markdowns								Average Stock
Purchases								PLN ACT
End Month Stock								Turnover
Future Sales	Feb	Mar	Apr					PLN 3.93 ACT
								WOS/STS
								Mark-Up

EXCEL SPREADSHEET 11-A1.

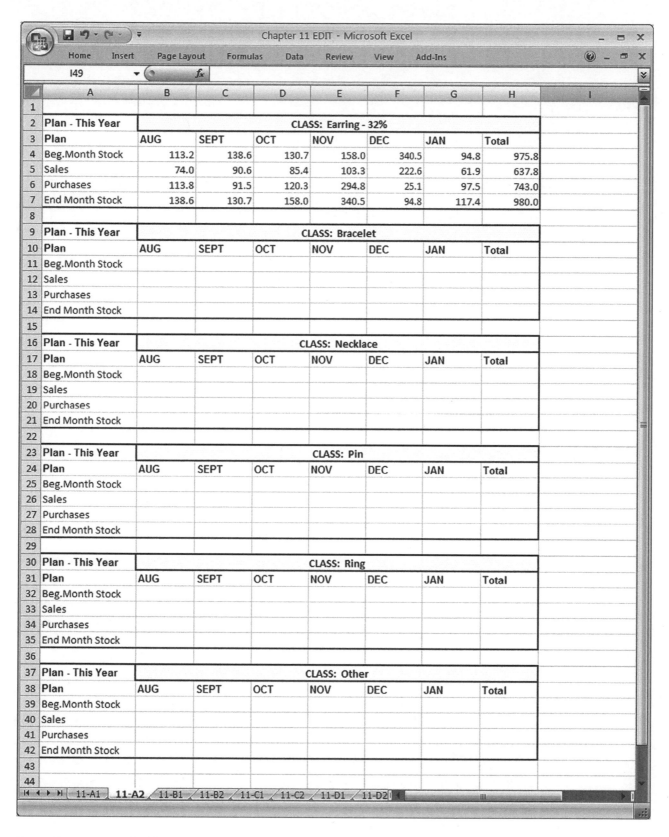

	A	B	C	D	E	F	G	H	I
1									
2	**Plan - This Year**	CLASS: Earring - 32%							
3	**Plan**	AUG	SEPT	OCT	NOV	DEC	JAN	Total	
4	Beg.Month Stock	113.2	138.6	130.7	158.0	340.5	94.8	975.8	
5	Sales	74.0	90.6	85.4	103.3	222.6	61.9	637.8	
6	Purchases	113.8	91.5	120.3	294.8	25.1	97.5	743.0	
7	End Month Stock	138.6	130.7	158.0	340.5	94.8	117.4	980.0	
8									
9	**Plan - This Year**	CLASS: Bracelet							
10	Plan	AUG	SEPT	OCT	NOV	DEC	JAN	Total	
11	Beg.Month Stock								
12	Sales								
13	Purchases								
14	End Month Stock								
15									
16	**Plan - This Year**	CLASS: Necklace							
17	Plan	AUG	SEPT	OCT	NOV	DEC	JAN	Total	
18	Beg.Month Stock								
19	Sales								
20	Purchases								
21	End Month Stock								
22									
23	**Plan - This Year**	CLASS: Pin							
24	Plan	AUG	SEPT	OCT	NOV	DEC	JAN	Total	
25	Beg.Month Stock								
26	Sales								
27	Purchases								
28	End Month Stock								
29									
30	**Plan - This Year**	CLASS: Ring							
31	Plan	AUG	SEPT	OCT	NOV	DEC	JAN	Total	
32	Beg.Month Stock								
33	Sales								
34	Purchases								
35	End Month Stock								
36									
37	**Plan - This Year**	CLASS: Other							
38	Plan	AUG	SEPT	OCT	NOV	DEC	JAN	Total	
39	Beg.Month Stock								
40	Sales								
41	Purchases								
42	End Month Stock								
43									
44									

Sheet tabs: 11-A1, **11-A2**, 11-B1, 11-B2, 11-C1, 11-C2, 11-D1, 11-D2

EXCEL SPREADSHEET 11-A2.

Home | Insert | Page Layout | Formulas | Data | Review | View | Add-Ins

M29

	A	B	C	D	E	F	G	H	I
1	Actual - Last Year								
2	Plan	Aug	Sept	Oct	Nov	Dec	Jan	Total	Actual Markdown
3	Beg.Month Stock	300	325	350	400	450	400		$262 %49.4
4	Sales	45	100	75	80	120	110	530	Sales Change % +5.3
5	Markdowns	10	36	20	16	40	140	262	Average Stock
6	Purchases	80	161	145	146	110	25	667	PLN ACT $342.9
7	End Month Stock	325	350	400	450	400	175		Turnover
8									PLN ACT 1.46
9	Future Sales	Feb	March	April					WOS/STS/FM
10		60	80	85					PLN ACT
11									
12									
13									
14	Plan - This Year								
15	Plan	Aug	Sept	Oct	Nov	Dec	Jan	Total	Actual Markdown
16	Beg.Month Stock								$ % 48.6
17	Sales								Sales Change % -3.3
18	Markdowns								Average Stock
19	Purchases								PLN ACT
20	End Month Stock								Turnover
21	Future Sales	Feb	March	April					PLN 2.05 ACT
22									WOS/STS/FM
23									
24									Mark-Up
25									
26									
27									

11-A1 | 11-A2 | 11-B1 | 11-B2 | 11-C1 | 11-C2 | 11-D1 | 11-D2 | Sheet1

EXCEL SPREADSHEET 11-B1.

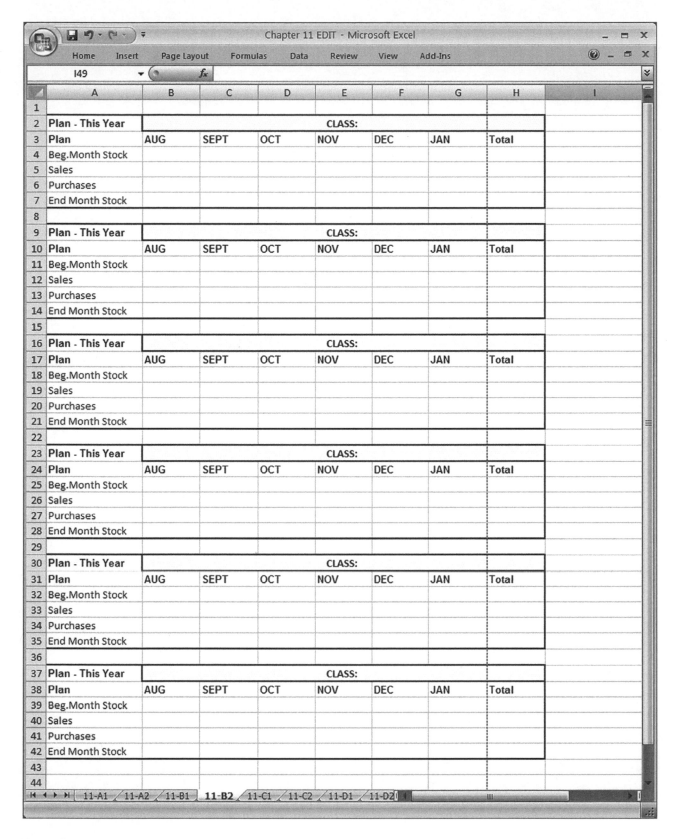

EXCEL SPREADSHEET 11-B2.

Actual - Last Year

Plan	Aug	Sept	Oct	Nov	Dec	Jan	Total	Actual Markdown
Beg.Month Stock	152	185	202	250	330	95		$257 %40.4
Sales	53	78	85	100	225	95	636	Sales Change % +6.0
Markdowns	25	12	10	50	100	60	257	Average Stock
Purchases	111	107	143	230	90	180	861	PLN ACT $190.6
End Month Stock	185	202	250	330	95	120		Turnover
								PLN ACT 3.34
Future Sales	Feb	Mar	April					WOS/STS/FM
	72	95	80					PLN ACT

Plan - This Year

Plan	Aug	Sept	Oct	Nov	Dec	Jan	Total	Actual Markdown
Beg.Month Stock								$ %39.9
Sales								Sales Change % +5.8
Markdowns								Average Stock
Purchases								PLN ACT
End Month Stock								Turnover
Future Sales	Feb	Mar	April					PLN 3.36 ACT
								WOS/STS/FM
								Mark-Up 62.3%

Excel Spreadsheet 11-C1.

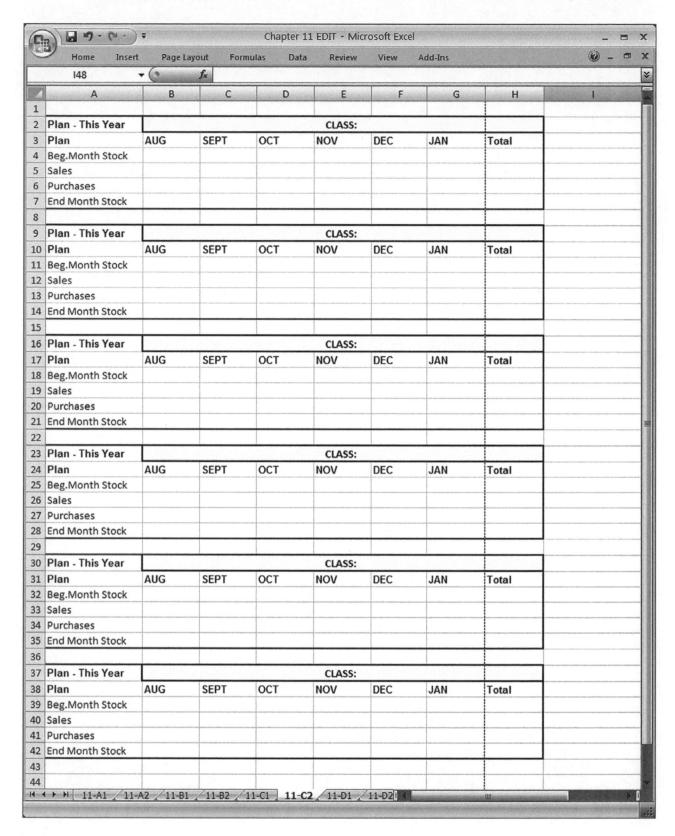

EXCEL SPREADSHEET **11-C2.**

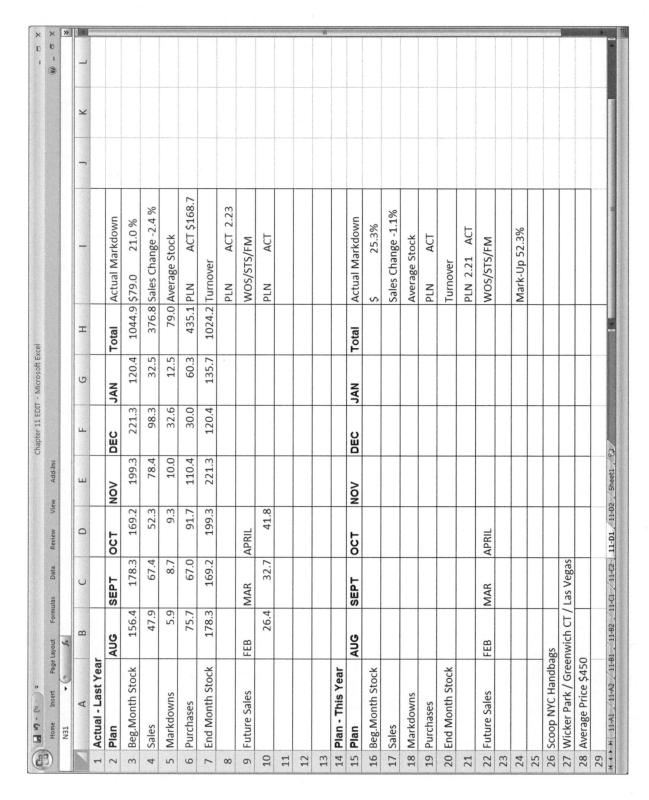

Actual - Last Year

Plan	AUG	SEPT	OCT	NOV	DEC	JAN	Total	Actual Markdown
Beg.Month Stock	156.4	178.3	169.2	199.3	221.3	120.4	1044.9	$79.0 21.0 %
Sales	47.9	67.4	52.3	78.4	98.3	32.5	376.8	Sales Change -2.4 %
Markdowns	5.9	8.7	9.3	10.0	32.6	12.5	79.0	Average Stock
Purchases	75.7	67.0	91.7	110.4	30.0	60.3	435.1	PLN ACT $168.7
End Month Stock	178.3	169.2	199.3	221.3	120.4	135.7	1024.2	Turnover
								PLN ACT 2.23
Future Sales	FEB	MAR	APRIL					WOS/STS/FM
	26.4	32.7	41.8					PLN ACT

Plan - This Year

Plan	AUG	SEPT	OCT	NOV	DEC	JAN	Total	Actual Markdown
Beg.Month Stock								$ 25.3%
Sales								Sales Change -1.1%
Markdowns								Average Stock
Purchases								PLN ACT
End Month Stock								Turnover
								PLN 2.21 ACT
Future Sales	FEB	MAR	APRIL					WOS/STS/FM
								Mark-Up 52.3%

Scoop NYC Handbags
Wicker Park / Greenwich CT / Las Vegas
Average Price $450

EXCEL SPREADSHEET 11-D1.

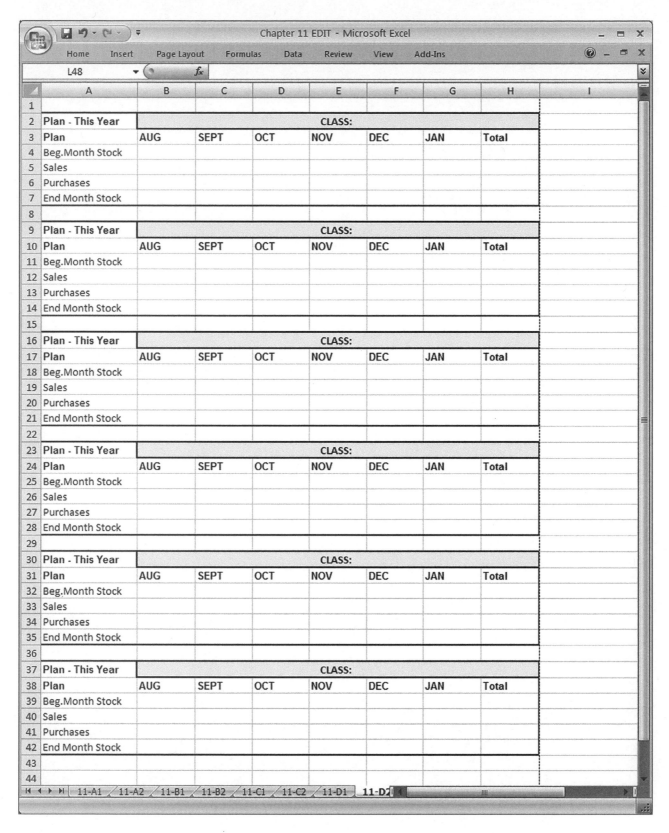

Excel Spreadsheet 11-D2.

ACTUAL - Last Year

Plan	Aug	Sept	Oct	Nov	Dec	Jan	Total			
Beg.Month Stock	$738.2	$899.3	$1,263.6	$1,435.9	$2,773.4	$654.3	$7,764.7	**Actual Markdown**	$918.0	19.3%
Sales	$452.9	$551.7	$775.2	$880.9	$1,701.5	$401.4	$4,763.6	**Sales Change %**	-2.2%	
Sales % Total	9.5%	11.6%	16.3%	18.5%	35.7%	8.4%	100.0%			
Markdowns	$42.6	$48.7	$65.8	$85.9	$472.4	$202.6	$918.0	**Average Stock**		
Markdown % Total	4.6%	5.3%	7.2%	9.4%	51.5%	22.1%	100%	PLN	ACT	
Purchases	$656.5	$964.7	$1,013.3	$2,304.4	$54.7	$363.6	$5,357.2	$1,294.5	$1,168.4	
End Month Stock	$899.3	$1,263.6	$1,435.9	$2,773.4	$654.3	$413.9	$7,440.3	**Turnover**		
								PLN	ACT	
Future Sales	Feb	Mar	April					3.68	4.08	
	$253.9	$310.6	$298.7					**WOS/STS**		
								PLN	ACT	
								1.63	1.47	
								Avg. Month Sales		
								$793.9		

Plan - This Year

Plan	Aug	Sept	Oct	Nov	Dec	Jan	Total			
Beg.Month Stock	$746.6	$911.7	$1,281.0	$1,453.9	$2,805.7	$660.2	$7,859.2	**Actual Markdown**	$915.3	19.1%
Sales	$455.3	$555.9	$781.1	$886.6	$1,710.8	$402.5	$4,792.2	**Sales Change %**	0.6%	
Sales % Total	9.5%	11.6%	16.3%	18.5%	35.7%	8.4%	100.0%			
Markdowns	$42.5	$48.6	$65.6	$85.6	$471.0	$202.0	$915.3	**Average Stock**		
Markdown % Total	4.6%	5.3%	7.2%	9.4%	51.5%	22.1%	100%	PLN	ACT	
Purchases	$662.8	$973.8	$1,019.6	$2,324.0	$36.3	$363.3	$5,379.8	$1,312.9	$1,182.6	
End Month Stock	$911.7	$1,281.0	$1,453.9	$2,805.7	$660.2	$418.9	$7,531.5	**Turnover**		
Future Sales	Feb	Mar	April					PLN	ACT	
	$255.4	$312.5	$300.5					3.65	4.05	
								WOS/STS		
								PLN	ACT	
								1.64	1.48	
								Avg. Month Sales		
								$798.7		
								Mark-Up	58.3%	

EXCEL SPREADSHEET 11-J1.

Unique Jewelry REVISED 6.09 [Compatibility Mode] - Microsoft Excel

Plan - This Year

CLASS: EARRING - 38%

Plan	AUG	SEPT	OCT	NOV	DEC	JAN	Total
Beg. Month Stock	$ 283.7	$ 346.4	$ 486.8	$ 552.5	$ 1,066.2	$ 250.9	$ 2,986.5
Sales	$ 173.0	$ 211.2	$ 295.8	$ 336.9	$ 650.1	$ 153.0	$ 1,821.0
Purchases	$ 251.9	$ 370.1	$ 387.5	$ 883.1	$ 13.8	$ 138.0	$ 2,044.3
End Month Stock	$ 346.4	$ 486.8	$ 552.5	$ 1,066.2	$ 250.9	$ 159.2	$ 2,862.0

Plan - This Year

CLASS: BRACELET - 18%

Plan	AUG	SEPT	OCT	NOV	DEC	JAN	Total
Beg. Month Stock	$ 134.4	$ 164.1	$ 230.6	$ 261.7	$ 505.0	$ 118.8	$ 1,414.7
Sales	$ 81.9	$ 100.1	$ 140.6	$ 159.6	$ 307.9	$ 72.5	$ 862.6
Purchases	$ 119.3	$ 175.3	$ 183.5	$ 418.3	$ 6.5	$ 65.4	$ 968.4
End Month Stock	$ 164.1	$ 230.6	$ 261.7	$ 505.0	$ 118.8	$ 75.4	$ 1,355.7

Plan - This Year

CLASS: NECKLACE - 21%

Plan	AUG	SEPT	OCT	NOV	DEC	JAN	Total
Beg. Month Stock	$ 156.8	$ 191.4	$ 269.0	$ 305.3	$ 589.2	$ 138.6	$ 1,650.4
Sales	$ 95.6	$ 116.7	$ 164.0	$ 186.2	$ 359.3	$ 84.5	$ 1,006.4
Purchases	$ 139.2	$ 204.5	$ 214.1	$ 488.0	$ 7.6	$ 76.3	$ 1,129.7
End Month Stock	$ 191.4	$ 269.0	$ 305.3	$ 589.2	$ 138.6	$ 88.0	$ 1,581.6

Plan - This Year

CLASS: PIN - 12%

Plan	AUG	SEPT	OCT	NOV	DEC	JAN	Total
Beg. Month Stock	$ 89.6	$ 109.4	$ 153.7	$ 174.5	$ 336.7	$ 79.2	$ 943.1
Sales	$ 54.6	$ 66.7	$ 93.7	$ 106.4	$ 205.3	$ 48.3	$ 575.1
Purchases	$ 79.5	$ 116.9	$ 122.4	$ 278.9	$ 4.4	$ 43.6	$ 645.6
End Month Stock	$ 109.4	$ 153.7	$ 174.5	$ 336.7	$ 79.2	$ 50.3	$ 903.8

Plan - This Year

CLASS: RING - 8%

Plan	AUG	SEPT	OCT	NOV	DEC	JAN	Total
Beg. Month Stock	$ 59.7	$ 72.9	$ 102.5	$ 116.3	$ 224.5	$ 52.8	$ 628.7
Sales	$ 36.4	$ 44.5	$ 62.5	$ 70.9	$ 136.9	$ 32.2	$ 383.4
Purchases	$ 53.0	$ 77.9	$ 81.6	$ 185.9	$ 2.9	$ 29.1	$ 430.4
End Month Stock	$ 72.9	$ 102.5	$ 116.3	$ 224.5	$ 52.8	$ 33.5	$ 602.5

Plan - This Year

CLASS: OTHER - 3%

Plan	AUG	SEPT	OCT	NOV	DEC	JAN	Total
Beg. Month Stock	$ 22.4	$ 27.3	$ 38.4	$ 43.6	$ 84.2	$ 19.8	$ 235.8
Sales	$ 13.7	$ 16.7	$ 23.4	$ 26.6	$ 51.3	$ 12.1	$ 143.8
Purchases	$ 19.9	$ 29.2	$ 30.6	$ 69.7	$ 1.1	$ 10.9	$ 161.4
End Month Stock	$ 27.3	$ 38.4	$ 43.6	$ 84.2	$ 19.8	$ 12.6	$ 225.9

EXCEL SPREADSHEET 11-J2.

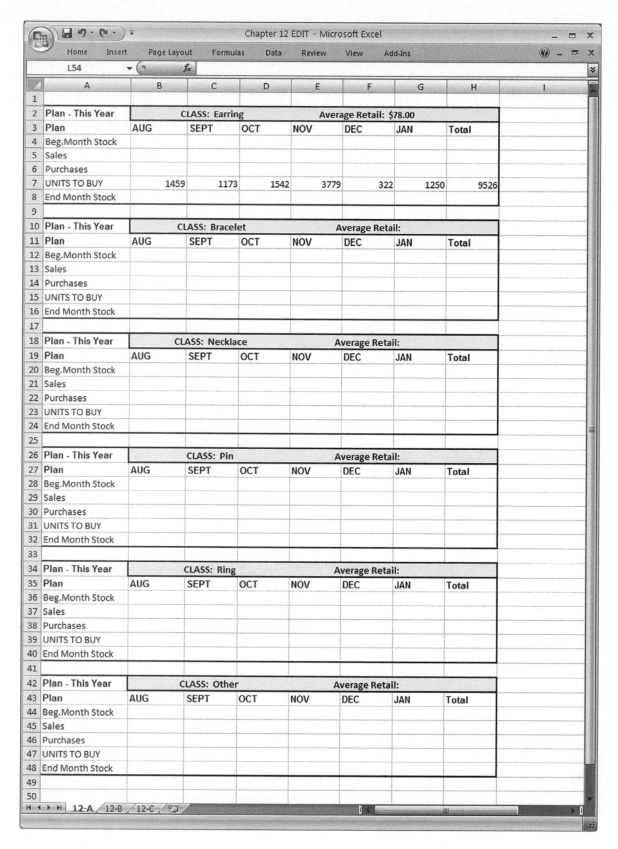

EXCEL SPREADSHEET 12-A.

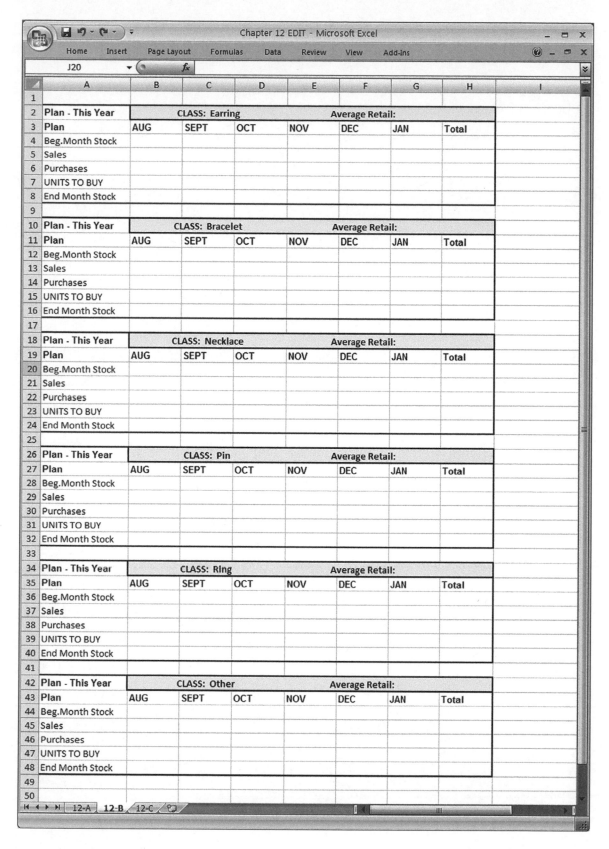

EXCEL SPREADSHEET 12-B.

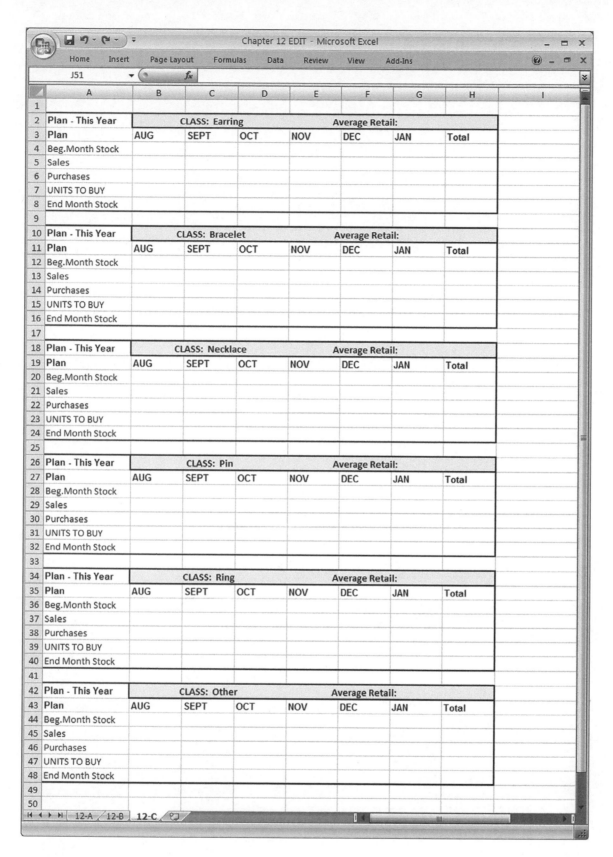

EXCEL SPREADSHEET 12-C.

Excel spreadsheet — Unique Jewelry REVISED 6.09 [Compatibility Mode] - Microsoft Excel

Plan – This Year

CLASS: EARRING – 38% — Average Retail $83.00

Plan	AUG	SEPT	OCT	NOV	DEC	JAN	Total
Beg.Month Stock	$283.7	$346.4	$486.8	$552.5	$1,066.2	$250.9	$2,986.5
Sales	$173.0	$211.2	$296.8	$336.9	$650.1	$153.0	$1,821.0
Purchases	$251.9	$370.1	$387.5	$883.1	$13.8	$138.0	$2,044.3
UNITS TO BUY	3.034	4.459	4.668	10.640	0.166	1.663	
End Month Stock	$346.4	$486.8	$552.5	$1,066.2	$250.9	$159.2	$2,862.0

Plan – This Year

CLASS: BRACELET – 18% — Average Retail $190.00

Plan	AUG	SEPT	OCT	NOV	DEC	JAN	Total
Beg.Month Stock	$134.4	$164.1	$230.6	$261.7	$505.0	$118.8	$1,414.7
Sales	$81.9	$100.1	$140.6	$159.6	$307.9	$72.5	$862.6
Purchases	$119.3	$175.3	$183.5	$418.3	$6.5	$65.4	$968.4
UNITS TO BUY	0.628	0.923	0.966	2.202	0.034	0.344	
End Month Stock	$164.1	$230.6	$261.7	$505.0	$118.8	$75.4	$1,355.7

Plan – This Year

CLASS: NECKLACE – 21% — Average Retail $225.00

Plan	AUG	SEPT	OCT	NOV	DEC	JAN	Total
Beg.Month Stock	$156.8	$191.4	$269.0	$305.3	$589.2	$138.6	$1,650.4
Sales	$95.6	$116.7	$164.0	$186.2	$359.3	$84.5	$1,006.4
Purchases	$139.2	$204.5	$214.1	$488.0	$7.6	$76.3	$1,129.7
UNITS TO BUY	0.619	0.909	0.952	2.169	0.034	0.339	
End Month Stock	$191.4	$269.0	$305.3	$589.2	$138.6	$88.0	$1,581.6

Plan – This Year

CLASS: PIN – 12% — Average Retail $86.00

Plan	AUG	SEPT	OCT	NOV	DEC	JAN	Total
Beg.Month Stock	$89.6	$109.4	$153.7	$174.5	$336.7	$79.2	$943.1
Sales	$54.6	$66.7	$93.7	$106.4	$205.3	$48.3	$575.1
Purchases	$79.5	$116.9	$122.4	$278.9	$4.4	$43.6	$645.6
UNITS TO BUY	0.925	1.359	1.423	3.243	0.051	0.507	
End Month Stock	$109.4	$153.7	$174.5	$336.7	$79.2	$50.3	$903.8

Plan – This Year

CLASS: RING – 8% — Average Retail $68.00

Plan	AUG	SEPT	OCT	NOV	DEC	JAN	Total
Beg.Month Stock	$59.7	$72.9	$102.5	$116.3	$224.5	$52.8	$628.7
Sales	$36.4	$44.5	$62.5	$70.9	$136.9	$32.2	$383.4
Purchases	$53.0	$77.9	$81.6	$185.9	$2.9	$29.1	$430.4
UNITS TO BUY	0.780	1.146	1.200	2.734	0.043	0.427	
End Month Stock	$72.9	$102.5	$116.3	$224.5	$52.8	$33.5	$602.5

Plan – This Year

CLASS: OTHER – 3% — Average Retail $61.00

Plan	AUG	SEPT	OCT	NOV	DEC	JAN	Total
Beg.Month Stock	$22.4	$27.3	$38.4	$43.6	$84.2	$19.8	$235.8
Sales	$13.7	$16.7	$23.4	$26.6	$51.3	$12.1	$143.8
Purchases	$19.9	$29.2	$30.6	$69.7	$1.1	$10.9	$161.4
UNITS TO BUY	0.326	0.479	0.501	1.143	0.018	0.179	
End Month Stock	$27.3	$38.4	$43.6	$84.2	$19.8	$12.6	$225.9

EXCEL SPREADSHEET 12-J.

Actual / Forecast

Plan	Aug PLAN	Aug ACTUAL	Sept PLAN	Sept ACTUAL	Oct PLAN	Oct FCST	Nov PLAN	Nov FCST	Dec PLAN	Dec FCST	Jan PLAN	Jan FCST	Total
Beg. Month Stock	301.8	310.2	367.4	366.7	347.1	311.0	420.0		906.9		254.4		2597.6
Sales	195.2	187.6	238.6	268.2	225.4		272.7		588.9		165.2		1686.0
Markdowns	36.4	41.3	22.1	25.7	18.7		22.9		122.1		32.8		255
Purchases	297.2	285.4	240.4	238.2	317		782.5		58.5		256.5		1952.1
End Month Stock	367.4	366.7	347.1	311.0	420.0		906.9		254.4		312.5		2608.3
$ (OVER) / Under		0.7		36.1									

	PLAN		FORECAST	
	Actual Markdown		Actual Markdown	
	$255.0	/ 15.1%	$	/ %
	Sales Change +6.2%		Sales Change	%
	Average Stock 255		Average Stock	
	PLN 432.3	ACT 415.7	PLN	ACT
	Turnover		Turnover	
	PLN 3.90	ACT 4.06	PLN	ACT
	WOS/STS		WOS/STS	
	PLN 1.54	ACT 1.48	PLN	ACT
	Average Sales		Average Sales	
	$	281.0		

Future Sales

	Feb	Mar	Apr
	202.9	151.3	142.7

EXCEL SPREADSHEET 13-A.

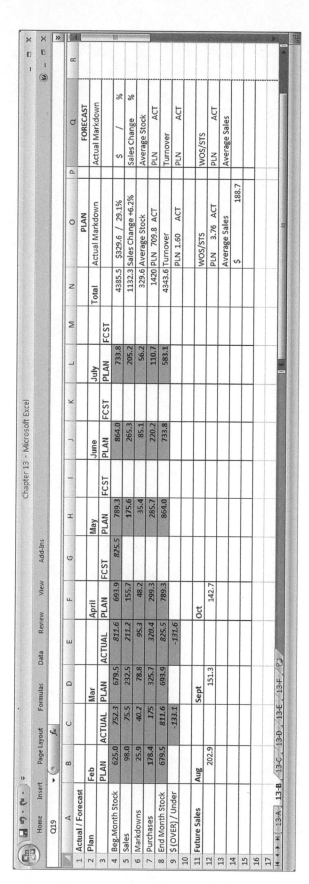

Home | Insert | Page Layout | Formulas | Data | Review | View | Add-Ins

Q19

Actual / Forecast

Plan	Feb		Mar		April		May		June		July			Total	PLAN		FORECAST	
	PLAN	ACTUAL	PLAN	ACTUAL	PLAN	FCST	PLAN	FCST	PLAN	FCST	PLAN	FCST		Total	Actual Markdown		Actual Markdown	
Beg.Month Stock	625.0	752.3	679.5	811.6	693.9	825.5	789.3		864.0		733.8			4385.5				
Sales	98.0	75.5	232.5	211.2	155.7		175.6		265.3		205.2			1132.3	$329.6 / 29.1%		$ /	%
Markdowns	25.9	40.2	78.8	95.3	48.2		35.4		85.1		56.2			329.6	Sales Change +6.2%		Sales Change	%
Purchases	178.4	175	325.7	320.4	299.3		285.7		220.2		110.7			1420	Average Stock		Average Stock	
End Month Stock	679.5	811.6	693.9	825.5	789.3		864.0		733.8		583.1			4343.6	PLN 709.8 ACT		PLN ACT	
$(OVER)/Under		-133.1		-131.6											Turnover		Turnover	
															PLN 1.60 ACT		PLN ACT	
Future Sales	Aug		Sept		Oct										WOS/STS		WOS/STS	
	202.9		151.3		142.7										PLN 3.76 ACT		PLN ACT	
															Average Sales		Average Sales	
															$ 188.7			

13-A / 13-B / 13-C / 13-D / 13-E / 13-F

Excel Spreadsheet 13-B.

Home | Insert | Page Layout | Formulas | Data | Review | View | Add-Ins

S28

Actual / Forecast

Plan	Aug PLAN	Aug ACTUAL	Sept PLAN	Sept ACTUAL	Oct PLAN	Oct FCST	Nov PLAN	Nov FCST	Dec PLAN	Dec FCST	Jan PLAN	Jan FCST	Total
Beg.Month Stock	301.8	310.2	367.4	366.7	347.1	311.0	420.0	392.5	906.9	758.6	254.4		2597.6
Sales	195.2	187.6	238.6	268.2	225.4	248.9	272.7	301.6	588.9		165.2		1686.0
Markdowns	36.4	41.3	22.1	25.7	18.7	21.2	22.9	55.2	122.1		32.8		255
Purchases	297.2	285.4	240.4	238.2	317	351.6	782.5	722.9	58.5		256.5		1952.1
End Month Stock	367.4	366.7	347.1	311.0	420.0	392.5	906.9	758.6	254.4		312.5		2608.3
$ (OVER) / Under		0.7		36.1		27.5		148.3					

PLAN

Total	Actual Markdown	
2597.6	$255.0 / 15.1%	
1686.0	Sales Change +6.2%	
255	Average Stock	PLN 432.3 ACT 415.7
1952.1	Turnover	PLN 3.90 ACT 4.06
2608.3	WOS/STS	PLN 1.54 ACT 1.48
	Average Sales	$ 281.0

FORECAST

Actual Markdown	
$ / %	
Sales Change %	
Average Stock	PLN ACT
Turnover	PLN ACT
WOS/STS	PLN ACT
Average Sales	

Future Sales

	Feb	Mar	Apr
	202.9	151.3	142.7

December Sales

	Plan	Actual
Week 1	$88.3	106.2
Week 2	$100.1	120.3
Week 3	$117.8	
Week 4	$253.2	
Week 5	$29.5	

13-A | 13-B | 13-C | 13-D | 13-E | 13-F

EXCEL SPREADSHEET 13-C.

Q23

Actual / Forecast

Plan	Aug PLAN	Aug ACTUAL	Sept PLAN	Sept ACTUAL	Oct PLAN	Oct FCST	Nov PLAN	Nov FCST	Dec PLAN	Dec FCST	Jan PLAN	Jan FCST	Total	PLAN Actual Markdown		FORECAST Actual Markdown	
Beg.Month Stock	301.8	310.2	367.4	366.7	347.1	373.9	420.0		906.9		254.4		2597.6	$255.0 / 15.1%	%	$ /	%
Sales	195.2	187.6	238.6	218.7	225.4		272.7		588.9		165.2		1686.0	Sales Change +6.2%		Sales Change	%
Markdowns	36.4	41.3	22.1	25.7	18.7		22.9		122.1		32.8		255	Average Stock		Average Stock	
Purchases	297.2	285.4	240.4	251.6	317		782.5		58.5		256.5		1952.1	PLN 432.3 ACT 415.7		PLN ACT	
End Month Stock	367.4	366.7	347.1	373.9	420.0		906.9		254.4		312.5		2608.3	Turnover		Turnover	
$ (OVER) / Under		0.7		-26.8										PLN 3.90 ACT 4.06		PLN ACT	

Future Sales

	Feb	Mar	Apr			WOS/STS	WOS/STS
	202.9	151.3	142.7			PLN 1.54 ACT 1.48	PLN ACT
						Average Sales	Average Sales
						$ 281.0	

Excel Spreadsheet 13-D.

Sheet tabs: 13-A | 13-B | 13-C | 13-D | 13-E | 13-F

Actual / Forecast

Plan	Feb PLAN	Feb ACTUAL	Mar PLAN	Mar ACTUAL	April PLAN	April FCST	May PLAN	May FCST	June PLAN	June FCST	July PLAN	July FCST	Total
Beg. Month Stock	68.4	89.9	99.9	121.1	122.4		124.2		103.6		87.7		606.2
Sales	25.7	23.9	30.3		24.7		47.9		35.8		25.2		189.6
Markdowns	8.1	8.1	10.0		9.2		15.3		13.6		11.2		67.4
Purchases	65.3	63.2	62.8		35.7		42.6		33.5		55.2		295.1
End Month Stock	99.9	121.1	122.4		124.2		103.6		87.7		106.5		644.3
$ (OVER) / Under		-21.2											

PLAN / FORECAST — Actual Markdown

	PLAN	FORECAST
Actual Markdown	$67.4 / 35.5%	$ / %
Sales Change	+7.9%	%
Average Stock	PLN 101.8 ACT	PLN ACT
Turnover	PLN 1.86 ACT	PLN ACT
WOS/STS	PLN 3.22 ACT	PLN ACT
Average Sales	$ 31.6	$

Future Sales

	Aug	Sept	Oct
	31.4	35.8	37.9

Sheet tabs: 13-A, 13-B, 13-C, 13-D, 13-E, 13-F

EXCEL SPREADSHEET 13-E.

| | Feb | | Mar | | April | | May | | June | | July | | | PLAN | | FORECAST |
Actual / Forecast	PLAN	ACTUAL	PLAN	ACTUAL	PLAN	FCST	PLAN	FCST	PLAN	FCST	PLAN	FCST	Total	Actual Markdown		Actual Markdown
Plan													**Total**	Actual Markdown		Actual Markdown
Beg.Month Stock	65.2	63.9	71.7		84.5		138.9		134.7		119.2		614.2	$135.5 / 40.5%		$ / %
Sales	15.3		22.7		40.5		75.3		95.1		85.9		334.8	Sales Change -2.3%		Sales Change %
Markdowns	18.9		12.4		9.1		9.6		25.2		60.3		135.5	Average Stock		Average Stock
Purchases	40.7		47.9		104.0		80.7		104.8		135.7		513.8	PLN 103.3 ACT		PLN ACT
End Month Stock	71.7		84.9		138.9		134.7		119.2		108.7		658.1	Turnover		Turnover
$ (OVER)/Under														PLN 3.24 ACT		PLN ACT
Future Sales	Aug		Sept		Oct									WOS/STS		WOS/STS
	31.4		35.8		37.9									PLN 1.85 ACT		PLN ACT
														Average Sales		Average Sales
														$ 55.8		

EXCEL SPREADSHEET 13-F.

Line #	Item Entry	Cost	Retail	Mark-up		Explanation
1	BOP	$279.4	$670.0	58.3%	BMU	Includes all stock
2	Purchase Receipts	$354.0	$885.0	60.0%	IMU	IMU is the initial mark-up on new merchandise
3	Freight	$3.5				Usually calculated as a percentage of cost receipts, 1%
4	Stock Available	$636.9	$1,555.0	59.0%	CMU	Total lines 1 thru 3, calculate cummulative markup (CMU)
	Subtract					
6	Sales		$800.0			Total sales for the period - month or season
7	Markdowns		$131.0			Total markdowns for the period - month or season
8	Shortage		$38.0			Total shortage dollars for the period - month or season
9	Employee Discount		$14.0			Total employee discount for the period - month or season
10	EOP	$240.3	$586.0	59.0%	CMU	Subtract line 6 thru 9 from line 4, calculate CMU for EOP cost
11	Cost of Goods Sold	$396.6				Subtract line 10 from line 4
12	Net Sales		$800.0			Same as line 6
	Subtract					
13	Cost of Good Sold	$396.6				Same as line 10 only entered on retail side
14	Workroom	$0.5				Calculated as a known dollar amount or percent of sales
	Add					
15	Cash Discount	$1.0				Discounts negotiated with vendors for early payment
16	Gross Margin $	$403.9				Line 12 minus lines 13 and 13, add line 15
17	Gross Margin %	50.5%				Line 16 / Line 12

EXCEL SPREADSHEET 14-A.

Line #	Item Entry	Cost	Retail	Mark-up			Explanation
1	BOP	$279.4	$670.0	58.3%	BMU		Includes all stock
2	Purchase Receipts	$354.0	$885.0	60.0%	IMU		IMU is the initial mark-up on new merchandise
3	Freight	$3.5					Usually calculated as a percentage of cost receipts, 1%
4	Stock Available	$636.9	$1,555.0	59.0%	CMU		Total lines 1 thru 3, calculate cummulative markup (CMU)
	Subtract						
6	Sales		$800.0				Total sales for the period - month or season
7	Markdowns		$131.0				Total markdowns for the period - month or season
8	Shortage		$38.0				Total shortage dollars for the period - month or season
9	Employee Discount		$14.0				Total employee discount for the period - month or season
10	EOP	$240.3	$586.0	59.0%	CMU		Subtract line 6 thru 9 from line 4, calculate CMU for EOP cost
11	Cost of Goods Sold	$396.6					Subtract line 10 from line 4
12	Net Sales		$800.0				Same as line 6
	Subtract						
13	Cost of Good Sold		$396.6				Same as line 10 only entered on retail side
14	Workroom		$0.5				Calculated as a known dollar amount or percent of sales
	Add						
15	Cash Discount		$1.0				Discounts negotiated with vendors for early payment
16	Gross Margin $		$403.9				Line 12 minus lines 13 and 13, add line 15
17	Gross Margin %		50.5%				Line 16 / Line 12
	Subtract Expenses						
18	Net Advertising		$78.0				Net dollar amount spent on advertising after vendor co-op
19	Supply Chain		$1.8				Calculated as .5% of cost purchase receipts
20	Selling/Store Processing		$1.1				Calculated as .3% of cost purchase receipts
21	Storage		$0.2				Calculated as a known dollar amount based on actual storage needs
22	Interest on Inventory		$10.6				Varies with interest rates, calculate at 3% of cost purchase receipts
23	Headquarters		$8.0				Calculated as 1% of retail sales
24	Contribution $		$304.2				Line 16 minus lines 18 through 23
25	Contribution %		38.0%				Line 25 / Line 12

EXCEL SPREADSHEET 14-B.

Line #	Item Entry	Cost	Retail	Mark-up		Explanation
1	BOP		$3,644.0	55.7%	BMU	Includes all stock
2	Purchase Receipts		$4,060.0	57.8%	IMU	IMU is the initial mark-up on new merchandise
3	Freight					Usually calculated as a percentage of cost receipts, 1.2%
4	Stock Available				CMU	Total lines 1 thru 3, calculate cummulative markup (CMU)
	Subtract					
6	Sales		$5,138.0			Total sales for the period - month or season
7	Markdowns		$1,686.0			Total markdowns for the period - month or season
8	Shortage		$256.2			Total shortage dollars for the period - month or season
9	Employee Discount		$92.5			Total employee discount for the period - month or season
10	EOP				CMU	Subtract line 6 thru 9 from line 4, calculate CMU for EOP cost
11	Cost of Goods Sold					Subtract line 10 from line 4
12	Net Sales					Same as line 6
	Subtract					
13	Cost of Good Sold					Same as line 10 only entered on retail side
14	Workroom		$1.2			Calculated as a known dollar amount or percent of sales
	Add					
15	Cash Discount		$5.9			Discounts negotiated with vendors for early payment
16	Gross Margin $					Line 12 minus lines 13 and 13, add line 15
17	Gross Margin %					Line 16 / Line 12

EXCEL SPREADSHEET 14-C.

Line #	Item Entry	Cost	Retail	Mark-up		Explanation
1	BOP		$3,644.0	55.7%	BMU	Includes all stock
2	Purchase Receipts		$4,060.0	57.8%	IMU	IMU is the initial mark-up on new merchandise
3	Freight					Usually calculated as a percentage of cost receipts, 1.2%
4	Stock Available				CMU	Total lines 1 thru 3, calculate cummulative markup (CMU)
	Subtract					
6	Sales		$5,138.0			Total sales for the period - month or season
7	Markdowns		$1,686.0			Total markdowns for the period - month or season
8	Shortage		$256.2			Total shortage dollars for the period - month or season
9	Employee Discount		$92.5			Total employee discount for the period - month or season
10	EOP				CMU	Subtract line 6 thru 9 from line 4, calculate CMU for EOP cost
11	Cost of Goods Sold					Subtract line 10 from line 4
12	Net Sales					Same as line 6
	Subtract					
13	Cost of Good Sold					Same as line 10 only entered on retail side
14	Workroom		$1.2			Calculated as a known dollar amount or percent of sales
	Add					
15	Cash Discount		$5.9			Discounts negotiated with vendors for early payment
16	Gross Margin $					Line 12 minus lines 13 and 13, add line 15
17	Gross Margin %					Line 16 / Line 12
	Subtract Expenses					
18	Net Advertising		$22.6			Net dollar amount spent on advertising after vendor co-op
19	Supply Chain					Calculated as .5% of cost purchase receipts
20	Selling/Store Processing					Calculated as .3% of cost purchase receipts
21	Storage		$0.0			Calculated as a known dollar amount based on actual storage needs
22	Interest on Inventory					Varies with interest rates, calculate at 3% of cost purchase receipts
23	Headquarters					Calculated as 1% of retail sales
24	Contribution $					Line 16 minus lines 18 through 23
25	Contribution %					Line 25 / Line 12

EXCEL SPREADSHEET 14-D.

Line #	Item Entry	Cost	Retail	Mark-up		Explanation
1	BOP		$1,593.2	62.3%	BMU	Includes all stock
2	Purchase Receipts		$938.4	71.0%	IMU	IMU is the initial mark-up on new merchandise
3	Freight					Usually calculated as a percentage of cost receipts, 1.9%
4	Stock Available				CMU	Total lines 1 thru 3, calculate cummulative markup (CMU)
	Subtract					
6	Sales		$1,512.3			Total sales for the period - month or season
7	Markdowns		$510.2			Total markdowns for the period - month or season
8	Shortage		$101.7			Total shortage dollars for the period - month or season
9	Employee Discount		$25.6			Total employee discount for the period - month or season
10	EOP				CMU	Subtract line 6 thru 9 from line 4, calculate CMU for EOP cost
11	Cost of Goods Sold					Subtract line 10 from line 4
12	Net Sales					Same as line 6
	Subtract					
13	Cost of Good Sold					Same as line 10 only entered on retail side
14	Workroom		$0.9			Calculated as a known dollar amount or percent of sales
	Add					
15	Cash Discount		$2.3			Discounts negotiated with vendors for early payment
16	Gross Margin $					Line 12 minus lines 13 and 13, add line 15
17	Gross Margin %					Line 16 / Line 12

EXCEL SPREADSHEET 14-E.

Line #	Item Entry	Cost	Retail	Mark-up		Explanation
				Mark-up		**Explanation**
1	**BOP**		$1,593.2	62.3%	BMU	Includes all stock
2	**Purchase Receipts**		$938.4	71.0%	IMU	IMU is the initial mark-up on new merchandise
3	**Freight**					Usually calculated as a percentage of cost receipts, 1.9%
4	**Stock Available**				CMU	Total lines 1 thru 3, calculate cummulative markup (CMU)
	Subtract					
6	**Sales**		$1,512.3			Total sales for the period - month or season
7	**Markdowns**		$510.2			Total markdowns for the period - month or season
8	**Shortage**		$101.7			Total shortage dollars for the period - month or season
9	**Employee Discount**		$25.6			Total employee discount for the period - month or season
10	**EOP**				CMU	Subtract line 6 thru 9 from line 4, calculate CMU for EOP cost
11	**Cost of Goods Sold**					Subtract line 10 from line 4
12	**Net Sales**					Same as line 6
	Subtract					
13	**Cost of Good Sold**					Same as line 10 only entered on retail side
14	**Workroom**		$0.9			Calculated as a known dollar amount or percent of sales
	Add					
15	**Cash Discount**		$2.3			Discounts negotiated with vendors for early payment
16	**Gross Margin $**					Line 12 minus lines 13 and 13, add line 15
17	**Gross Margin %**					Line 16 / Line 12
	Subtract Expenses					
18	**Net Advertising**		$125.8			Net dollar amount spent on advertising after vendor co-op
19	**Supply Chain**					Calculated as .5% of cost purchase receipts
20	**Selling/Store Processing**					Calculated as .3% of cost purchase receipts
21	**Storage**		$0.0			Calculated as a known dollar amount based on actual storage needs
22	**Interest on Inventory**					Varies with interest rates, calculate at 3.5% of cost purchase receipts
23	**Headquarters**					Calculated as 1% of retail sales
24	**Contribution $**					Line 16 minus lines 18 through 23
25	**Contribution %**					Line 25 / Line 12

EXCEL SPREADSHEET 14-F.

Line #	Item Entry	Cost	Retail	Mark-up			Explanation
1	BOP			58.3%	BMU		Includes all stock
2	Purchase Receipts			62.0%	IMU		IMU is the initial mark-up on new merchandise
3	Freight						Usually calculated as a percentage of cost receipts, 1.9%
4	Stock Available				CMU		Total lines 1 thru 3, calculate cummulative markup (CMU)
	Subtract						
6	Sales						Total sales for the period - month or season
7	Markdowns						Total markdowns for the period - month or season
8	Shortage						Total shortage dollars for the period - month or season
9	Employee Discount						Total employee discount for the period - month or season
10	EOP				CMU		Subtract line 6 thru 9 from line 4, calculate CMU for EOP cost
11	Cost of Goods Sold						Subtract line 10 from line 4
12	Net Sales						Same as line 6
	Subtract						
13	Cost of Good Sold						Same as line 10 only entered on retail side
14	Workroom						Calculated as a known dollar amount or percent of sales
	Add						
15	Cash Discount						Discounts negotiated with vendors for early payment
16	Gross Margin $						Line 12 minus lines 13 and 13, add line 15
17	Gross Margin %						Line 16 / Line 12
	Subtract Expenses						
18	Net Advertising						Net dollar amount spent on advertising after vendor co-op
19	Supply Chain						Calculated as .3% of cost purchase receipts
20	Selling/Store Processing						Calculated as .7% of cost purchase receipts
21	Storage						Calculated as a known dollar amount based on actual storage needs
22	Interest on Inventory						Varies with interest rates, calculate at 1.5% of cost purchase receipts
23	Headquarters						Calculated as 2% of retail sales
24	Contribution $		$2,296.8				Line 16 minus lines 18 through 23
25	Contribution %		47.9%				Line 25 / Line 12

EXCEL SPREADSHEET 14-J.

INDEX

Page numbers followed by "f" refer to figures; page numbers followed by "t" refer to tables.